Thomas De Quincey

Edinburgh Critical Studies in Romanticism
Series Editors: Ian Duncan and Penny Fielding

**Available Titles**
*A Feminine Enlightenment: British Women Writers and the Philosophy of Progress, 1759–1820*
JoEllen DeLucia

*Reinventing Liberty: Nation, Commerce and the Historical Novel from Walpole to Scott*
Fiona Price

*The Politics of Romanticism: The Social Contract and Literature*
Zoe Beenstock

*Radical Romantics: Prophets, Pirates, and the Space Beyond Nation*
Talissa J. Ford

*Literature and Medicine in the Nineteenth-Century Periodical Press:* Blackwood's Edinburgh Magazine, *1817–1858*
Megan Coyer

*Discovering the Footsteps of Time: Geological Travel Writing in Scotland, 1700–1820*
Tom Furniss

*The Dissolution of Character in Late Romanticism*
Jonas Cope

*Commemorating Peterloo: Violence, Resilience, and Claim-making during the Romantic Era*
Michael Demson and Regina Hewitt

*Dialectics of Improvement: Scottish Romanticism, 1786–1831*
Gerard Lee McKeever

*Literary Manuscript Culture in Romantic Britain*
Michelle Levy

*Scottish Romanticism and Collective Memory in the British Atlantic*
Kenneth McNeil

*Romantic Periodicals in the Twenty-First Century: Eleven Case Studies from* Blackwood's Edinburgh Magazine
Nicholas Mason and Tom Mole

*Godwin and the Book: Imagining Media, 1783–1836*
J. Louise McCray

*Thomas De Quincey: Romanticism in Translation*
Brecht de Groote

**Forthcoming Titles**
*Romantic Environmental Sensibility: Nature, Class and Empire*
Ve-Yin Tee

*Romantic Pasts: History, Fiction and Feeling in Britain and Ireland, 1790–1850*
Porscha Fermanis

*Romantic Networks in Europe: Transnational Encounters, 1786–1850*
Carmen Casaliggi

*Romanticism and Consciousness*
Richard Sha and Joel Faflak

*Death,* Blackwood's Edinburgh Magazine *and Authoring Romantic Scotland*
Sarah Sharp

Visit our website at: www.edinburghuniversitypress.com/series/ECSR

# Thomas De Quincey

Romanticism in Translation

Brecht de Groote

EDINBURGH
University Press

Edinburgh University Press is one of the leading university presses in the UK. We publish academic books and journals in our selected subject areas across the humanities and social sciences, combining cutting-edge scholarship with high editorial and production values to produce academic works of lasting importance. For more information visit our website: edinburghuniversitypress.com

© Brecht de Groote, 2021, 2023

Edinburgh University Press Ltd
The Tun – Holyrood Road
12(2f) Jackson's Entry
Edinburgh EH8 8PJ

First published in hardback by Edinburgh University Press 2021

Typeset in 10.5/13 Sabon by
Servis Filmsetting Ltd, Stockport, Cheshire

A CIP record for this book is available from the British Library

ISBN 978 1 4744 8389 6 (hardback)
ISBN 978 1 4744 8390 2 (paperback)
ISBN 978 1 4744 8391 9 (webready PDF)
ISBN 978 1 4744 8392 6 (epub)

The right of Brecht de Groote to be identified as the author of this work has been asserted in accordance with the Copyright, Designs and Patents Act 1988, and the Copyright and Related Rights Regulations 2003 (SI No. 2498).

# Contents

| | |
|---|---|
| Acknowledgements | vii |
| De Quincey and Translation: A Timeline | viii |
| Abbreviations | x |
| Introduction: Dark Interpreter | 1 |
| 1. [I] Wrote This: Authorship, Translatorship | 14 |
| 2. How to Write English: The Transnationalism of a National Style | 56 |
| 3. Translating (against) Kant: A Translator's Idealism | 99 |
| 4. The Ghost of Cutler's Stockings: The Idea of Translation | 147 |
| Coda: A Yearning for Translation | 179 |
| Bibliography | 187 |
| Index | 198 |

*Mrs Dangle*     Mr Dangle, here are two very civil gentlemen trying to make themselves understood, and I don't know which is the interpreter.
*Mr Dangle*      Egad, I think the interpreter is the hardest to be understood of the two.¹
*Mr Coleridge*   [T]hese forces should be assumed to be both alike infinite, both alike indestructible. The problem will then be to discover the result or product of two such forces.²
*Mr De Quincey*  The unit itself that should facilitate [...] becomes itself elusive of the mental grasp: it comes in as an interpreter; and (as in some other cases) the interpreter is hardest to be understood of the two.³
*Mr Benjamin*    If the original does not exist for the reader's sake, how could the translation be understood on this premise? [...] There is a philosophical genius that is characterised by a yearning for that language which manifests itself in translation.⁴

---

[1] Richard Brinsley Sheridan, *The Critic: Or, a Tragedy Rehearsed: A Farce*, ed. G. A. Aitken (London: J. M. Dent, 1897), 31–2.
[2] BL, 299.
[3] System of the Heavens, 15.401.
[4] Walter Benjamin, 'The Task of the Translator: An Introduction to the Translation of Baudelaire's *Tableaux Parisiens*', *Illuminations*, trans. Harry Zorn (London: Pimlico, 1999), 71; 76.

## *Acknowledgements*

This book has been a long time in the making and remaking. It has travelled with me as I have moved in and out of various positions and institutions, and I have accordingly taken on many debts. I can only begin to repay them by recording them here. At the three universities I have called home during the writing of this book – Leuven, Edinburgh and Ghent – I wish to single out Tom Toremans and Ortwin de Graef, as well as Laura Cernat, Bernard De Clerck, Raphaël Ingelbien, Lieve Jooken, Tom Mole, Désirée Schyns, Frederik Van Dam, Sonia Vandepitte, Willow Verkerk and Pieter Vermeulen. For their suggestions and encouragement during the writing of this book and the development of projects that have flowed from it, I wish to pay tribute to several generous friends in Romanticism and beyond. They are Jessica Allen-Hansen, Fred Burwick, Jim Chandler, David L. Clark, Éric Dayre, Stephanie Dumke, Svend Erik Larsen, Angela Esterhammer, Cassandra Falke, Jacques Khalip, Fiona McIntosh-Varjabédian, Rob Morrison, Emma Peacocke, Martin Procházka, Neil Ramsey, Chuck Rzepka, Matt Sangster, Diego Saglia, Phil Shaw and Judith Thompson. I also wish to thank the series editors, Ian Duncan and Penny Fielding, for their guidance and patience. Finally, none of what I struggle to say in the following pages would have been written if not for the person to whom I owe the greatest debt of all – Sebastiaan: all this is more dear for thy sake.

# De Quincey and Translation: A Timeline

| | |
|---|---|
| 1521–2 | Luther translates the New Testament |
| 1760 | Macpherson begins publishing his Ossianic poems |
| 1781–90 | Kant, *Critiques* |
| 1785 | De Quincey born in Manchester |
| 1794 | Schiller, *Esthetische Erziehung* |
| 1795–6 | Goethe, *Wilhelm Meisters Lehrjahre* |
| 1798 | Wordsworth and Coleridge, *Lyrical Ballads* |
| 1800 | Schelling, *System des transcendentalen Idealismus* |
| 1802 | Hölderlin, *Brief an Böhlendorf* |
| 1803 | De Quincey begins writing his *Diary* |
| 1804 | Kant dies |
| | Jean Paul, *Vorschule der Aesthetik* |
| | Wasianski, *Immanuel Kant in seinen letzten Lebensjahren* |
| 1805 | Schiller dies |
| 1808–9 | De Quincey edits Wordsworth's *Concerning the Convention of Cintra* |
| 1817 | Coleridge, *Biographia Literaria* |
| 1818 | De Quincey becomes editor for the *Westmorland Gazette* |
| 1821 | 'Confessions of an English Opium-Eater' |
| | 'Jean Paul Frederick Richter' |
| 1823 | 'Letters to a Young Man, Whose Education has been Neglected' |
| | 'On the Knocking at the Gate in Macbeth' |
| | Alexis begins publishing *Walladmor* |
| 1823–4 | Translations of six short stories by Friedrich Laun (allegedly) |
| 1824 | 'Analects from John Paul Richter' |
| | 'Kant on National Character, in Relation to the Sublime and the Beautiful' |
| | Carlyle, *Wilhelm Meister's Apprenticeship* |

|  |  |
|---|---|
|  | 'Wilhelm Meister' |
|  | 'Abstract of Swedenborgianism: By Immanuel Kant' |
|  | 'Idea of a Universal History on Cosmo-Political Plan, by Immanuel Kant' |
|  | 'Walladmor: Sir Walter Scott's German Novel' |
| 1825 | *Walladmor* |
| 1826–7 | 'Gallery of the German Prose Classics' Nos. I through III |
| 1830 | 'Kant in his Miscellaneous Essays' |
| 1832 | Goethe dies |
| 1833–4 | Carlyle, *Sartor Resartus* |
| 1834 | Coleridge dies |
| 1834–5 | 'Samuel Taylor Coleridge' |
| 1839 | 'The English Language' |
| 1839–41 | 'Autobiography of an English Opium-Eater' |
| 1840 | 'Style' Nos. I through IV |
| 1841 | 'Goethe' |
|  | 'Schiller' |
| 1845 | 'Suspiria de Profundis' |
|  | 'On Wordsworth's Poetry' |
| 1849 | 'The English Mail-Coach: Or, the Glory of Motion' |
| 1850 | 'On the Present Stage of the English Language' |
| 1852 | 'Sir William Hamilton, with a Glance at his Logical Reforms' |
| 1853 | 'How to Write English' |
| 1850 | Wordsworth dies |
|  | American edition of De Quincey's collected works |
| 1853 | British edition of De Quincey's collected works; De Quincey begins reworking several of his writings |
| 1859 | De Quincey dies in Edinburgh |
| 1860 | Baudelaire, *Les Paradis Artificiels* |
| 1923 | Benjamin, 'Die Aufgabe des Übersetzers' |
| 1983 | De Man, '"Conclusions" on Walter Benjamin's "The Task of the Translator"' |
| 1995 | Berman, *Pour une critique des traductions: John Donne* |
| 1996 | Iser, 'The Emergence of a Cross-Cultural Discourse' |

# Abbreviations

Unless otherwise indicated, all references are to works by De Quincey, more specifically the most recent critical edition of his *Collected Works* (Pickering & Chatto, 2000–3). Notes indicate volumes and page numbers in this edition. Particularly frequent references are abbreviated as follows.

| | |
|---|---|
| AB | 'Autobiography of an English Opium-Eater' |
| BL | Coleridge, *Biographia Literaria* |
| C 1821 | 'Confessions of an English Opium-Eater', 1821 version |
| C 1822 | Appendix to 'Confessions' |
| C 1856 | 'Confessions of an English Opium-Eater', 1856 version |
| D | *Diary* |
| EMC | 'The English Mail-Coach, or the Glory of Motion' |
| ER | 'Elements of Rhetoric' |
| HWE | 'How to Write English' |
| KME | 'Kant in his Miscellaneous Essays' |
| LD | 'The Last Days of Immanuel Kant' |
| LJ | Wasianski, *Die letzte Jahre Immanuel Kants* |
| LYM | 'Letters to a Young Man Whose Education has been Neglected' |
| M | 'Wilhelm Meister' |
| R | 'Jean Paul Frederick Richter' |
| S | 'Style' Nos. I through IV |
| SdP | 'Suspiria de Profundis' |
| SGG | *Selections Grave and Gay* |
| SEL | 'On the Present Stage of the English Language' |
| TEL | 'The English Language' |
| W | *Walladmor* |
| WA | Alexis, *Walladmor* |
| WH | 'Sir William Hamilton, with a Glance at His Logical Reforms' |
| WL | 'Walladmor: Sir Walter Scott's German Novel' |

# Introduction: Dark Interpreter

### The Story of a Translator

This is the story [*une fiction*] of an individual [...] who would abolish in himself the boundaries, the classes, the exclusions, not by syncretism, but by the simple act of discarding of that old spectre: *logical contradiction*; who would mix all languages, no matter if they were reputed to be incompatible; who would mutely bear every accusation of illogicality, of infidelity [...] This man would be the reject of our society: tribunals, the school, the asylum; conversation would make him into a stranger: who endures contradiction without shame? Now this antihero exists. Thus the Biblical myth is reversed/returns [*se retourne*], the confusion of tongues is no longer a punishment, the subject gains access to bliss by a cohabitation of languages, *which work side by side*: the text that gives pleasure is a joyous Babel.[1]

A strange void sits at the core, or somewhere near the core, of Tilottama Rajan's seminal study *Dark Interpreter: The Discourse of Romanticism*, published in 1980 – a void which this book contends is representative of a broader neglect in Romantic studies, and which it hopes to dispel by asserting the pivotal importance of translation and De Quincey's unique qualifications to begin clarifying the centrality of translation to Romantic thought. For her title, Rajan adverts to a figure that originates in the work of a lesser personality amongst the British Romantics. Having thus highlighted the metaphor and its creator, however, she barely discusses either. The figure's inventor, Thomas De Quincey, features at most interstitially, as an occasional aside to the discussion of the larger presences that surround him. As a gloss on her arresting title, Rajan offers an excerpt from the 'Suspiria de Profundis', De Quincey's sequel to his 'Confessions of an English Opium-Eater', perhaps his most famous (and certainly his most infamous) publication. The 'Suspiria' is composed of rhapsodic reflections on various themes and topics, including a longish section on a class of spectral apparitions which De Quincey dubs 'dark interpreters'.² Fittingly, this illuminating extract does not actually feature in the essay as it was published by De Quincey in 1845. Instead, Rajan chooses her excerpt from lines stricken from the text as it was initially printed, perhaps because their author or publisher considered them too lurid for publication, prompted as they are by a brutal murder that 'leaves the room [. . .] floating in blood'.³ The dark interpreter as De Quincey originally described him is now only to be found in the annotative apparatus of scholarly editions.

De Quincey lends Rajan's monograph its title even as the latter largely remains blind to the orientation that it might receive from him. The reader is plainly meant to deduce that the monograph's titular image is a figure for the antinomian constitution of Romantic writing that Rajan lays bare: its compulsion, that is, incessantly to assert and unmake its ambitions as it confronts new realities. De Quincey's interpreter, however, is a design both sprawling and profound, a multitudinous thing constructed out of multiple antitheses and parallelisms. In addition to allegorising the ironical play between mimesis and antimimesis that Rajan argues characterises all Romantic discourse, it also functions to allegorise De Quincey's attempt to understand the writing he practises: a form that partakes of a wide range of genres, and positions itself at the unstable intersection of various discourses, including the philosophical essay, the review, the Gothic novel, the prose poem, and the auto/biography. The dark interpreter and similarly constituted personages are difficult to parse because they allegorise a writerly programme intent on reinventing writing by incorporating a multitude of voices and styles. The interpreter darkly highlights a blind spot in Romantic writing and Romanticist criticism – that only those texts may be said to speak, and to open themselves to critical engagement, that can be ascribed to a singular creative voice. This book pursues De Quincey's figures and practices of interpretation in order to complicate this understanding of Romantic writing. Ultimately, it aims to persuade readers of De Quincey of his extraordinary investment in translation. More broadly, it also seeks to persuade literary critics of the value in attending more closely to peripheral modes like translation, and to persuade scholars of translation to nuance their current tendency to overprivilege contextual factors by studying the translated text on its own terms: that is to say, as a cultural phenomenon that is pulled towards asserting its autonomy and self-sufficiency even as it remains conscious of its inherent derivativeness.

De Quincey explores the literary potential of writing from the perspective of an interpreter in three related senses. First, he interprets the past in order to write the autobiographies and biographies which continue to be central to his critical reputation. Second, he interprets others' texts in order to produce the critical reviews and essays which lay the foundation for his contemporary notoriety and his enduring importance to Romanticists. And third, he interprets texts in foreign languages, rendering them into English, and thereby gradually establishing a theory of translation which ultimately grows to encompass his entire philosophy of writing. De Quincey's achievements in the former two senses of interpretation have been comprehensively covered by Romanticist scholarship. Barring a few luminous exceptions, among them Frederick Burwick's work, the third is almost wholly absent from De Quincey studies, to say nothing of Romantic studies. The near-absence of De Quincey's dark interpretion of Romanticism in Rajan's book and the body of scholarship that it may be seen to represent finally resolves itself to the following question: what position does translation occupy in Romantic literature and culture? It is this question – what does translation *do* in (for, to, with, through) Romantic thought and writing? – that this book addresses by attending to De Quincey's considerable but understudied output of works touching on matters of translation.

Translation pervades Romantic-period culture, both as a pragmatic means of organising interlinguistic imports of useful forms and insights and as an imaginative structure through which writers map their positions on the national and international plane. British Romanticism, in particular, often frames itself, and has accordingly often been framed, as a highly self-conscious import from Germany that is thence exported to other nations. Translation is one of the central constituents, this book would argue, of what it means to write, think, and act romantically – and what it means to profess to its scholarly study. And yet translation largely tends to toil underground in Romantic studies: the 'invisibility of the translator' that was rather rashly diagnosed by Lawrence Venuti as a phenomenon born of Romantic prejudices continues to disproportionately affect Romantic studies, especially in the Anglosphere.[4] The cosmopolitan, even proto-globalist character of the period that coined the concept of world literature has now been so thoroughly described and assessed that it amounts to a critical given. Work on European Romanticism has long been joined by transatlantic studies, and has recently seen a further expansion to global and planetary perspectives. It is now far more difficult to imagine, however, the publication of a book like René Wellek's 1931 *Immanuel Kant in England*, which exactingly traces the measurable influence of a single author, the eponymous German philosopher, through a critical inventory of translators and translations. A recent, otherwise illuminating book like Evan Gottlieb's *Romantic Globalism* notably never once takes up issues of translation.[5] This neglect of translation is not entirely a matter of shifting paradigms and methods. Along with several other fields, within and without literary and cultural studies, Romanticist scholarship largely operates to a working hypothesis akin to a metempsychotic perfusion of ideas in Hegelian fashion, enthusiastically drawing leylines of influence while evading an examination of how such theorised networks of *Geist* might operate on a mechanical level. It is generally considered sufficient to read Schelling in conjunction with Coleridge, in other terms, and to leave as incidental the trajectories of this presumptive influence. The frame that Rajan constructs for her own revelatory analysis is exemplary in this regard. In a three-part gesture that continues to inform Romantic studies to the present day, especially in the theoretically inclined byways of the field, she establishes a critical triad, reciprocally reading British writers and German thinkers through the common language of French theory. Translation – literally, the act of carrying across – hardly features as an explicit concern, yet the critic's own activity is eminently translatorial, imagining itself either to operate through a third term that mediates between German and English, or to cultivate a double vision through which one language may be made to reveal another. The lack of attention for translation as such is all the more striking in that translation might afford an impetus to push forward the unfinished project of Romanticism as it is rearticulated by theory. If a necessary part of this rearticulation involves (as Rajan suggests in a retrospective on her work published in 2012) an exploration of those Romantics who are, like the theorists that have followed in their footsteps, 'in search of a genre', and if this requires situating criticism on what is described as 'the threshold of an age of prose, not wanting to give up on the spirit of poetry yet not quite knowing how to carry it forward', a useful frame may well be found in the underexamined site of literary knowing called translation.[6] Much as translation describes a process between languages that does not itself acquire the status of a separable idiom, translation is not a genre, but something near it; a 'mode', as Walter Benjamin puts it,[7] readily transforming itself into whatever form the occasion requires – not quite a theory, moreover, in that it remains tied to practical implementation, but something near it.

The site of literary knowing under investigation in the present book is traversed by translators and theorists of translation. Thomas De Quincey, the book's case study (occasionally accompanied by other writers caught between translatorship and authorship), occupies a zone intersected by French, German and British Romanticism. The previous paragraphs have sketched out this book's theoretical argument, a fuller articulation of which is reserved for the coda (the analysis as such leaves such deliberations largely implicit). Other motives also inform the present study, not least the development of a perspective on De Quincey's persona and oeuvre that has yet to receive its full due. De Quincey's life as handed down to us through his writing, this book contends, is suffused by translation and is designed to be read as such, much more so than has been acknowledged even amid numerous critical passes at his work – biographic, psychoanalytic, deconstructive, postcolonial, rhetorical. Translation extends its influence even into works that address topics seemingly remote from matters of language and communication. De Quincey, this monograph hopes to show, devotes his entire career to developing translation into a master figure for Romanticism. Or, as he might have argued, had he been a better critic of his own writings, translation was always already central to (post-)Romantic endeavours, to its writing, thinking and acting: De Quincey merely uncovers its centrality. In translation, he detects a principle that allows him to recuperate his acute sense of belatedness, of inferiority and minority, into a paradoxically creative and original stance that grants literary writing a practical resolution to the theoretical quandaries that beset the poetics, aesthetics and philosophies through which Romantic writers and thinkers, and post-Romantic authors after them, frame their authority. In short, in ceding the prerogatives of authorship and adopting the humbler garb of the translator, De Quincey discerns a principle that allows him to translate, and thereby to overcome, the quandaries of theory into a textual practice.

'I shall be charged with mysticism, Behmenism, quietism, &c. but *that* shall not alarm me', De Quincey proclaims in his 'Confessions', predicting the kaleidoscope of readings that have been brought to bear on his oeuvre.[8] Perhaps to the alarm of some readers, this book adds another. In rereading De Quincey through the filter of translation, it stages an intervention in Romantic and translation studies as these fields are presently constituted. Addressing the former, it hopes to demonstrate that translation is far more than the necessary but unexciting auxiliary to the cross-border communication that shaped national and local Romanticisms. This book suggests that translation generates ideas fundamental to Romantic writing and its legacies: in translation's logic of interlinguistic exchange, writers locate a practice through which they may appreciate and redefine the stakes and mechanisms of their writing and thinking, which may be roughly summarised as a structure of interlinguistic, intercultural and inter-discursive negotiation. This book, in short, addresses the 'relationship between aesthetics, rhetoric, and translation' which Tom Toremans has noted stands in urgent 'need of closer investigation'.[9]

A keener appreciation of the practical and figural functions of translation is a particularly pressing concern amid the surge of critical interest in cosmopolitanism and its links to networks and practices of communication, in which one of the key questions of cosmopolitanism – the question of linguistic difference – has remained underdeveloped. This book joins David Simpson in 'arguing for the potential of translation as a focus concept' that might overcome the unspoken linguistic 'limits of cosmopolitanism'.[10] In recent years, answers to such under-resolved questions have begun to arrive from various quarters. Diego Saglia's energising *European Literatures in Britain 1815–1832: Romantic Translations*, which cites De Quincey's essay on Jean Paul by way of overture (see this book's Chapter 2), suggests translation is poised for a restoration to its proper position, even if Saglia cannot help commenting on his 'slightly unorthodox remit' in conducting a survey of Romantic translation in a British context.[11] Like Saglia's study, the present book aims to consider translation in its own right, as a form of writing whose purely practical purposes invite close consideration of what it means to write English in an international community of nations and languages – and, ultimately, what it means to write at all. However, its focus is less on the political and historical dimensions of a national-through-transnational imaginary (as in Saglia) than it is on questions of authorship, language, philosophy and aesthetics. It asks, then: What *style* is imparted to the text once it has recognised the vitalising impact of translation? Does the translational text adopt a distinct mode, as Benjamin has it, and how is the reader to parse that mode? This study also takes a cue from Kristina Mendicino's *Prophecies of Language* in analysing translation as a mode, structure and figure deserving of a thoroughgoing, theoretically grounded engagement. Like Mendicino, the present monograph implicitly adopts a deconstructive or post-structuralist perspective, albeit judiciously admixed with critical theory and phenomenology. Finally, in offering an analysis focused on a single author (and translator), this book makes a point similar to Paul Hamilton's *Coleridge and German Philosophy*: that is, that an author's translatorial output deserves to be critically considered on the same footing as the more evidently creative work. As Hamilton does for Coleridge, the following chapters focus on De Quincey's negotiation of German idealism for the benefit of a British audience. De Quincey's preference for a broad portfolio and speed of publication over profundity and thoroughness, however, has enforced consideration of a more extensive range of topics.

To translation studies, the present work hopes to demonstrate the import of a Romanticist perspective. If a book like Wellek's is now scarcely imaginable in Romantic studies, the situation is even more dire in translation studies. Treatises like Antoine Berman's 1984 *The Experience of the Foreign*, which carefully traces modern conceptions of translation and foreignness to a handful of mostly German nineteenth-century translators and theorists of translation, have become vanishingly rare. While influenced by the insights of recent scholarship on translation, this book also strikes a path akin to Berman's: a path that runs athwart the two main traditions of literary translation studies – one defunct even at the time of Berman's writing; one going strong even now – polemically outlined by Berman in his unfinished *Toward a Translation Criticism*, posthumously published in 1995.[12] This work, then, does not seek to conduct a reactionary study in contrasts: its aim is not to orchestrate a series of face-offs between originals and their translations so as to evaluate the latter.[13] When such exercises are not performed in order to demonstrate the irreplicable genius of the original, as Shelley does in his *Defence of Poetry*, they may hold considerable pedagogic value. This book, however, does not seek to police the standards of taste, although several of the nineteenth-century writers it considers would have constrained the criticism of translation, if not all criticism, to this function. Other than research focused on education, almost no scholarship on translation now follows this model. However, this book also differs from the dominant model in investigations of historical practices of translation in that it is not a study in the descriptive sociocultural mould, championed by Gideon Toury and Itamar Even-Zohar in partial imitation of Pierre Bourdieu, which continues to shape a preponderance of ongoing translational research. While this sociological model of translation boasts as distinct advantages over its subjective, largely ad hoc and source-oriented predecessor a more even-handed and theoretically reflective method of enquiry, it tends to a purely external description of translation in which literature finds itself reduced to one form of exchange among many, and in which the key function of criticism, the deliberative reading of texts, is wholly neglected – in which, in short, the text is eclipsed by a context which is endowed with determinative agency. In its quest for 'translation norms',[14] for a set of principles that encode the deviations of the translated texts, and in its explanatory recourse to the cultural, social and especially ideological pressures that act on the depersonalised translator, this approach finds it difficult to conceive of translation as a literary mode, instinct with a capacity to redouble on itself and thereby gain a measure of autonomy. So strictly does the sociology of translation insist on reading its objects in terms of power relations that it loses track of the textual artefact; so vocally does it separate itself from a (small-r) romantic attachment to questions of aesthetics and individuality that key questions fall outside its ambit, chiefly relating to the writer's aesthetic and poetic ambitions.

In complement to these two perspectives, a third can be asserted, which combines the accomplishments and insights of literary criticism and translation studies into a mutually enriching perspective. What emerges from this cold fusion is a literary criticism adapted for translated literature, as well as a form of translation studies equipped to tackle questions of poetics, aesthetics and stylistics. This monograph advocates, in short, a method for the analysis of translation that is itself in interdisciplinary translation. It is likely that these two approaches will never fully meld: their premises sit at right angles, with the one positing the text as endowed with an inalienable autonomy, and the other reading it chiefly as an instrument of communication, to be read in terms of its origination, purpose and context. It is, however, precisely through this struggle between production and reproduction, autonomy and derivation, centrality and peripherality, that translations and translators define themselves. For Berman, the conciliation of literary criticism and translation studies is made possible by attending to the figure of the translator – the writer, never quite an author, whose existence is premised on achieving an uneasy balance between languages. In contrast to both translation studies and literary criticism, both of which typically find it difficult to ponder the connections between writers as biographical beings, textual functions, and instances of production, Berman urges close attention to the figure of the interpreter. *Cherchez le traducteur*: read the translator for their 'Idea' of translation, Berman urges, capitalising that term to signal its Platonic charge, and invoking an ambition not far removed from the Prague-School interest in literariness that gave rise to modern literary studies. Read the translation, that is, for the translator – and read the translator for the overarching concept of translation to which his acts of translation collectively aspire, with the aim of imparting to his oeuvre-in-translation, and even to his writings not apparently in translation, the coherency of a project.[15] To the extent that the present work quixotically strives to locate De Quincey, it elaborates on Berman's prolegomena to a criticism of translation. While for his own test case, Berman focuses on a series of interpreters engaged in adapting John Donne for a French-speaking readership, this book focuses on a single translator. In thus narrowing its scope, this book hopes to offer an account of translation and translatorship that is more sustained than Berman's; more intent, moreover, on tracking how the translator situates their work athwart the dichotomies through which literature ordinarily positions itself, and on noting those instances in which the translator symbolises his practice of translation.

This book also seeks to ponder Romantic ideologies of translation in their various flavours, and thereby to apply a vital corrective to Berman. If the latter has a fault, albeit one shared with numerous scholars of translation, it is his uncritical affiliation with those Romantic writers eager to revalue the cultural stakes of translation. Hearkening to the theories of Hölderlin, Humboldt, Schelling, and others, who idealise translation as the saviour of Western or German culture, Berman is so eager to reverse decades of neglect, so earnestly engaged in uplifting unfairly maligned translators, that a careful analysis of this hyper-positive discourse is sidelined. Just as the tradition of dismissing translators as fundamentally treacherous, shifty, or at any rate merely peripheral merits careful critique, so does its counterpart. The Romantic translator, this book will demonstrate, constructs for himself an identity just as much as the authors of the primary material that he translates – this identity, however, has an altogether different inflection, in that it is forever troubled by its inherent secondariness. In writing on a Romantic like De Quincey, steeped in prejudices that trouble his attempts to claim authority and reputation through translation, this book cultivates a revelatory distance with respect to its subject's gestures and performances. In contrast to Berman, it aims at producing less a *criticism* of translation than a *critical theory* of translation. That is, it seeks to facilitate a reciprocal exchange between literary criticism and translation studies that takes its interpretative energy from, and ultimately propels itself towards, a descriptive perspective anchored in a scrupulously theoretical stance. It does so by reading De Quincey as a translator – by reading his work in and on translation, and by reading across his entire oeuvre in light of his output as a translator and a theorist of translation. Moreover, in reading De Quincey through a translational lens, the present work provides an outline for a critical theory of translation as the latter manifests in British Romanticism and beyond.

This introduction does not pretend to be a theoretical preface in full possession of all references and implications. Nor will the book's coda spell out a general theory in a list of numbered postulates. Translations, like the translators that produce them, are things that must *act* – that must perform themselves. The same applies to a critical theory of translation. What follows is a four-part series of acts, each building on the ones previous to it, and each demonstrating the transformative impact of De Quincey's poetics of translation on his navigation of the discourses of Romanticism.

## A Quadrangle of Interpreters

Tacitly shaped throughout by the critical-theoretical perspective outlined in the previous section and further explicated in this book's coda, the following pages conduct a four-movement exploration of De Quincey's work in and on translation. De Quincey's writings will be shown to resonate to an amphibolic logic such as can only be attained in and through translation. Translation, that is, provides De Quincey with a set of structures through which he endeavours to resolve a number of quandaries at once foundational and disruptive to his sense of himself as a writer and thinker. These dilemmas are chiefly related to issues of identity, stylistics, philosophy and economics. Each of these four touchstones provides a focus for one of the following chapters, which trace De Quincey's efforts to overcome the problems vexing these discourses by applying the structures of translation to them. Through a series of analogising and allegorising gestures, De Quincey projects onto a range of issues the paradox that energises and bedevils the concept and practice of translation – that is, the irresolvable chasm that yawns between creation and imitation. This is a two-part process that involves, first, the dichotomisation of a particular discourse or discipline and, second, the reconfiguration of the resulting dichotomies into chiastic patterns of exchange. The first chapter establishes this basic structure by charting De Quincey's navigation of the distinctions between translatorship and authorship. Applying and extending the insights acquired from this first reading, the second chapter attends to the chiastic pseudo-philology De Quincey designs in response to the rifts between native and foreign systems of language. Chapter 3 ponders his proposals for a hyperactive philosophy that might satisfactorily remedy the Kantian separation of experience into the noumenal and the phenomenal by attending to the disjunction he institutes between meaningful and material aspects of expression. Chapter 4 revisits the distinction between author and translator in order to examine De Quincey's take on the antagonism between aesthetics and economics. Finally, by way of envoi, the coda to this stacked series of cases proposes a path towards a more fully fledged critical theory of translation.

In the best version of a project along the lines the present monograph has set itself, a forbiddingly wide range of Romantic and post-Romantic authors would be studied in detail, all making their distinct contributions. Even a book that chooses to limit its scope to the extraordinary role played by translation in British Romanticism alone would have to examine a kaleidoscopic collection of writers, most notable amongst them James Macpherson, Charlotte Smith, Samuel Taylor Coleridge, Thomas Carlyle, Percy Bysshe Shelley and Henry Crabb Robinson. Just about every Romantic writer translated, and often translated with abandon, in a fantastic variety of ways. Of course, a reconstruction of Romantic translation on such a kaleidoscopic scale would be an interminable undertaking. The present monograph limits itself to Thomas De Quincey, who takes pride of place as a representative exponent of the much broader Romantic-era effort to examine and revaluate translation. At appropriate junctures, relevant contemporary voices will be introduced to assist in the elucidation of De Quincey's methods. Given De Quincey's pivotal role in the development of British Romanticism and his much-advertised interest in German letters, the writers that will be especially prominent in the construction of a context to De Quincey's exploits are Coleridge, Carlyle, Hölderlin, Kant, Schiller and Jean Paul.

The first chapter stages a series of close readings of De Quincey's early work and its structural characteristics, sourcing these to a project to design himself as a minor creature belatedly arriving to Romanticism long after its creative options have been exhausted. For his own authorship, De Quincey resolves to stay a median course, paradoxically grounding his claims to authorship in an unparalleled capacity to imitate, rather than create, if to imitate a great range of voices and styles, switching between these as occasion or fancy demands. It is this propensity for a constant reconfiguration of personality that De Quincey expands into a stylistic principle under the header of impassioned prose, a style he credits with the potential to achieve the impossible feat of commingling prose and poetry into a third mode of writing. This impassioned prose is revealed to revolve around problems of language that find their resolution in practices of translation. In short, De Quincey's early career may be read as an increasingly urgent exploration of translation, both as a poetical principle and as a means to gain a foothold in British Romanticism. Translation emerges as the organising term in the author's self-performance, explaining much of De Quincey's jockeying for supremacy with Coleridge and Carlyle. If he singles out these two, it is because they most closely approximate him in proposing translation as a practical mode of access to the fabled *tertium aliquid* – a structure, that is, through which to overcome the aporetic oppositions that incapacitate modern writing and thinking.

Chapter 2 ponders the stylistic and linguistic implications of De Quincey's poetical architectonics, expanding the first chapter's notes on impassioned prose. This chapter examines De Quincey's career-spanning endeavour to reconstruct English into a truly national language and style, a project which requires that the national idiom be maintained in a constant state of translation. Prompted by a vague sense of civilisational exhaustion, and building on Enlightenment theories regarding the origins and evolution of language, De Quincey designs a pseudo-comparative model of the English language in which the latter is charged with functioning as the fulcrum in a chiastic system of interlinguistic comparison and cultural transfer. Much as the interpreter occupies a central position in the conversion of source into target, English is to be repositioned as a universal medium of translation that assumes centre stage in the traffic between other languages and their respective styles. Among the modern languages, the two privileged idioms in this scheme of perpetual translation are French and German, with the latter receiving particular emphasis due to the extraordinary vitality of its literature and philosophy. Arguing that languages and nations evince a natural teleology, De Quincey claims that it is the destiny of English to translate itself into a mediatory position. Much like Rome in the ancient world, which appropriated the best aspects of other languages and cultures, the British nation is certain to bestow upon itself a new lease of life in premising itself on translation. Moreover, in arrogating to itself traits of every language, it will render itself so flexible as to transform into the lingua franca of choice, assuming global predominance in cultural and political matters. In thus yoking together style, language, identity and politics, translation grounds a novel aesthetic ideology of Britishness and Empire.

The next chapter tracks De Quincey's propulsion of translation to an additional level of complexity. Spurred by his contempt for transcendental thought, De Quincey locates in translation a set of structures that contain a mode of thinking and being that offers a potent rejoinder to Kantian philosophy. While he initially welcomes Kant's division of experience and expression into a meaningful or spiritual language and a material or sensuous realm, he soon signals significant reservations regarding the German philosopher's tacit prioritisation of the former over the latter. Through mischievous translations of texts on and by Kant and a series of critical essays, De Quincey undercuts the philosopher, demonstrating the absurdities of his tenets if left underdeveloped. As an alternative, De Quincey offers an idealism premised on the constant vacillation enshrined in his chiastic theory of translation: an architecture founded on incessant code-switching, at whose centre the unattainable ideal of a fully synthetic translation may fleetingly be gleaned.

The fourth and final chapter provides a detailed account of De Quincey's most intrepid and most entertaining foray into translation, his work on the German *Walladmor*, a pseudo-translation of Scott by the German author Willibald Alexis. Alexis's text ignites a furious critical debate amongst various stakeholders that bring to the fore the vexing questions circling around the fraught status of translated literature. Sensing the opportunities such confusion affords, De Quincey commences a protracted engagement with the text, culminating in a parodic translation of Alexis's pseudo-translation that envisages an infinity of further reciprocal acts of translation. It is out of this hypothesised construct that the ideal emerges towards which De Quincey's oeuvre in and on translation labours: the ultimate translation attains to a purity and autonomy that allows it to shed any need for a primordial original. In the final analysis, translation emerges as a mode of thinking and writing that achieves a dignity and force all its own, instinct with a poetics and aesthetics to which it alone can lay claim.

Finally, the book closes with a coda which proffers an outline for a critical theory of translation that may aid in future studies of Romantic and post-Romantic translators. Reweaving the strands of this book's four-part analysis, this concluding section abstracts from the observations on De Quincey's translatorial oeuvre a basic theory through which to document writers' literary, stylistic, political and philosophical ambitions in reading their writing through the structures of translation.

## Notes

1. Roland Barthes, *Le plaisir du texte* (Paris: Seuil, 1973), 9–10. Translation mine.
2. Tilottama Rajan, *Dark Interpreter: The Discourse of Romanticism* (Ithaca: Cornell University Press, 1980), 198; 5.
3. Thomas De Quincey, *The Posthumous Works of Thomas De Quincey: Edited from the Original Mss., with Introductions and Notes*, ed. Alexander H. Japp (London: William Heinemann, 1891), 1.13.
4. See Lawrence Venuti, *The Translator's Invisibility: A History of Translation*, 2nd edn (London: Routledge, 2008).
5. Evan Gottlieb, *Romantic Globalism: British Literature and Modern World Order, 1750–1830* (Columbus: Ohio State University Press, 2014).
6. Tilottama Rajan, 'Romanticism and the Unfinished Project of Deconstruction', *European Romantic Review* 23, no. 3 (2013): 297.
7. Walter Benjamin, 'Task', 70.
8. C 1821, 2.203.
9. Tom Toremans, '*Sartor Resartus* and the Rhetoric of Translation', *Translation and Literature* 20 (2011): 61–2.
10. David Simpson, 'The Limits of Cosmopolitanism and the Case for Translation', *European Romantic Review* 16, no. 2 (2005): 151.
11. Diego Saglia, *European Literatures in Britain, 1815–1832: Romantic Translations* (Cambridge: Cambridge University Press, 2019), xvi.
12. Antoine Berman, *Toward a Translation Criticism: John Donne*, trans. and ed. Françoise Massardier-Kennedy (Kent, OH: Kent State University Press, 2009), 4–5; 36–48.
13. Henri Meschonnic, 'Propositions pour une poétique de la traduction', *Langages* 7, no. 28 (1972): 49–54.
14. Gideon Toury, *In Search of a Theory of Translation* (Tel Aviv: Porter Institute for Poetics and Semitics of Tel Aviv University, 1980), 141.
15. Berman, *Toward a Translation Criticism*, 46.

## Chapter 1

# [I] Wrote This:
# Authorship, Translatorship

### Being Lesser

'TOO LATE.' When Thomas De Quincey writes his essay on 'The English Mail-Coach', a rhapsodic meditation on the boons and pitfalls of modern media, he has the eponymous postal carriage heave into the narrative 'sculptured with the hours, and with the dreadful legend TOO LATE'. De Quincey confronts the 'dreadful knell of these words' throughout his career, constantly seeking to reclaim his sense of belatedness as a positive foundation for his authorship.[1] His autobiographical work accordingly centres on the declaration, allegedly at seven years old, that he is late even to his own life – '[l]ife is finished! Finished it is!'[2] In his essays, too, De Quincey devotes particular attention to his tardy arrival to the literary movement with which he most seeks to affiliate. Born in 1785, well behind the authors for whom he professes the greatest admiration, deferring the publication of his first major text until 1822, and dragging out his career into the late 1850s,[3] he is forever in pursuit of more luminous figures like Wordsworth, Coleridge, Southey and Scott; so much so that he has been claimed to straddle Romanticism and Victorianism.[4] De Quincey's position has been oxymoronically characterised as supremely subordinate, a 'flame in sunlight' forever to be outshone by larger personalities, against whose outsize profile he can barely cut a figure.[5] Yet even though he easily blurs into the background, his peripherality also affords a strange safeguard against oblivion: he continues to be a fixture of Romantic anthologies and surveys, not often considered in his own right, but considered nevertheless – 'secure but secondary', as Margaret Russett summarises his complicated canonical status. De Quincey, moreover, is keenly aware of the protections afforded by secondariness. His minority is as much imposed as it self-inflicted, as much the outcome of critical assessment as it is of his own calculated attempts at gaining a foothold in the Romantic movement. 'Critical discourse', as Russett remarks, 'reiterates the rhetorical structure of the minor text.'[6] The present chapter examines the ways in which De Quincey actively crafts an authorial profile premised on minority, as it is this performance of secondariness that lays the groundwork for his fascination with translation. As a form of writing that fluctuates between tacitly accepting its inherent derivativeness and subtly rebelling against its modest status, translation proves highly apposite to De Quincey's complicated relationship with British Romanticism.

If De Quincey's authorship proves so hazy, it is largely because he leans into his peripherality, openly dissembling his authority by filtering his voice through a variety of characters.[7] De Quincey, as Baudelaire observes in *Les Paradis Artificiels*, a freewheeling translation of the 'Confessions' and the 'Suspiria' designed to frenchify the opium-eater into a decadent *poète maudit*, is an early example of the *flâneur*.[8] In the 'Confessions', the work that most puts him on the literary map, De Quincey comes forward as 'a sombre and solitary walker', Baudelaire observes; portraying himself ever to be 'bobbing along amongst on the surf of the crowds [*le flot mouvant des multitudes*]', haphazardly chancing on incidents that develop without any active participation on his part.[9] Styling himself 'of necessity a peripatetic, or a walker of the streets', 'a Catholic creature [. . .] standing in equal relation to high and low', De Quincey recollects that he 'would wander forth, without much regarding the direction or the distance, to all the markets and the parts of London to which the poor resort',[10] dipping in and out of the lives of others. His empathy initially appears almost absolute: '[I]f wages were a little higher or expected to be so, or the quartern loaf a little lower, or it was reported that onions and butter were expected to fall, I was glad.'[11] Whereas Baudelaire emphasises the positive aspects of *flânerie*, describing the practice of 'being both himself and other people, at will' as a restorative 'bath in the crowds [*un bain de multitude*]', to De Quincey, being possessed of a talent for expansive sympathy is an ambivalent thing. Baudelaire only hints at negative aspects when he touches on the resemblance of the *flâneur* to 'those lost souls which wander in search of a body'.[12] De Quincey, by contrast, observing himself in the third person, finds that the 'crowds become an oppression to him'.[13] Like Keats, another Romantic who writes of his fears that 'the identity of every one in the room begins so press upon me that I am in a very little time annihilated',[14] to De Quincey, the many always press too close, transforming from objects of attraction into a negatively sublime ocean 'paved with innumerable faces upturned to the heavens – faces imploring, wrathful, despairing, surging upwards by thousands, by myriads, by generations, by centuries'.[15] Nearing suffocation, the opium-eater is compelled to move on, to new objects of study. '[H]e was', as Virginia Woolf observes, 'incapable of a sustained [. . .] interest in the affairs of other people', delighting in crowds but only ever momentarily so; writing 'sympathetically, but at a distance [. . .] Nothing must come too close. [. . .] A mist must lie upon the human face.'[16] It is true that 'while there is no one quite like Thomas De Quincey, Thomas De Quincey was quite like everyone',[17] but it is only true when his many performances of ventriloquism are considered in isolation. De Quincey hides his own voice behind and between the incidents ostensibly at the focus of his narrative, dramatising the 'ineluctable becoming, rather than fixed Being' that structures his fraught sense of himself.[18]

De Quincey's serial urban encounters allegorise his meandering trajectory through the texts and authors that surround him: his procedure is often to channel his writing through other people's work. Despite his youthful fascination for Thomas Chatterton, his aim is not to participate in the contemporary vogue for literary counterfeiting. This practice, he writes in a note on Macpherson's Ossianic poems, is to be rejected with 'unqualified scorn [. . .] Heavens! what poverty: secondly, what monotony: thirdly, what falsehood of imagery!'[19] De Quincey refuses to disguise his texts as the creations of another writer, fictional or otherwise: while he dabbles in the games of identity employed by many Romantic texts, he only does so when his aliases reliably link back to him, or to one of the personae he seeks to establish.[20] His favourite nom de plume is the English Opium-Eater. His second option, the nondescript X. Y. Z. under which he publishes most of his translations, is similarly claimed as his by the 'Confessions'. '[I]n popular estimation', he writes, in a self-subverted show of mock-modesty, 'I am X. Y. Z. Esquire.'[21] A third, much rarer moniker, *Grasmeriensis Teutonizans*, the German student of Grasmere, adorns the translation most pivotal to his own conception of literature.[22] De Quincey's texts, in short, teeter between claiming authority and admitting the extent of their derivation. This double focus renders it exceedingly difficult to separate De Quincey's dispersed authorial presence from those writers he emulates, and many readers have accordingly suspected that '[n]othing ever happened to De Quincey that he had not read about first'.[23] Such misgivings have long clung to De Quincey: René Wellek notes a 'fundamental insincerity',[24] approvingly quoting the philosopher J. H. Stirling's assessment that De Quincey

> fell a martyr to the tone of the day – a tone that *sounded* only genius, genius, let me have flight, let us have the unexampled, the inconceivable, the unutterably original. To have the credit of being up in German metaphysicians, Latin schoolmen, Thaumaturgic Platonists, Religious mystics etc., this too lay

in the order of the day. But to be up in such things meant only to be able to read in them.[25]

Others have alleged plagiarism. Albert Goldman bluntly asserts that 'what De Quincey has done must be regarded as plagiarism of the most flagrant sort'.[26] If such accusations are not more common, it is because De Quincey pre-empts them, flagging sources with exaggerated care and charging other writers with having committed sins far more egregious than his own. More importantly, he also handles his sources creatively, generally prioritising the artful infusion of stylistic and philosophical principles over simply larding his texts with pilfered phrases and ideas. When De Quincey writes *of* Kant, he writes *like* Kant, in extraordinarily long sentences full of hyperfine metaphysical speculation. When he is commissioned to author a piece for *Blackwood's*, he substitutes metaphysical detachment for ultra-Tory thundering, the very picture of 'a disconsolate or uncompromising John Bull'.[27] When he writes for *Tait's*, he morphs into a passionate proponent of reform, applauding the Revolution and embracing Shelley as his 'brother Oxonian'.[28] 'A few days ago', De Quincey records at age seventeen, 'I became fully convinced that one leading trait in my mental character... is – *Facility of impression.*'[29]

While De Quincey's exercises in emulation initially appear playful, he only ever briefly keeps up each of his bouts of mimicry. Just as the 'tyranny of the human face'[30] besets his impressions of metropolitan multitudes, his bookish exploits leave him overwhelmed by an anxiety of influence carried to the highest pitch.[31] De Quincey repeatedly styles himself an inveterate reader, 'a boy so passionately fond of books' that he gathers an extensive library of rare volumes, 'the only article of property in which I am richer than my neighbours [...] about five thousand',[32] but he also offers much less enthusiastic reflections on the burdens of reading to sublime excess. Recalling his subscription to an encyclopaedia of maritime history projected to run for a high number of volumes, he imagines their delivery through the language of negative infinity previously deployed to describe the thronging London masses, capturing his growing distress through a homology of indebtedness, debt, and guilt – a triple *Schuld*:

> Very soon I had run ahead of my allowance, and was about three guineas in debt. There I paused; for deep anxiety now began to oppress me as to the course in which this mysterious (and indeed guilty) current of debt would finally flow. [...] Amongst the books which I had bought [...] was a general history of navigation, supported by a vast body of voyages. [...] Now, when I considered with myself what a huge thing the sea was, and that so many thousands of captains, commodores, admirals, were eternally running up and down it [...] I began to fear that such a work tended to infinity. [...] Then

rose up before me this great opera-house 'scena' of the delivery. There would be a ring at the door. A waggoner in the front, with a bland voice, would ask for, 'a young gentleman who had given an order to their house.' Looking out, I should perceive a procession of carts and wagons [. . .] Men would not know my guilt merely, they would see it.[33]

De Quincey's autobiographical texts present an author hounded by crowds, creditors and competitors; all elements that serve as indices of a darkly enjoyable but deeply dangerous dependency on forces beyond himself. Inverting his apparent inability to honour the Romantic imperative of radical originality into the basis for a literary persona, De Quincey enters his texts as an artist who surrenders his entire being to the pursuit of art, in that his considerable need for aesthetic aids – chief among them his books and his opium – always threatens to drown out his own voice; always threatens to outpace his physical tolerance and his capacity to secure adequate funds. De Quincey may constantly be seen to count his dwindling monies, often 'endur[ing] the extremity of personal privation [. . .] no stockings, no shoes, no neck-handkerchief, no coast, waist-coat, or hat [. . .] constantly barefoot' in order to afford some vital book or an inspirational vial of laudanum.[34] All too often, his destitution is too real, but in performing it so publicly, he invites contemporaries to read his financial and social marginality as an extension of his literary peripherality.

The first traces of De Quincey's ambivalent relationship with books and texts emerge in the journal that he keeps at age seventeen, from mid-April to 24 June 1803. While the diary is generally read as a private record, a status which it partly derives from its remaining unpublished until 1927, it sits midway between a personal and public document, and is best understood as a dress rehearsal for his future career. The diary starts off as a meditation on the benefits of bodily discipline, in which De Quincey oscillates between the first and third person, then morphs into a book of drafted letters, and finally assumes the form a fairly conventional, fully first-person journal, albeit one that chiefly revolves around meticulous notes on the various works read by the diarist. De Quincey is especially attracted to Southey. A reading session of the latter's 1801 *Thalaba*, for instance, invites a careful consideration of a handful of lines culled from the text, practised passages of epic poetry, a plan for an 'Arabian drama', and imitative reflections on the poet's style.[35] This early interest in Southey, ahead of the authors with whom De Quincey associates a few years later, may be explained in part by his fascination for a man regarded as an 'unabashed textual pirate'[36] or 'counterfeit poet',[37] notorious amongst his peers for his borrowings from the *Lyrical Ballads*. Moreover, in importing references to another author, and in so visibly integrating this author's style into his own text, De Quincey begins to graft a poetics of creation on a rhetoric of imitation. In a continuation of the split between the first- and third-person perspectives the diary opens with, he signposts his sources even in his descriptions of apparently trivial events and ideas. Indeed, most of the experiences he logs in significant detail are both channelled through and occasioned by books. Such passages are typically presented as immediate, visceral reactions to a text, and generally proceed from a self-quotation which is subsequently retooled into a more carefully considered response. 'I just said – "My imagination feels, like Noah's dove, from the ark of my mind ... and finds no place on earth to rest the sole of her foot except Coleridge – Wordsworth and Southey."' Or, '[l]ast night in lecto b. [volume] 12 and 1, I said [. . .] "and this was the y$^e$ burden of his song"'. Even more explicit instances of self-referentiality will occasionally appear: 'took 4th volume of "*Acc. Sp.*" [*Accusing Spirit*, a Gothic novel by Mary Pilkington] – read 165 pages; – wrote this'.[38] In thus situating his experiences in a network of dependencies, De Quincey performatively downgrades his creative impact on his own compositions, and even on the incidents of his own life, to the status of annotation and imitation. His own voice is present, but it is constrained; reduced to that of a reader observing himself as he comments on other people's texts. There is an author here, but he requires critical recovery – in a word, '[I] wrote this.'[39] So indeterminate is the sense of self that De Quincey broadcasts that the very spelling of his name varies wildly even to the present day, with some opting for the lowercase *d* which he insisted upon for its aristocratic flavour; others resisting such airs by maintaining the capital *D*; and others still calling him Quincey.

Not for De Quincey, then, the self-evident authority on which are founded the works of his literary heroes. Even as he praises Herodotus, Milton and Jean Paul for their confident presence in their texts, the 'ear-piercing violence' of their voices, he studiously refrains from thus asserting himself. Acting on a pseudo-historiographic theory that great intellects group together in circles which tend to appear at wide historical intervals, he associates not with the latest such grouping of brilliant talents, '[t]he age commencing with Cowper' – that is, the Romantic 'volcanic eruption of the British genius [that] has displayed enormous power and splendour'. Instead, he affiliates with the troughs between the peaks. This role is figured through the somewhat undignified image of a dumb-bell, in which De Quincey grants himself the function of the connecting bar – seemingly supplementary to the two weights at either end, yet ultimately integral to the construction of the whole. Equating his role to that of a minor writer like Isocrates, whose only claim to noteworthiness is that he happens to straddle the two far greater ages of

Pericles and Alexander, he maps out his literary career as one meekly led in the long shadow of genius:

> [n]ow, reader, it is under this image of the dumb-bell we couch an allegory. Those globes at each end are the two systems or separate clusters of Greek Literature; and that cylinder which connects them is the long man that ran into each system, binding the two together. Who was that? It was Isocrates. Great we cannot call him in conscience; and, therefore, by way of compromise, we call him long [. . .] He narrowly escaped being a hundred years old; and, though that did not carry him from centre to centre, yet, as each system might be supposed to protend a radius each way of twenty years, he had, in fact, a full personal cognisance (and pretty equally) of the two systems, remote as they were, which composed the total world of Grecian Genius. [. . .] True, he never practised himself, for which lie had two reasons: 'My lungs,' he tells us himself, 'are weak'; and, secondly, 'I am naturally, as well as upon principle, a coward.' [. . .] But he, feeling himself wanted, laid his length down like a railroad exactly where he could be useful – with his positive pole towards Pericles, and his negative pole towards Alexander.[40]

'Great we cannot call him [. . .] we call him long': De Quincey is no more than a relay between other, greater writers, between past and future; ultimately, between styles and languages not fully his own. Here, in short, is a man who would be understood to be predestined by his very constitution to discipleship, not leadership; to recomposition rather than production – much less a man than a function; a structurally required connection. In one of his occasional bouts of delirium, Charles Lloyd, another lesser writer of the period, comments perceptively on this paradoxically demonstrative poetics of self-erasure, describing De Quincey as a 'nobody, a nonentity; you have no being. [. . .] you do not exist at all. It is merely appearance, and not reality.'[41] The following sections examine the ways in which De Quincey designs himself as an unreal presence by performing himself as a compound of multiple presences that betrays a measure of personality only in the capacity to switch between these presences. What follows is a somewhat familiar story, told from an unfamiliar angle – the narrative, that is, of De Quincey's interaction with Wordsworth and Coleridge: a complicated story of push and pull that is here read for its prefiguration of a programme of translation that inverts affects of secondariness into authority.

### Squaring the Wordsworth Circle

Of all the authors to whom De Quincey attaches himself, one stands out; so much so that the mere mention of his name merits a triple exclamation mark. When he assesses in his diary which writers are most important to him, De Quincey sorts twelve exceptional inspirations into a hierarchy culminating in the Lake Poets, among whom Wordsworth reigns supreme. The attainments of 'Edmund Spenser; William Shakespeare; John Milton' thus lead into the overwhelming brilliance of 'Robert Southey; S. T. Coleridge; William Wordsworth!!!'[42] It is through his precocious admiration for the latter that he shapes much of his authorial profile, framing his beginnings through his ceaseless quest for admittance into the Wordsworth circle,[43] and defining the later phase of his professional life through his Isocrates-like curation of its legacy.[44] A significant portion of the *Diary* is devoted to practised overtures through the medium of an introductory letter, first drafted on 13 May, anxiously redrafted on 30 May, and finally despatched the day after – all events sufficiently momentous to invite blow-by-blow entries ('Write – copy – seal – take to office'). The resulting letter reads as a set piece in Wordsworthian rhetoric: De Quincey tailors his message to the receiver, mimicking the style, phraseology and poetics that he has gleaned from the *Lyrical Ballads* and its 1800 preface. He portrays himself as a young disciple in need of fatherly counsel, 'some guide who might assist to develope & to tutor my new feelings'. He identifies as 'but a boy' in the 'Winander' mould, 'maintained from my infancy in the Love of Nature' – solitary in sensitivity; unpolished and unschooled yet remarkably attuned to the moral truths inherent in natural beauty. In an effort to drive home this plea for recognition, he grandiosely caps off his servile missive by swearing fealty:

> I have no other motive for soliciting your ~~friendship~~ notice than what (I should think) every man, who has read and felt the 'Lyrical Ballads,' must have in common with me. [. . .] I am but a boy and have therefore formed no connection which could draw you one step farther from the sweet retreats of poetry to the detested haunts of men [. . .] you will never find anyone more zealously attached to you [. . .] than he who now bends the knee before you. And I will add that, to no man on earth except yourself and one other (a friend of your's [Coleridge]), would I thus lowly and suppliantly prostrate myself.[45]

Crucially, De Quincey here introduces himself as a reader recently converted to the superiority of the Wordsworthian vision. '[F]rom some frequent meditation on some characters of our own, & some ancient story, & afterwards on some of the German drama, I began to model my conduct on theirs.' At length, however, he learned he must relinquish any 'hope of elevating my name in authority' such sources had spuriously instilled in him. He has discovered his vocation is not to be an author, but a reader, and specifically a reader of Wordsworth; always in search of the 'purer & more permanent pleasure' gleaned during 'my long & lonely rambles through many beautiful scenes' which best find their expression in the *Lyrical Ballads*.[46]

De Quincey's stage-managed overture proves well judged. While Wordsworth's poetics proceed from an egotistic impulse, from a withdrawn and self-reliant contemplation of nature, they simultaneously encompass a significant dependence on friends, family and disciples.[47] Wordsworth's self-stated 'wish' is 'to be considered as a Teacher, or as nothing',[48] or, as Coleridge remarks, to be 'living wholly among *Devotees*'.[49] 'Though solitary and self-isolated', as Stephen Parrish argues, 'he was rarely self-sufficient; both his literary taste and his self-confidence were nourished by drawing compulsively upon the energies and talents of other people.'[50] Wordsworth's reply to De Quincey, written shortly after he received the latter's missive on 27 July, strikes exactly the paternal tone invited by De Quincey's deferential attitude. While he cautiously notes that '[m]y friendship is not in my power to give', and warns against renouncing the 'proper influence of other writers', he stresses that he feels 'kindly disposed' towards his admirer. He even appends an extended postscript in which he invites his young aficionado to visit him at Dove Cottage, and gruffly apologises for any apparent 'coldness' in the preceding text, which he claims derives from his dislike of letter-writing.[51] This gracious response was enough to keep De Quincey awake all night 'from mere excess of pleasure through a long night in June 1803', and to spark an even more enthusiastic letter, in which the young Wordsworthian further tailors his communication to the limits and terms set out by Wordsworth.[52] Even though he has a copy of his letter in his diary, he pretends that '[w]hat foolish thing I said of friendship, I cannot now recollect'; assures his correspondent that '[n]othing, I am sure, was farther from my intention than to breathe a syllable of disrespect against our elder poets'; and begs him that 'you will not give yourself the trouble of writing oftener than you feel disposed'.[53] This second letter meets with Wordsworth's full approval, triggering an epistolary conversation that would continue, albeit eventually interrupted by very long intermissions due to cooling affections, until shortly before Wordsworth's death in 1850.[54] Even in the earliest phase of their acquaintance, the connection proves promising enough for Wordsworth to sign off as '[y]our very affectionate friend' as early as his second reply, and to soften his somewhat imperious tone by insisting that he did 'not mean to preach: I speak in simplicity and tender apprehension, as one lover of Nature and of Virtue speaking to another'.[55] As John Jordan comments, '[t]hat friendship which he had sagely said was the "growth of time and circumstance" had come in two letters!'[56]

While De Quincey enthusiastically accepts Wordsworth's standing invitation to Grasmere, assuring him that 'the bowers of paradise could hold no such allurement', their meeting would not transpire until November 1807.[57] This means that they meet after De Quincey has undergone the formative experiences detailed in the 'Confessions' – his rain-sodden walking tour of Wales, his months of homeless destitution in London, and the start of his addiction to opium. He arrives a child of nature no more. Moreover, he draws up at Dove Cottage not as an unconnected naïf, but as the chaperone of Coleridge's wife and children. When the Wordsworths welcome De Quincey 'like one of our own Family', however, they ignore these hints of gathering difference, incorporating him in the character in which he first presented himself. He continues to be regarded as an excellent specimen of the type of reader targeted by the *Lyrical Ballads*, and precisely the sort of minor character the narrative of Romantic genius requires: 'a remarkable instance of the power of my brother's poems over a lonely and contemplative mind, unwarped by any established taste [. . .] – a pure and innocent mind!', as Dorothy describes him. De Quincey is so much the lesser presence that his inferiority is projected onto his stature, which is recurrently characterised as 'very diminutive in person, which, to strangers, makes him appear insignificant'.[58] 'Little Mr De Quincey' soon develops into a standard hypocorism – 'so courteous, yet so weak and poor [. . .] Poor little De Quincey!'[59] As such, when he takes up the tenancy of Dove Cottage in 1808, on the suggestion of the Wordsworths who had vacated the house in search of roomier lodgings, he does so in presumed continuation of his subordination – not, that is, in order to claim a central locus of British Romanticism as his own, but as what Robert Morrison aptly calls a 'custodian',[60] tasked with ensuring that the original occupants might have 'almost a home still at the old and dearest spot of all'. Similarly, when De Quincey is asked to contribute to Wordsworth's *Concerning the Convention of Cintra*, a book-length essay on the 1808 treaty between the British and the French that had ignited the poet's patriotic fury, he is employed not for his literary talents but as a glorified amanuensis.[61] Wordsworth represents the duties he entrusts to his protégé to be relatively modest: he has simply asked his student to hurry the manuscript to the London publishers and see it through the proofing stage. De Quincey has free rein only in minor matters, like the book's punctuation, which Wordsworth declares he 'had never attended and had of course settled no scheme of it in my own mind'. As such, 'I deputed that office to Mr De Quincey', ominously adding '*Hinc illae lacrymae!*'[62]

Ensconced in the Wordsworth Circle, De Quincey soon appears powerless to resist the dynamic of attraction and repulsion that patterns every instance of his reliance on external inspirations. The *Cintra* episode presents the clearest signs of the tensions to come. Having taken up his assignment with gusto, De Quincey finds himself thrown between maintaining his role as a selfless tributary to Wordsworth's greatness and asserting a separable voice of his own, if only by affiliating with alternative voices. As such, while he occasionally risks playing up his discretion to amend Wordsworth's manuscript, magnifying his duties to the 'editing [of] a pamphlet', he simultaneously dissembles his growing hunger to establish an authorial identity of his own, averring an almost existential hesitation to intervene even in trivial issues. What, for instance, he asks William, Dorothy and Mary in a flurry of increasingly frantic letters, is 'the most learned and *ineffable* orthography': 'Ghenghis – Genghis – or Genghiz Khan or Khân?' At times, De Quincey writes to Mary, he is sorely tempted to intercalate unsanctioned material, stopping himself only when he recalls his sacred charge to hew to Wordsworth's directives. His realisation that 'I had used language which could not be reconciled with Mr. Wordsworth's direction' so dismays him that he returns to the text and reverses his emendations of 'several parts of it'.[63] Such performances increasingly fail to ingratiate him with William, however. '[T]hat he has failed is too clear', the latter writes, 'and not without great blame on his own part (being a man of great ability and the best feelings, but, as I have found, not fitted for smooth and speedy progress in business.)'[64] These emerging frictions notwithstanding, the *Convention* will ultimately see print, albeit several weeks behind schedule. While the delay is injurious to the sales of a text designed to make a timely intervention in public debate, and casts significant doubt on De Quincey's professed eagerness to learn at Wordsworth's feet, their relationship is not yet irreparably ruptured. Still, De Quincey recognises its deterioration, casting the closest period of their acquaintance as a thing of the past when he notes in a letter that he was once 'honoured with a place in your ~~friendship~~ good opinion'.[65]

As De Quincey seeks to reduce his subordination to Wordsworth, even the last vestiges of mutual 'good opinion' are eroded. 'The commentator', as Leslie Stephen summarises the drive behind De Quincey's work, is 'seeking to eclipse the text', albeit in a conflicted fashion – tentatively, like a guilty thing; never to such an extent that a unified or authoritative voice may be seen to emerge.[66] His first act is to cast off his position as a placeholder tenant, ordering the chopping of the orchard near Dove Cottage in 1811 and thereby indelibly stamping the hallowed nucleus of the Wordsworth Circle with his own presence. 'What do you say to de Q's having polled the Ash Tree & cut down the hedge all round the orchard', Hutchinson fumes, adding that Dorothy 'is so hurt and angry that she can never speak to him more: & truly it was a most unfeeling thing when he knew how much store they set by that orchard'. The qualities that initially granted De Quincey access are now dismissed as negatives, with his bookishness coming in for particular scorn. Hutchinson comments that De Quincey 'lives only for himself and his Books', and Dorothy notes that 'Mr de Quinceys [sic] Books have literally turned their master & his whole family out of doors.'[67]

With the 1821 publication of the 'Confessions', De Quincey applies his efforts at separation to his writing, which had hitherto consisted of a few articles published in the *Westmorland Gazette* in the course of his editorship of the journal from 1818 to 1819, a position he had been granted on Wordsworth's recommendation.[68] While the 'Confessions' continue to abide by the prescriptions of the *Ballads*, most notably in that they emphasise the dignity of characters at the margins of society, many of the text's key features are in defiance of the lyrical revolution. De Quincey appears precisely the sort of writer that Wordsworth takes aim at when he laments the anti-literary forces the serious poet presently finds arrayed against him – 'a multitude of causes unknown to former times' which 'are now acting with a combined force to blunt the discriminating powers of the mind, and [. . .] reduce it to a state of almost savage torpor'. Wordsworth writes that 'the encreasing accumulation of men in cities' is a force inimical to great literature, and De Quincey decides to style himself an urban writer, helplessly drawn to the metropolis, one of the first of that species in British literature. Wordsworth rails against stooping to the level of the crowd by satisfying their 'craving for extraordinary incident' through a 'rapid communication of intelligence', and De Quincey publishes his work almost solely through the periodical press, cultivating an air of off-the-cuff composition by mixing the newspaper article, the philosophical essay and the private diary. Most egregiously of all, in insubordination of Wordsworth's proselytising against the use of 'gross and violent stimulants' as a means to 'excite[] [. . .] the human mind', De Quincey barrels onto the public stage as an addict obsessed with logging in minute detail the transformative effects of laudanum, interspersing observations on the impact of other soporifics and analeptics.[69] Noting these differences, De Quincey compresses them into a question of national affiliation, protesting his puzzlement at seeing his 'Confessions' infected by foreign ideas at variance with Wordsworth's solidly English brand of writing:

> Nothing, indeed, is more revolting to English feelings than the spectacle of a human being obtruding on our notice his moral ulcers or scars [. . .] and for any such acts of gratuitous self-humiliation [. . .], we must look to French literature, or to that part of the German which is tainted with the spurious

and defective sensibility of the French. [...] Guilt and misery shrink, by a natural instinct, from public notice [...] as if [...] wishing (in the affecting language of Mr Wordsworth)
   Humbly to express
   A penitential loneliness.[70]

The 'Confessions' may have been penned by an emphatically '*English* Opium-Eater', but its writer's national affections are divided, partaking of French and French-*via*-German sensibilities in addition to English values. The opium-eater is Wordsworth's parodic double on a multitude of levels: forever closely in pursuit of his original, occasionally attempting to overtake the latter, yet all the while denying such intentions.

De Quincey fully pushes through his para-Wordsworthian stance in his *Recollections of the Lakes and the Lake Poets*, the name retrospectively applied to a series of articles published from 1834 through 1840 in which he documents his sojourn in the Lake District and his acquaintance with the Lake Poets.[71] Naturally, as the chief target for his youthful bardolatry and subsequent rebellion, Wordsworth is granted pride of place.[72] Having described the particulars of their first meeting, which is cast as an electrifying event, and having devoted several solemn paragraphs to the poet's *vita*, De Quincey proceeds to give his estimation of the Wordsworths, constantly offsetting appreciation with vicious criticism. Dorothy is said to be afflicted by 'a considerable obliquity of vision', yet her eyes are possessed 'of vesper gentleness'. Her ocular defect 'ought to have been displeasing or repulsive; yet, in fact, it was not'. William is decidedly ungainly: he is, 'upon the whole, not a well-made man'. And yet, De Quincey declares in a fit of pseudo-phrenology, his face exhibits a 'very good likeness' to Milton's, foretelling his destiny as a poet for the ages.[73] A terrific amount of Wordsworth's poetry has been written in what is assuredly 'a wrong key, and [...] [on] a false basis'. *The Excursion*, in particular, is a painfully protracted exercise in fumbling diction in which the poet versifies with all the grace of 'a cow dancing a cotillon'. And yet, despite its limping turns of phrase, Wordsworth's oeuvre is credited with having revealed 'many a truth into life [...] which previously had slumbered indistinctly for all men'.[74] When he looks back on his *Recollections* in 1845, De Quincey continues his double-dealing, at once affirming a 'deep respect [...] a more than filial devotion', and admitting that his reminiscences of Wordsworth are tainted by unspecified slight.[75] 'I acknowledge myself to have been long alienated from Wordsworth', he muses; 'sometimes even I feel a rising emotion of hostility – nay, something, I fear, too nearly akin to vindicative [sic] hatred.'[76] It is from such complex emotions that De Quincey will develop his amphibolic poetics.

One more significant personality must be discussed to chart the translational structures through which he will seek to position his writing. In effect, De Quincey gains in autonomy by shuttling between a Wordsworthian and a Coleridgean alter ego.

## Coleridgean Quandaries

While De Quincey seizes on a wide range of authors to refract his own voice, his uses and abuses of Wordsworth are the most visible. In demonstratively cutting himself free from Wordsworth's overbearing presence, however, he is seen to veer exceedingly close to another writer whose career is largely defined by his complicated relationship with Wordsworth. Contemporary observers are quick to trace several parallels between Coleridge and De Quincey, noting especially their common interest in the practical and poetical uses of addiction.[77] Coleridge predates De Quincey by a significant margin in the literary exploration of opium-eating, having come under its spell in 1804 and having begun to harness its tropological potential in 1816.[78] As such, when De Quincey's own dependency encroaches on his professional obligations, his acquaintances naturally frame such eccentricities through the Coleridgean precedent. To the Wordsworths and their wider circle, this comparison further damages De Quincey's already precarious standing: reading 'a bad account of him from Wordsworth', Crabb Robinson remarks in 1816 that '[i]t appears that he has taken to opium, and, like Coleridge, seriously injured his health'.[79] Other, less publicly visible points of approximation include a shared fascination with abstruse German philosophy, the construction of an authorial persona by abandoning poetry for criticism, and the exploration of stylistic and philosophical questions through the mode of translation. While striking, all these and further points of resonance are hard to pursue, both because little record remains of the two men's epistolary exchanges,[80] and because their work strategically de-emphasises any similarities, each instead shaping their authorship through the looming figure of Wordsworth.[81] It is also the centrality of Wordsworth that imparts to Coleridge's and De Quincey's interaction a quality of relative equality, liberating De Quincey from the dynamic of subordination and rebellion that emerges when he enters into a mentor/disciple dynamic. When De Quincey engages with Wordsworth, he maintains him in his role as the quintessential poet, casting his own work as a rebellious exploration of ideas that his idol has only touched upon. When he positions himself vis-à-vis Coleridge, by contrast, he does so to arrogate key aspects of the latter's persona, excusing his out-Coleridgeing of Coleridge by pointing up the latter's inability to inhabit his own identity.

As in his dealings with Wordsworth, De Quincey prepares the complication of his association with Coleridge in the private sphere before he extends his oedipal efforts into his writing. In 1807, the year of the *Cintra* episode, he offers Coleridge a significant tranche of his patrimony to offset the latter's debts. Initially portraying the sum as a donation, and ensuring that the money reaches the poet semi-anonymously, he unsuccessfully requests reimbursement in 1821, and publicly comes forward as Coleridge's munificent patron in 1834. Acting on the homology of literary and financial indebtedness on which he bases many of his performative flourishes, De Quincey converts his loan into an inverted relationship of obligation. This tactic also affects the way in which the 'Confessions' define their position with respect to Coleridge. While De Quincey repeatedly pays tribute to the latter in naming him the sole 'subtle thinker' presently alive in Britain,[82] his 'Confessions' also signal their ambition to better their instruction in presenting a protagonist who does succeed in using opium to creative ends.[83] Contemporary readers consequently note the text's close resemblance to Coleridge as well as its far greater qualities: Crabb Robinson describes the text as 'a fragment of autobiography in emulation of Coleridge's diseased egotism'.[84]

In the opening salvo of the *Recollections*, published a year before the Wordsworth sequence, De Quincey seeks to distinguish his attainments from Coleridge's even further. So violently does he train his rhetorical fire on Coleridge that these articles have been characterised as exercises in 'literary assassination',[85] or as a 'generous contribution to [the] critique of the Romantic authorial personality'.[86] True to form, De Quincey cushions his blows by including professions of undying admiration. Declaring his subject 'the largest and most spacious intellect [. . .] that has yet existed amongst men', he notes that his own literary education has purposely followed 'the same track as Coleridge – that track in which few of any age will ever follow us, such as German metaphysicians, Latin schoolmen, thaumaturgic Platonists, religious Mystics'.[87] And yet he also argues that '[t]o *him* I owed nothing at all'.[88] As such, he considers himself free to broach such scandalous topics as Coleridge's marital misery, opining that it is precisely this matrimonial 'weight of dejection' that spurred Coleridge into his abstractions: 'the restless activity of Coleridge's mind, in chasing abstract truths, and burying himself in the dark places of human speculation, seemed to me, in a great measure, an attempt to escape out of his personal wretchedness'. Such being the impetus for his thought, Coleridge could not but prove hopeless at providing a pragmatic exposition of his ideas, so attached was he to the pursuit of philosophy purely for the sake of prolonging his respite from Mrs Coleridge. Drawing on the interlocking tropes of laudanum, lucre and literature, De Quincey goes on to portray his subject as an addict given over to depraved consumption, ingesting opium, money and foreign literature 'not as a relief from bodily pains or nervous sensations', nor as a means of writing better literature, 'but as source of luxurious sensations', pursued solely to shield him from reality.

Not much has been preserved of Coleridge's and Wordsworth's responses to De Quincey's jockeying. Coleridge is no longer alive when the *Recollections* start hitting *Tait's*, but those efforts at self-manifestation that he does live to witness elicit a brief skirmish through competing essays. Having previously, with a 'peculiar emphasis of horror',[89] warned De Quincey against using opium, both as a means to combat pain and to anchor a literary persona, he responds to the 'Confessions' by declaring the latter 'a wicked book, a monstrous exaggeration'.[90] By way of counterblast, he publishes an opium article of his own, the 'Literary Correspondence', choosing for his venue *Blackwood's*, a conservative periodical sharply opposed to De Quincey's Whiggish *London Magazine* platform.[91] The comparison of the 'Confessions' and the 'Correspondence' was infinitely to De Quincey's advantage. While the latter was widely deemed 'too dull to be read' and 'mostly unintelligible',[92] the 'Confessions' solidified De Quincey as the *only* Opium-Eater – even *Blackwood's* own 'Noctes Ambrosianae' use the name as De Quincey's sobriquet. For his part, Wordsworth attacks De Quincey's 'obnoxious publication' for its rank treachery. De Quincey, he writes in an indignant letter to Coleridge's literary executor, is a literary parasite, draining inspiration from suitably brilliant hosts. He purposely 'sought following [sic] [Coleridge] into different parts of England', but clearly did so only to 'abuse[] [his] confidence, & in certain particulars pervert[] the communication made to him'. While Wordsworth briefly muses on the advisability of countering the article through a public 'letter of caution, or remonstrance', he instead resolves to deprive the Quinceyan leech of sustenance, henceforth refusing to acknowledge their connection. 'I have never read a word of his infamous production nor ever shall', he writes, recounting the facts of their friendship in a manner calculated to diminish his accuser to a thankless stowaway. 'He was 7 months an inmate of my house [. . .] A man who has set such an example, I hold to be a pest in society, and of the most worthless of mankind. [. . .] The particulars shall never by me be recorded.'[93] And yet, their disdain notwithstanding, Coleridge and Wordsworth cannot help but respond in kind to De Quincey's equivocations, punctuating their contempt with touches of appreciation. Coleridge's notebooks contain several memoranda to contact De Quincey on various topics, and he declares himself so taken with the latter's 1832 novel *Klosterheim*, which he extravagantly claims possesses 'in purity of style and idiom [...] an excellence to which Sir W. Scott [...] appears to never have aspired' that he decides to write to 'my old friend'.[94] Similarly, shortly before his death, Wordsworth asks that the glossary to his *Guide through the District of the Lakes* be forwarded to De Quincey. 'I am still of opinion that it is very desirable that they should be looked over by Mr De Quincey' ('if he can be got at', he adds testily) – provided, however, that 'my name must on no account be used in the business'.[95] For his own part, De Quincey comes to define his authorship, such as it is, as a practice positioned between Coleridge and Wordsworth, variously declaring for either inspiration. And so to De Quincey.

### Man in the Middle

So who *is* De Quincey? Where do his gyrations leave his own profile, which increasingly appears impossible to delineate except by framing him in negative, through the greater men and women that surround him? 'What shall be *my* character? I have been thinking this afternoon', he puzzles in a diary entry dated 9 May 1803, weighing up his options: 'wild – impetuous – *splendidly* sublime? dignified – melancholy – *gloomily* sublime? or shrouded in mystery – supernatural – like the "ancient Mariner" – *awfully* sublime?' Throughout his work, De Quincey repeatedly pauses to ponder what style he might be able to claim as fully his, characterising his writing not so much in terms of invention as judiciously picking one's way through a system of choices that has long attained maturity. Too late (and too whimsical) to be Wordsworth, too early (and too self-conscious) to be Byron, too close for comfort to be Coleridge, and ultimately incapable of declaring any stably exclusive affiliation, he strikes a path that meanders between the directions in which he is pulled, cobbling an original poetics from a collection of unoriginal materials.

In a series of self-appraisals recorded on 1 and 2 May 1803, instigated by bouts of fevered nocturnal reading and announced as '[n]otes on my own character, begun this evening', De Quincey reports on his epiphanic realisation that there might be methods of circumventing the onerous necessity of restricting one's literary allegiances. As he peruses Carl Grosse's *The Dagger*, which he identifies as a translation ('Titlepage torn out; – Q. is it a translation from yᵉ German?'), he hits on a novel method of schematising the options available to authors. He elects theatre as a staging ground, opposing classical tragedy to the somewhat vaguely defined 'Romantic Drama'. While the former focuses on intense feeling, he writes, the latter exploits the play's formal possibilities. His own contributions to the theatre will build on the example of Southey's epic poem *Thalaba* and other literary greats like Wordsworth and Milton in order to achieve a cold fusion of tragic pathos and Romantic poetry:

> [l]ast night it struck me (in lecto) that, though pathos be proper to Tragedy, yet what hinders *imagery* (or *poetry*) from being cloathed in or applied to a dramatic form – and thus having the drama divided into two species – the 1st. that appropriated to pathos – or Tragedy; the 2nd. that appropriated to poetry – which may be termed and classified as the 'Romantic Drama' and a 3rd. species compounded of both. [. . .] *my* Arabian Drama will be an example of Pathos and Poetry united; – pathos 'not loud but deep' – Like God's own head. Milton's *Comus* is an example of this last sort. N.B. Observe that poetry (except in this and Sampson Agonistes has never been dramatised) . . . but always exhibited in a narrative form [punctuation *sic*]. In *pastoral* indeed this has been attempted [. . .] there is no good pastoral in the world but Wordsworth's '*Brothers*'; and that enchant<sup>g</sup> composition has more pathos (ah! *what* pathos!) than poetry in it.[96]

The mediatory style that De Quincey here half-proposes is presented as a deeply suspect thing. It is described through quotes spoken by the tragic heroes of *Macbeth* and 'The Ancient Mariner', both of them characters who fatally transgress against the laws of nature and man. Bitterly noting that he has 'lived long enough', Macbeth resolves to commit to the consequences of his regicide, foregoing the laurels of elder statesmanship for '[c]urses, not loud but deep'.[97] For his part, the tragic mariner is visited by a mercilessly bright sun upon his killing of the albatross, the star appearing to him 'nor dim nor red, / Like God's own head.'[98] The latter reference describes a sudden transport into a terrifying world of supernatural consequence, and points to a structure that at once founds itself on and transcends dichotomies. The former line points forward to De Quincey's 1823 essay 'On the Knocking at the Gate in Macbeth', which examines Shakespeare's transitions from 'the world of ordinary life' to 'the world of darkness' in which the regicide of Duncan occurs. What connects these two quotes is that both are premised on a dual scheme whereby an otherwise unnavigable boundary is traversed by antiheroes acting on irrational impulses for self-assertion. Shakespeare, moreover, De Quincey will reflect in a later essay, has an advantage over Coleridge in that he intuits the real goal of the fatal predisposition to shuttle between spheres, between the familiar and the alien, lies in those infinitesimal moments where movement is suspended, and two worlds stand side by side as equally valid options: those moments, that is, when a true medium is fleetingly achieved. *Macbeth* provides an illustration. 'From my boyish days I had always felt a great perplexity on one point in *Macbeth*', De Quincey recollects:

> [i]t was this: – the knocking at the gate, which succeeds the murder of Duncan, produced to my feelings an effect for which I could never account. [...] for many years I never could see why it should produce such an effect.

Even in 1823, no explanation is offered for the transfixing effect of the knocking at the gate, except to note briefly the attractiveness of grafting a poetics on the pauses for breath that separate the contrasting terms in a dichotomy. 'O, mighty poet!', De Quincey intones; 'Thy works are [...] like the phenomena of nature, like the sun and the sea, the stars and the flowers, – like frost and snow, rain and dew, hail-storm and thunder.'[99]

While it is difficult to see how De Quincey's initial notes on his future profile might be practically implemented, he is so taken with his scheme that he returns on 8 May 1803 to the structures of sublime dichotomy. He now applies its architecture to poetry. As he meditates on the differences 'between Southey and Burns ... and thence [...] the difference between Burns and other poets', he once again proclaims himself 'struck' by a sensational realisation. Like drama, poetry is characterised by a disjunction between its stylistics and aesthetics, a split that loosely rehashes the division between the beautiful and the sublime. This is a well-travelled distinction, thoroughly familiar to De Quincey from his reading of contemporary writers and eighteenth-century manuals of rhetoric. However, the hypothesised existence of a *third* branch of composition in which the beautiful and the sublime merge in a playful or 'humorous' manner can still be cast as a relatively recent thing, as yet underexplored and undertheorised.[100] The one exception, at least in British letters, is to be found in Gothic writing, which generates frissons by momentarily crossing the frontiers that separate the beautifully orderly from the sublimely chaotic:

> the love of nature (which is poetry) divides itself into two kinds – the home – hedge – lane – rose – hawthorn – violet – cuckoo – milkmaid – May – species, and the great awful torrid zone – boundless forest – mighty river – wild wild solitude species [...] This satisfied me with regard to Shakespeare and Burns, because I instantly became sensible that they possessed only the former species: so far – so well: but how to account for Southey [...] as to all his earlier pieces, it may be observe [*sic*] that they are not (at least what I have read or remember) *Poetry*; that is, they are not the ebullitions of a mind pursuing either the *first* or *second* species; but belong to the newly-discovered state or sometimes perhaps to the medium Ratcliffian kind which (I know not *why* in theory; but, in practice, it is evident) certainly admits of humour. –[101]

This is as yet a halting description of the ideal mode of writing, replete with half-answered questions, dashes, underscores, ellipses and parentheses, ending in the inelegant suspension of a long dash. More problematically, it is not entirely clear how De Quincey's aesthetic and stylistic categories ought to map onto one another. De Quincey will require an entire career to define his 'medium' mode of writing, which he primarily accomplishes by shifting his focus from singular genres like drama and poetry to the interaction *between* genres, and thence between languages and systems of thought.

De Quincey hits on an adequately comprehensive term only in 1853, when in the preface to his collected works he refers to his ideal style as 'impassioned prose'.[102] The crux of this impassioned style is already present in the excerpt above, in the brief but telling association of 'the newly-discovered state' with Southey and Ann Radcliffe, both names that serve as shorthand for the Gothic irruption of the astonishing into the normal. In singling out Radcliffe, De Quincey particularly invokes the commingling of poetry and prose that was considered to characterise her work. In his 1825 'Prefatory Memoir of the Author' attached to the collected edition of Radcliffe's novels, Walter Scott remarks on her curiously hybrid style, noting that she 'has a title to be considered the first poetess of romantic fiction', in that her 'prose fiction [. . .] introduc[es] a tone of fanciful description and impressive narrative, which had hitherto been exclusively applied to poetry',[103] even as her poetry 'partakes of the rich and beautiful colouring which distinguishes her prose composition'. The overall effect is compelling, if fundamentally uncanny: 'the English', Scott muses, 'is not adapted' to observing a double purpose.[104] Like Radcliffe's orchestration of an intrusion of poetry into prose and vice versa, De Quincey's 'impassioned prose' figures itself as 'a third, and in virtue of their aims, [. . .] a far higher class of composition'.[105] The resulting style has been characterised as 'stand[ing] across the boundary lines' of poetry and prose,[106] as 'prose in the age of poets',[107] or, more floridly, as a '*melange des genres*, "prose poetry" [. . .] a label prompted by the rich "poetic" quality of his diction as well as the beautiful orbicularity of his rhythmical periods'.[108]

If De Quincey is best figured as a 'bat, an ambiguous character, rising on the wings of prose to the borders of the true poetical region [. . .] doing in prose what every great poet does in verse',[109] how does one read such hybridised writing? Other than the problem inherent in capturing the essence of a mode that arises out of a collision of genres, and as such emerges only performatively and interstitially, much of the difficulty in describing or theorising impassioned prose resides in the assumption that it is De Quincey's invention. This, Stephen notes, is an attitude inspired by his brazen declaration that his experiments 'rang[e] under no precedents that I am aware in any literature'.[110] 'De Quincey implicitly puts forward a claim which has been accepted by all competent critics', Stephen remarks:

> [h]e declares that he has used language for purposes to which it hardly been applied by any prose writers. He alone of all human beings who have written since the world began, has entered a path, which the absence of rivals proves to be encumbered with some unusual obstacles.

An assertion as bold as this requires 'a short examination'.[111] De Quincey willingly supplies the material required for such an examination. Despite his protestations of radical originality, he repeatedly invokes authors who have pursued courses parallel to his, and to a much greater extent than Radcliffe or Southey. Names of particular importance include Wordsworth, Coleridge, Carlyle, Browne, Taylor, Herodotus and several German idealists. De Quincey's method in presenting these inspirations varies. While he is happy to pay homage to those authors who are either German or long-deceased (and preferably both), he is circumspect in praising his contemporary compatriots. Since they move towards a theory of literature that approximates his own, he clothes in understatement and disagreement his references to two key texts, Coleridge's 1817 *Biographia Literaria* and Carlyle's 1836 *Sartor Resartus*.

De Quincey, Coleridge and Carlyle all present their thoughts on a potential 'medium species of writing' in a loose fashion, casually hypothesising on the conditions of its emergence rather than offering any exact definition. Coleridge hits on the idea as he ponders Kant's illustration of the principles of transcendental philosophy through the laws of mathematical and physical calculation. The Romantic writer, Coleridge reflects, writes to precisely the same ends, and through precisely the same methods, as do philosophers, mathematicians and scientists. These four fields all seek to divide the world into 'two contrary forces, the one of which tends to expand infinitely, while the other strives to apprehend or find itself in this infinity'.[112] Mathematics divides the world into positive and negative numbers; physics into action and reaction; philosophy into idealism and materialism; and poetry, a new entry proposed by Coleridge, into the imagination and the fancy. Seductive though this progression of equivalences is, its neatness disguises a lack of development. It is unclear what the exact philosophical and literary correlates might be to the numbers and vectors that anchor Coleridge's theory. That is, what exactly are the discrete elements that the philosopher and the poet ought to play off in order to recreate the interaction of negative and positive numbers? More pressingly still, while numbers and vectors add up to definite results, to total sums and final motions, the third thing that ought to emerge from an interplay of the two fundamental elements of philosophy and literature remains nebulous. Coleridge's awkward movement from the realms of calculation to disputation and thence to composition is symptomatic: while he briefly notes that literary writing is better equipped than philosophy to settle the conflicts that beset modern thought, he can equate the two only by obfuscating their purported homology by way of an interruptive 'letter from a friend' that conceals his inability to shuttle between planes of thought. What remains is a text that has resigned itself to its paralysis:

> Now the transcendental philosophy demands; first, that two forces should be conceived which counteract each other by their essential nature [. . .]: secondly, that these forces should be assumed to be both alike infinite, both alike indestructible. The problem will then be to discover the result or product of two such forces [. . .] By what instrument this is possible the solution itself will discover, at the same time that it will reveal to and for whom it is possible. *Non omnia possumus omnes.* [. . .] as something must be the result of these two forces [. . .] and as rest or neutralisation can not be this result; no other conception is possible, but that the product must be a *tertium aliquid*, or finite generation. [. . .] Now this tertium aliquid can be no other than an interpenetration of the counteracting powers, partaking of both – Thus far had the work been transcribed for the press, when I received the following letter from a friend.

In averring himself unequal to his great task, Coleridge effectively bequeaths the final determination of the fabled *tertium aliquid* to another thinker. All he can do is offer a hard-won approximation. Whatever the third style turns out to be, it will assuredly be a derived phenomenon, arising not of its own accord, but from the push and pull between two original and greater systems – constantly recreating and redefining itself in a flickering succession of generations, and therefore only ever to be recognised at the moment of its emergence, refusing any sustained presence and eluding any a priori definition. Poetical prose, rationalist empiricism, fanciful imagination, materialist idealism or allegorical symbolism are no simple syntheses, but something at once more profound and more fleeting.

In his own investigations into the *tertium aliquid*, Carlyle pushes forward Coleridge's envoi by dedicating an entire novel to the coordination of what the *Biographia* had distinguished as the 'poetic' and the 'philosophical genius'.[113] *Sartor Resartus* adds two catalysts to Coleridge's schema of equivalences. First, Carlyle breathes life into what is otherwise an abstruse debate, dramatising the conflict between empiricism and rationalism by recoding it as a personified narrative. Secondly, he intuits that the *Biographia* is hobbled by its inability to name the units of force that carry the binary of imagination and fancy. He begins to fill this lacuna by specifying his text's structure as a meeting of mutually unintelligible voices and languages: the drama of Carlyle's novel resides in the many tribulations its protagonist, an unnamed editor-cum-translator, must face as he attempts to introduce to a sceptical British audience the life and work of a fictional German philosopher by the name of Diogenes Teufelsdröckh. Just as the editor endeavours to shuttle to and fro across the linguistic divide between German and English, so do the intercalated stories show his subject engaged in resolving the duality of materialist empiricism and rationalism. Diogenes Teufelsdröckh's name – literally, God-created Devil-dung –, which fuses irreconcilable languages and values into a single designation, expresses his predestination to this ambition. Having established this promising amphibolic structure across the two tiers of its narration, however, the novel soon proves unequal to its ambitions. Unable to move beyond the irreconcilable claims of empiricism and rationalism, Diogenes hurtles towards a crisis of dejection. At the same time, the editor finds the philosopher's life and thought impervious to any attempt at order, summary or translation. Notwithstanding its determination to improve on Coleridge, Carlyle's philosophical novel, too, collapses into a chronicle of its own impossibility. Lest its efforts run aground, the narrative rushes to orchestrate an unceremonious sublation of the contradictions that are fast overtaking it. Permitting Diogenes one final spoken statement, '[i]t is beginning [*Es geht an*]', the narrative has him retire, insisting that Diogenes has deduced an incommunicable procedure for resolving the conflict of reason and the senses by entirely irradiating the latter. In essence, the novel chooses to spirit itself away: the commencement of the exclusive reign of rationalism coincides with the end of the work of writing and thinking. While the novel briefly acknowledges the advantages of a mediatory style in productively engaging with the sublime clash of thought and sense, it is so frustrated in its efforts that it declares this 'centre of indifference' to be unproductive.[114] For Carlyle, German philosophy and the philosophical potential of translation were never again to become objects of sustained attention.

Following the defeat of the *Biographia* and *Sartor*, De Quincey's own engagement with the third style grows into a lifelong obsession: his work is marked by a ceaseless search for figures and structures that might assist him in defining its nature. Among such images, one might think of opium, which is described as interminably swinging between incommensurable properties. Opium is a 'dread agent of unimaginable pleasure and pain' that jolts into life the poet's imagination and simultaneously condemns him to crises of acedia; that dulls aches only to inflict greater suffering; and that reconciles body to mind only to shatter both. One might also think of De Quincey's celebrated definition of literariness through the opposition of knowledge and power, 'the most philosophical expression for literature and anti-literature'. True literature, he writes, is premised on 'a sublime antagonism [. . .] two worlds [. . .] brought face to face [. . .] mirrors of each other, semichoral antiphonies, strophe and antistrophe heaving with rival convulsions'.[115] Or of his politics, which vacillate between opposing creeds: as he queries of his doppelgänger Coleridge, 'were his propensities Conservative or Reforming? [. . .] as a philosopher, he was, according to circumstances, and according to the object concerned, all of these by turns.'[116] And so on: summaries of De Quincey's oscillations are standard features in the criticism on this author, often in cascades of divergent areas of interest connected only in their strikingly similar structuration. As one prototypical introduction to his work observes, he 'seem[s] to shift from a Tory blue to a colonial pink to a radical red [. . .]; he is a Romantic and a Victorian, compassionate and snobbish; a reader and a writer; a patient and a doctor; a literary giant and a wretched journalist; an addict and an agent'.[117] This talent for duplication was also noted by De Quincey's contemporaries. While his judgement receives some colour from the accusations made by the *Recollections*, Hartley Coleridge, eldest son of Samuel Taylor, articulates the frustration of many when during a stroll near Grasmere he confides in his interlocutor his exasperation:

'I will tell you what De Quincey is, he is an anomaly and a contradiction – a contradiction to himself, a contradiction throughout! He steals the aristocratic "de"; he announces for years the most aristocratic tastes, principles, and predilections, and then he goes and marries the uneducated daughter of a very humble, very coarse, and very poor farmer. He continues to be, in profession and in talk, as violent a Tory and anti-reformer as ever, and yet he writes for Tait. He professed almost an idolatry for Wordsworth and for my father, and quite a filial affection for Mrs Wordsworth, and yet you see how he is treating them! The fellow cannot even let Mrs Wordsworth's squint alone!'[118]

'Ups and downs you will see, heights and depths, in our fiery course together', De Quincey declaims in his 'Suspiria', 'such as will sometimes tempt you to look shyly and suspiciously at me, your guide, the ruler of the oscillations.'[119] Seeking to conquer their shyness, several readers have recognised that this propensity for Janus-faced performances ought to focus any interpretation of De Quincey. The earliest critical account to remark on De Quincey's mutability, George Gilfillan's 1852 *Second*

*Gallery of Literary Portraits*, attributes the 'want of unity and proper compactness amongst his various faculties [which] are all powerfully developed, but not properly balanced' to the influence of stimulants. He argues that these propel his writing from the 'calm, profound citations of De Quincey sober' towards 'the sublime ravings of De Quincey drunk'.[120] More than a century after Gilfillan, breaking a prolonged lull in critical engagement (excepting the archival and biographical work of John Jordan, David Masson and Alexander Japp), J. Hillis Miller reads De Quincey as the first in a line of modern authors who seek to compensate for the collapse of religious frames by demonstrating through their texts 'that there is a built-in law of compensation in man, in nature, and in history, whereby one power tends to call up its opposite and keep things in balanced motion'. Hence his hybrid style, since 'poetic prose [...] creates the most expanded continuum by oscillating between the most widely distant polar antagonists'.[121] On evaluating his monograph in its 1975 reprint, Miller recants the Pouletian premise that an oeuvre ultimately coalesces into an impression of its author's ego, announcing the start of a move towards deconstruction.[122] He revisits De Quincey only in 1999, however, in *Black Holes*, an experimental book which features essays by Miller and Manuel Asensi on facing pages. Asensi suggests De Quincey would be an ideal test case for Miller's concept of dissensus, which describes a mode of thought that forbears from enforcing a synthesis of incommensurable perspectives and instead encourages constant switches between them. Asensi describes De Quincey as an exemplar of boustrophedonic authorship: just as early Greek texts invert their writing direction between lines, reversing word order and mirroring individual characters as required, Asensi argues, so does De Quincey systematically alternate between writing with and against the grain, asking his readers to pivot along with his numerous volte-faces. What escapes the notice of Miller's and Asensi's pragmatic deconstructionism, however, perhaps because it threatens to complicate their critical project, is De Quincey's outspoken yearning for a medium state; for a fulcrum that centres and makes coherent his stabilising efforts. This shortcoming notwithstanding, it is regrettable that Miller's work is now rarely referenced in the scholarship on De Quincey: the majority of the scholarship on De Quincey presently favours a broadly historicist angle, an approach championed by Robert Maniquis in 1976.[123]

Amid the profusion of interpretations that have hitherto been proposed to adumbrate De Quincey's apparent contradictions, one paradigm remains to be explored. The next chapters will focus on De Quincey's figuration of his authorship through his translatorship, deploying a method at the intersection of the rhetorical focus of Miller and the historical expansion of Maniquis. Before moving to consider De Quincey's poetics and practice of translation in detail, a final pass is needed to map the concrete ways in which he deploys his translatorship to stake out a unique position among his contemporaries.

## Thomas De Quincey, Translator

De Quincey's decision to define his authorship through his translatorship explains why Wordsworth escapes the full brunt of the reviews that his one-time factotum brings to bear on Coleridge and Carlyle. Wordsworth certainly dabbled in translation, and indeed 'cared deeply about' the accuracy of his translations.[124] The translations Wordsworth does produce, however, fall outside the arena that De Quincey patrols most jealously, both because they are not pursued in furtherance of a literary persona and therefore often go unpublished, and because Wordsworth gives wide berth to German letters, instead preferring to focus almost exclusively on the classics.[125] More importantly, Wordsworth takes great care to offset his forays into translation by repeated affirmations of his distaste for the mode: throughout his work, he acts upon the Romantic doctrine that poetry ought to be constrained entirely to highly personal outpourings of emotions and thoughts.[126] In the Immortality Ode, he presents imitativeness as a crisis in the poet's development, to be surpassed without delay: the child's fall from a state of an all-encompassing imagination is precipitated by its move from self-articulation to reproduction, '[a]s if his whole vocation / Were endless imitation.'[127] For De Quincey, Wordsworth can be dealt with summarily; for instance, by way of an aside to a diatribe against Coleridge in which he notes that 'neither Wordsworth nor Coleridge could speak German with any fluency'.[128]

Having signalled grander aspirations than Wordsworth with his translation of *Wilhelm Meister's Apprenticeship*, Carlyle requires a sharper rejoinder. Perhaps deriving encouragement from Wordsworth's contempt for Goethe,[129] De Quincey launches a two-pronged assault, rubbishing *Wilhelm Meister* for its original defects as well as its errors of translation. He first targets Goethe, castigating him as an inept writer and thinker. '[T]he ultimate point we aim at', he writes in a review of the novel, 'is not to quarrel with the particular book, which has been the accidental occasion of bringing Goethe before us [. . .] our mark is Goethe himself.' De Quincey also charges Carlyle's translation with spoiling what few positive qualities Goethe had imparted to his disastrous publication. In his misapprehensions of the exact meaning of various German terms and his awkward transpositions of registers and dialects, Carlyle has ensured that if 'Goethe's original is bad', the translation is much worse in that it is insufficiently adapted to a British context. As such,

> even Goethe, however worthless in other respects, is not objectionable in the way in which the translation is so. He is no great master, nor was ever reputed a great master, of the idiomatic wealth of his own language; but he does not offend by provincialisms, vulgarisms, or barbarisms of any sort: with all of which the translation is overrun. [. . .] the translation too generally, by the awkward German air of its style, reminds us painfully that it *is* a translation.[130]

Recognising that De Quincey's review aims at painting its author as the sole authority in German matters, a strategy that runs against his own endeavour to lay claim to this position through periodical pieces like his 1825 'Life of Schiller', Carlyle commits his ire to several letters, each time dismissing the 'dwarf Opium-eater' as an indigent addict barely able to scrape by 'on the scanty produce of his scribble far off in Westmoreland'; a spiteful little creature who 'carries a laudanum bottle in his pocket, and the venom of a wasp in his heart'. Having discoursed at length on his critic's numerous vices, he warms to him when they meet socially in 1827 – an encounter that Carlyle is delighted to record causes De Quincey such discomfort that the latter 'grew pale as ashes at my entrance'. His own enthusiasm for the relatively low-profile vocation of translator having abated considerably following the échec of *Sartor Resartus*, he cedes the position to De Quincey, noting that his own career has brought him to genres which grant him an infinitely higher station. 'Poor little creature!' he writes of his critic; '[h]e is [. . .] extremely *washable away*'. Further dramatising his assumption of majority, Carlyle mimics De Quincey's double-edged loan to Coleridge, recording that he has gifted the former with a copy of Jean Paul's autobiography, and advised him to translate this text 'so he might raise a few pounds, and fence off the Genius of Hunger yet a little while'. Shortly after turning the opium-eater's sensitivity to self-performance against him, Carlyle strikes a more genuinely generous tone in inviting him to Craigenputtock so that they might found the 'Bog School', a pantisocratic commune set up in parody of the Lake Poets:

> Come, therefore, come and see us; for we often long after you: nay I can promise too that we are almost a unique sight in the British Empire; such a quantity of German Periodicals, and mystical speculation, embosomed in a plain Scottish Peat-moor [. . .] In idle hours, we sometimes project founding a sort of Colony here, to be called the 'Misanthropic Society'; the settlers all to be men of a certain philosophic depth, and intensely sensible of the present

state of Literature [...] Would *you* come hither, and be king over us; *then* indeed we had made a fair beginning, and the 'Bog School' might snap its fingers at the 'Lake School' itself, and hope to be one day recognised of all men.[131]

Carlyle's proposal for bogside balladeering was never to come to fruition. Even before *Sartor* soured Carlyle on German idealism, the two writers had begun to gravitate towards very different modes of writership, with De Quincey professing a much stronger commitment to the legacies of Romantic writing. Moreover, in sending a letter that alleges profound resonances, Carlyle does his request few favours. Having started his career as an upstart doppelgänger eager to assume primacy by claiming Coleridge's territory for himself, De Quincey was loath to have the manoeuvre repeated on him.

De Quincey's most formidable rival in opium throws the largest shadow in matters of translation, too: Coleridge accordingly comes in for the most sustained efforts to create distance. The *Recollections* do so most aggressively, seizing on Coleridge's hesitation to acknowledge his reliance on translation to advance De Quincey's claims to translatorial pre-eminence. Barely pausing to set up an introduction, the article rushes to reveal that Coleridge's entire critical output relies on ideas pilfered from others. To accuse another of plagiarism is to injure the aura of authenticity that is vital to authorial performances in British Romanticism: partly because of its efficacy, such charges had come to constitute a prime 'mode of critical attack'.[132] In addition, in backing up his accusation with exhibits, De Quincey can indirectly demonstrate his translational acuity. He accordingly stresses that he is first to notice the extent of Coleridge's indebtedness, as his barefaced theft 'could in prudence have been risked only by relying too much upon the slight knowledge of German literature in this country'.[133]

Devastating as the brand of plagiarism is, its deployment requires circumspection. In an 1823 instalment of the 'Noctes', *Blackwood's* has De Quincey's fictional alter ego exclaim that 'I have traced [Coleridge] through German literature, poetry, and philosophy, and he is, sir, not only a plagiary, but, sir, a thief, a *bone fide* most unconscientious thief.'[134] The real opium-eater is more cautious, biding his time until Coleridge's death and devoting significant space to denying any vulgar motives in publicising his findings, insisting that his prosecutorial zeal proceeds from a selfless concern to head off any 'unfriendly use' of the very discoveries he has paradocially been instrumental in broadcasting to the world. This strategy proves successful: when Sara Coleridge reads De Quincey's article, her first instinct is to hit back, but the benefit of a few days' contemplation of the piece persuades of her its gentility:

I bethink me that I have written too fiercely about the little Poppyman in the first fuzz of my fury & though I would not even at first have done him any harm I have done amiss in making such an elaborate picture of my wrathful emotions as rehearsing in fancy the retaliating upon him. He is a man of genius & learning the finest metaphysician, I should imagine, *now* living, & by nature & birth a thorough gentleman [. . .] he has performed an ungentlemanly thing in a gentlemanly manner.[135]

Other readers were less easily swayed by De Quincey's show of earnestness. Reflecting on the affair in 1840, Hartley Coleridge dismisses De Quincey's protestations of professional duty as so many instances of a 'hypocritical pretence of friendship or reluctance'.[136] Conscious of the outrage generated by his indelicate article, De Quincey in 1854 appends a retrospective note to the piece in which he runs through the contrary impulses that he alleges his attack endeavoured to balance. Initially pleading he has done Coleridge a kindness in offering a balanced report, he swiftly moves to argue their relationship was never subject to the moral demands of friendship:

> I have somewhere seen it remarked with respect to these charges of plagiarism, that, however incontrovertible, they did not come with any propriety or grace from myself as the supposed friend of Coleridge [. . .] My answer is this: *I* certainly was the first person (first, I believe, by some years) to point out the plagiarisms of Coleridge, and above all others that circumstantial plagiarism, of which it is impossible to suppose him unconscious [. . .] Secondly, in stating it at all, I did so (as at the time I explained) in pure kindness. Well I knew that, from the direction in which English philosophic studies were travelling, sooner or later these appropriations of Coleridge must be detected; and I felt that it would break the force of the discovery, as an unmitigated sort of police detection, if first of all it had been announced by one who, in the same breath, was professing an unshaken faith in Coleridge's philosophic power. [. . .] But thirdly, I must inform the reader, that I was not, nor ever had been, the 'friend' of Coleridge in any sense which could have a right to restrain my frankest opinions upon his merits.[137]

Claiming his overriding concern is to 'greatly *understate*[] the case against Coleridge', De Quincey in his 1834 article initially seems prepared to dismiss all cases of suspected plagiarism as instances of creative borrowing. Adducing representative samples of gratuitous appropriation harvested across the oeuvre under review, De Quincey pronounces them perfectly legitimate, in that they were undertaken not in order to profit from another writer's labour, but to improve on the original; or to pay homage to a text so well known that precise references would verge on pedantry; or, finally, to take no more than a slight 'original hint'. The *Biographia* is a different beast, however. Even though Coleridge prefaces his book by 'insisting on the impossibility that he could have borrowed arguments', and indeed signals significant personal investment in subtitling the work *Biographical Sketches of My Literary Life and Opinions*, he borrows so extensively that the work amounts to little more than 'barefaced plagiarism'. De Quincey stamps the *Biographia* a case of multiple compound 'robberies', professing his 'astonishment to find that the entire essay, from the first word to the last, is a *verbatim* translation from Schelling'. Betraying that at least one of his aims in disclosing Coleridge's larceny is to promote his own writership, he expresses especial offence at the 'dissertation upon the reciprocal relations of [. . .] the *subjective* and the *objective*',[138] whence Coleridge derives his thesis that the contrary forces underlying transcendental philosophy might be reconciled through the travails of an author attuned to the philosophical potential of style.

In excoriating Coleridge for his expropriations of Schelling, De Quincey blithely ignores the former's attempts to head off the 'charge of plagiarism'. Noting the parallels between the *Biographia* and several of Schelling's philosophical treatises, Coleridge pre-emptively proposes an alternative theory of influence, centred on a metempsychotic melding of minds. Coleridge antedates his idealist epiphany to a time before his acquaintance with Schelling, explaining any awkward echoes between his and Schelling's work by pointing to a quasi-mystical *Geist* certain to tell on all steeped in German thought. Having both partaken of Kantian fare, Schelling's and Coleridge's onward trajectory could not but have overlapped:

> It would be but a mere act of justice to myself, were I to warn my future readers, that an identity of thought, or even similarity of phrase, will not be at all times a certain proof that the passage has been borrowed from Schelling, or that the conceptions were originally learnt from him. [. . .] Nor is this coincidence at all to be wondered at. We had studied in the same school; been disciplined by the same preparatory philosophy, namely, the writings of Kant [. . .] Whether a work is the offspring of a man's own spirit, and the product of original thinking, will be discovered by those who are its sole legitimate judges, by better tests than the mere reference to dates. For readers in general, let whatever shall be found in this or any future work of mine, that resembles, or coincides with, the doctrines of my German predecessor, though contemporary, be wholly attributed to *him*: provided, that the absence of distinct references to his books, which I could not at all times make with truth as designating citations or thoughts actually derived from him; and which, I trust, would, after this general acknowledgment be superfluous; be not charged on me as an ungenerous concealment or intentional plagiarism.[139]

Having affirmed his obeisance to the Romantic creed of personal creativity by framing his weighing of his work's exact amount of derivativeness proceeds from a desire to do 'justice to myself', Coleridge swiftly moves to a second tactic. Sensing his obfuscation of the problem of origination might not dispel suspicion, he evades the juridical question by signing away his claims, even as he signals he is doing so against his better judgement, and indeed defers a precise tally of his debts to the deliberations of experts. While this somewhat tortuous apology fails to move De Quincey, it is deemed satisfactory by some readers – including Schelling. When the latter finds his own ideas repeated back to him in an English journal, he indicates his overruling emotion is one of gratification. While the German public have been slow to realise the importance of his systematisation of transcendental thought, here is proof of a British readership who are more appreciative of serious philosophy. What is more, Schelling credits Coleridge with effecting a popularisation of his most recondite ideas, paying him the compliment of borrowing a particularly useful term from the English translation:

> I borrow this term [i.e. *tautegorical*] from the famous Coleridge, the first of his countrymen to have understood and meaningfully used German poetry, science, and especially philosophy. The expression is located in what is incidentally a wonderful essay in the *Transactions of the R. Society of Literature*. I was particularly pleased by this essay, because it showed that one of my earlier writings, whose philosophical substance and importance were so little or rather not at all understood in Germany, has been understood by the talented Brit. I grant him with pleasure the borrowings from my works that were harshly, even too harshly judged by his countrymen due to the fact that my name was not mentioned. One should not hold such things against a truly congenial mind. The severity of this censure in England does prove, however, what value is laid there upon the ownership of ideas [*wissenschaftliche Eigentümlichkeit*], and how strictly the *suum cuique* is observed.[140]

Schelling here ascribes his insouciance in matters of copyright to German literary camaraderie, which he contrasts with a uniquely English ferocity in policing the sanctity of private property. His demonstratively careful citation of Coleridge and his explanation of the British hostility to appropriation point to an alternative code of amicable exchange: while the British hysteria over ownership leads to surreptitious theft, he suggests, the German model employs a model of productive cooperation.

When De Quincey critiques Coleridge, he invokes the quintessentially British virtue of the sanctity of private property. His true purpose, however, is to tempt readers into a comparison between Coleridge's literary and translational powers and those boasted by his biographer, who *can* handle his opium, and who *does* reference his inspirations. 'As I have never allowed myself to covet any man's ox nor his ass, nor anything that is his, still less would it become a philosopher to covet other people's images, or metaphors', he writes in a typically demonstrative performance of authorial probity: '[h]ere, therefore, I restore to Mr Wordsworth this fine image [...] I borrowed it for one moment [...] which being done, the reader is witness that I now pay it back instantly by a note made for that sole purpose.'[141] De Quincey further sharpens the contrast between himself and his competitor as as he considers the root causes of Coleridge's thieving tendencies. Coleridge, De Quincey insists, did not steal because because he wanted for ideas – he is not a member of the tribe of hacks described as the 'thousands of feeble writers [who] [...] subsist by Plagiarism',[142] and did not 'borrow *in forma pauperis*', since he manifestly

> spun daily, and at all hours [...] from the loom of his own magical brain, theories more gorgeous by far, and supposed by a pomp and luxury of images such as neither Schelling – no, nor any German that ever breathed, not John Paul – could have emulated in his dreams.[143]

Coleridge's compulsive thievery is argued to proceed from psychological rather than creative motives.[144] He is portrayed as the literary equivalent of a fabulously wealthy man so besotted with his own riches that he has fallen prey to 'that maniacal propensity which is sometimes well known to attack enormous proprietors and millionaires for acts of petty larceny'. Or, De Quincey muses, lest his account grow too complimentary in crediting his target with great stores of mental power, perhaps a more apposite analogy may be found in the annals of pathopsychology, or even in the pockets of an enterprising toddler:

> Many cases have crossed me in life of people, otherwise not wanting in principle, who had habits, or at least hankerings, of the same kind. And the phrenologists, I believe, are well acquainted with the case, its signs, its progress, and its history. [...] [D]id [the reader] ever amuse himself by searching the pockets of a child – three years old, suppose – when buried in slumber after a long summer's day of out-o'-doors intense activity? I have done this; and, for the amusement of the child's mother, have analysed the contents, and drawn up a formal register of the whole. Philosophy is puzzled, conjecture and hypothesis are confounded, in the attempt to explain the law of selection which *can* have presided in the child's labours; stones remarkable only for weight, old rusty hinges, nails, crooked skewers stolen when the cook had turned her back, rags, broken glass, tea-cups having the bottom knocked out, and loads of similar jewels, were the prevailing articles in this *procès-verbal*. [...] Such in value were the robberies of Coleridge; such their usefulness to himself or anybody else.

Not only does Coleridge lack the fortitude to assume the role of a creative author; he is also unequal to playing the alternative part of the Romantic translator, even if he is the first Romantic to glean the role's literary potential. While he recognises the transformative potential of translation, if only to impart some vigour to his moribund imagination, he is unable to manage his muses. His writing therefore exhibits a nearly pathological inability to face up to its origination in translation, and this, in turn, renders him unable to orchestrate a transfusion of the foreign into the native. This leaves his texts overburdened by badly integrated artefacts from his reading; his style 'disfigured by German modes of thinking, and by a German taste'. The implication is clear: De Quincey, another incorrigible hoarder of quotable phrases, rises above Coleridge in that his borrowings, as a result of his skill in counterbalancing his lacklustre creativity with a superior ability to acknowledge and pay off his debts, embody a quality only seen in Coleridge's very best work, in which

> by a judicious amplification of some topics, and by [a] far deeper tone of lyrical enthusiasm, the dry bones of the German outline have been awakened [. . .] into the fulness of life. It is not, therefore, a *paraphrase*, but a *recast* of the original.[145]

By his own reckoning, De Quincey translates selflessly – that is, in order to present worthwhile insights to an English readership, rather than to enhance his own writings. More importantly, in adapting the foreign text to British preferences, he improves on the original by reconceiving its style. It is on this capacity that De Quincey founds his claims to ownership and authorship, arguing that

> [i]t was a paper in this sense mine, that from me it had received form and arrangement; but the materials belonged to a learned German [. . .] No German has any conception of style. I therefore did him the favour to wash his dirty face [. . .] but the substance was drawn entirely from this German book.[146]

In short, not Coleridge but De Quincey is the 'Grasmeriensis Teutonizans', as he signs his best article on German literature and the benefits of translation – the Germanising Grasmerian, or, less awkwardly, the German student of Grasmere. De Quincey's campaign to become Britain's pre-eminent German scholar proves persuasive: not only does he usurp Coleridge's association with opiated writing; before long, his mastery of German thought is widely contrasted favourably with Coleridge's. Thomas Hood imagines him much as he might Coleridge, ever verging on being overwhelmed by exotic sources: the crucial qualification which is seen to apply only to the younger upstart, however, is that De Quincey always steadies himself. He is 'at home, quite at home, in the midst of a German Ocean of *Literature*, in a storm, – flooding all the floor, the tables and the chairs, – billows of books, tossing, tumbling, surging open'.[147] Descriptions like these betoken De Quincey's success in capturing a position for himself in the constellation of writers he is aching to join. Through his increasingly visible translatorship, he comes forward as a securely secondary figure, located in the peripheries of Wordsworth, Coleridge and Carlyle yet insistently different from each. More mercurial than Wordsworth, more dependable than Coleridge, and more thoroughly committed to upholding Romantic sensibilities than Carlyle, De Quincey emerges as his own creature, if perhaps only intermittently so.

The comments that De Quincey scatters throughout his review of Carlyle and his retrospectives of Wordsworth and Coleridge are the first indications of his desire to build translation into the foundation for his authorship. From these essays, a programme for translation emerges; animated by an early intuition that the structures of translation may ground a voice, a style and a philosophy: if each of these can be demonstrated to operate as a dichotomy, the productive resolution of duality that translation proposes must equally hold. Even if it is necessarily derived, belated, even ancillary, translation possesses all the dignity of a separable mode of Romantic genius – indeed, if De Quincey is to be believed, translation is the culminating point of Romanticism. This chapter has followed De Quincey as he expands translation from a practice which grants him a unique presence amongst the British Romantics, if one partly wrested from Coleridge and Carlyle, into a redefinition of the nature of authorship. The next chapter follows De Quincey as he applies the dyadic structure of translation to problems of style, carrying translation into the very heart of writing.

### Notes

1. EMC, 16.421; 16.432. In keeping with De Quincey's directions, published as a prefatory note to 'The Vision of Sudden Death', I regard the latter as an integral part of 'The English Mail-Coach' essay.
2. Autobiographic Sketches, 19.3.
3. While De Quincey had long prepared for his career as an author, both by practising his writing in his 1803 *Diary* and by associating with the Wordsworth circle, he defers publishing his work until 1818, when he takes up the editorship of the *Westmorland Gazette*; his next publication is his 1821 'Confessions of an English Opium-Eater'. His very final exploit is an article on the defence of India, published in 1858.
4. See Joel Faflak, 'De Quincey Collects Himself', *Nervous Reactions: Victorian Recollections of Romanticism*, ed. Joel Faflak and Julia M. Wright (Albany: SUNY Press, 2004), 23–46.
5. Edward Sackville-West, *A Flame in Sunlight: Life and Work of Thomas De Quincey* (London: Cassell, 1936).

6. Margaret Russett, *De Quincey's Romanticism: Canonical Minority and the Forms of Transmission* (Cambridge: Cambridge University Press, 1997), 1; 3.
7. For scholarship on Baudelaire's translation of De Quincey, see Éric Dayre, 'Baudelaire, traducteur de Thomas De Quincey, une prosaïque comparée de la modernité', *Romantisme* 29, no. 4 (1999): 31–51; and François Lallier, 'Traduire *Les confessions d'un anglais mangeur d'opium*', *Traductions, Passages: Le domaine anglais*, ed. Stephen Romer (Tours: Presses Universitaires François-Rabelais, 1993), 69–75.
8. On De Quincey's prescient development of *flânerie*, see Emily B. Stanback, 'Peripatetic in the City: De Quincey's *Confessions of an English Opium-Eater* and the Birth of the *Flâneur*', *Literature Compass* 10, no. 2 (2013): 146–61.
9. Charles Baudelaire, *Les paradis artificiels, opium et haschisch* (Paris: Poulet-Malassis and de Broise, 1860), iii. Translation mine.
10. C 1821, 2.25; 2.49.
11. C 1856, 2.202–3.
12. Charles Baudelaire, 'Les foules', *Petits poèmes en prose [Le spleen de Paris]*, *Œuvres complètes de Charles Baudelaire* (Paris: Michel Lévy, 1869), 4.31–2. Translation mine.
13. C 1821, 2.50; 2.70.
14. John Keats, 27 October 1818 [Letter 30], *Letters of John Keats*, ed. Stanley Gardner (London: University of London Press, 1965), 121–2.
15. C 1821, 2.70.
16. Virginia Woolf, 'De Quincey's Autobiography', *Collected Essays* (London: Hogarth, 1967), 4.1. On De Quincey, Woolf, and the representation of individuality in the era of the crowd, see Ortwin de Graef, 'Shaft Which Ran: Chinese Whispers with Auerbach, Buck, Woolf, and De Quincey', *Fear and Fantasy in a Global World*, ed. Susana Araújo, Marta Pacheco Pinto and Sandra Bettencourt (Amsterdam: Brill/Rodopi, 2015), 320–1.
17. Frances Wilson, *Guilty Thing: A Life of Thomas De Quincey* (London: Bloomsbury, 2016), 7.
18. Julian Wolfreys, 'Otherwise in London or, the Essence of Things: Modernity and Estrangement in the Nineteenth-Century Cityscape', *Victoriographies* 5, no. 1 (2015): 25.
19. S, 12.275.
20. On De Quincey's propensity for artful pseudonym, see Robert Morrison, 'De Quincey and the Opium-Eater's Other Selves', *Romanticism* 5, no. 1 (1999): 87–103.
21. C 1821, 2.53.
22. R, 3.27.
23. Margaret Russett, 'Wordsworth's Gothic Interpreter: De Quincey Personifies "We Are Seven"', *Studies in Romanticism* 30, no. 3 (1991): 349.
24. René Wellek, *Immanuel Kant in England 1793–1838* (Princeton: Princeton University Press, 1931), 180.
25. J. H. Stirling, *Jerrod, Tennyson and Macaulay, With Other Critical Essays* (Edinburgh: Edmonston & Douglas, 1886), 187. Emphasis mine.
26. Albert Goldman, *The Mine and the Mint: Sources for the Writings of*

*Thomas De Quincey* (Carbondale: Southern Illinois University Press, 1965), 9.
27. Robert Morrison, 'Red De Quincey', *The Wordsworth Circle* 29, no. 2 (1998): 133.
28. 'Gilfillan', 15.293–4. For further examples, see Morrison, 'Red De Quincey', 134–5.
29. D, 153.
30. C 1821, 2.70.
31. On Thomas De Quincey's antiquarian interests, see Deirdre Lynch, '"Wedded to Books": Bibliomania and the Romantic Essayists', *Romantic Circles Praxis Series*, February 2004. Available at < https://romantic-circles.org/praxis/libraries/lynch/lynch.html> (last accessed 10 March 2019); and Josephine McDonagh, 'De Quincey and the Secret Life of Books', *Thomas De Quincey: New Theoretical and Critical Directions*, ed. Robert Morrison and Daniel Sanjiv Roberts (London: Routledge, 2008), 123–42.
32. C 1821, 2.16; 2.60.
33. SdP, 15.163–7.
34. Cited in Horace Ainsworth Eaton, *A Biography of Thomas De Quincey* (Oxford: Oxford University Press, 1936), 386–7.
35. D, 160–1; 147; 154.
36. Christopher Smith, 'Robert Southey and the Emergence of *Lyrical Ballads*', *Romanticism on the Net* 9, February1998. Available at <https://ronjournal.org/s/330> (last accessed 11 March 2019). Smith's article also provides an inventory of the poems Southey lifted from the *Lyrical Ballads*.
37. Wilson, *Guilty Thing*, 108.
38. D, 209; 151; 162.
39. For a detailed analysis of De Quincey's attempt to regain his sense of self through rhetorical gestures, see Alina Clej, *A Genealogy of the Modern Self: Thomas De Quincey and the Intoxication of Writing* (Stanford: Stanford University Press, 1995), ch. 8.
40. S, 12.37; 12.52; 12.59.
41. James Hogg, *De Quincey and His Friends: Personal Recollections, Souvenirs and Anecdotes* (London: Sampson Low, Marston & Co., 1895), 78–9. While something of a standard feature in De Quincey biographies, the provenance of this quote is unclear. Hogg notes that he has taken the incident from 'Notes of Conversations by Richard Woodhouse – happily preserved by Dr Garnett (of the British Museum), in his admirable edition of "The Confessions" (Parchment Library), before the original MS. perished in a fire.' (ix)
42. D, 145–6.
43. For detailed accounts of De Quincey's approach to Wordsworth, see John E. Jordan, *De Quincey to Wordsworth: A Biography of a Relationship* (Berkeley: University of California Press, 1962), 1–47, and Russett, *De Quincey's Romanticism*, 14–91.
44. De Quincey's curatorship of Romantic afterlives is a neglected perspective in Tom Mole's *What the Victorians Made of Romanticism: Material Artefacts, Cultural Practices, and Reception History* (Princeton: Princeton University Press, 2017). Hints towards a project on this topic can be

found in Julian North, 'Intertextual Sociability in Victorian *Lives* of the Romantic Poets: Thomas De Quincey's "Lake Reminiscences" and Edward John Trelawny's *Recollections of the Last Days of Shelley and Byron*', *Life Writings* 14, no. 2 (2017): 155–69.
45. D, 187–88; see also Jordan, *De Quincey to Wordsworth*, 30–1; for De Quincey's draft, see 28–32.
46. Jordan, *De Quincey to Wordsworth*, 37.
47. See Thomas McFarland, *Romanticism and the Forms of Ruin: Wordsworth, Coleridge, the Modalities of Fragmentation* (Princeton: Princeton University Press, 1981), 137–216.
48. Dorothy and William Wordsworth, *The Letters of Dorothy and William Wordsworth: The Middle Years*, ed. Ernest de Selincourt (Oxford: Clarendon, 1967), 1.370.
49. Samuel Taylor Coleridge, *Collected Letters of Samuel Taylor Coleridge*, ed. Earl Leslie Griggs (London: Clarendon, 1956), 2.1013.
50. Stephen Mayfield Parrish, *The Art of the Lyrical Ballads* (Cambridge, MA: Harvard University Press, 1973), 46–7.
51. Thomas De Quincey, *De Quincey Memorials, Being Letters and Other Records Here First Published*, ed. Alexander H. Japp (London: Heinemann, 1891), 1.121.
52. AB, 10.235.
53. Jordan, *De Quincey to Wordsworth*, 32; 35.
54. Some sixty letters by De Quincey to Wordsworth have survived. Jordan's *De Quincey to Wordsworth* attempts a chronology with conjectures as to what has gone missing.
55. Wordsworth, *Letters*, 2.1.370.
56. Jordan, *De Quincey to Wordsworth*, 76; 19.
57. Jordan, *De Quincey to Wordsworth*, 34.
58. Wordsworth, *Letters* 2.1.195; 2.1.180; 2.1.159.
59. Thomas Carlyle and Jane Welsh Carlyle, 18 November 1827, *The Carlyle Letters Online*, ed. Brent E. Kinser (Durham, NC: Duke University Press: 2007–16), 4.287–93. References to De Quincey's diminutive stature are so common among his contemporaries as to be something of an epithet: Southey calls him 'Little Mr De Quincey', and adds that he 'wish[es] he were not so little' (*Letters of Robert Southey: A Selection*, ed. M. H. Fitzgerald (Oxford: Oxford University Press, 1912), 152). Thomas Hood describes him as 'almost boyish [. . .] from a peculiar delicacy of complexion and smallness of features' (Thomas Hood, *Prose and Verse* (New York: Wiley and Putnam, 1845), 1: 87). The association continues to the present day: see Nicholas Spice, 'Little Mr De Quincey', *London Review of Books*, 18 May 2017: 3–8.
60. Robert Morrison, *The English Opium-Eater: A Biography of Thomas De Quincey* (London: Weidenfeld & Nicolson, 2009), 154.
61. Wordsworth, *Letters* 2.1.346; 245. For the political context of Wordsworth's essay, see Richard Gravil, 'Wordsworth as Partisan', *Concerning the Convention of Cintra* by William Wordsworth, ed. Richard Gravil and W. J. B. Owen (Tirril: Humanities-Ebooks, 2009), 17–30. Jordan, *De Quincey to Wordsworth*, 60–202, provides a detailed description of the back-and-forth between De Quincey and Wordsworth

as they attempted to prepare *Cintra* for the press. Further valuable background is provided by John Edwin Wells, 'The Story of Wordsworth's "Cintra"', *Studies in Philology* 18, no. 1 (1921): 15–76.
62. Wordsworth, *Letters*, 1.320.
63. Jordan, *De Quincey to Wordsworth*, 199; 138; 199.
64. Wordsworth, *Letters*, 1.319.
65. Jordan, *De Quincey to Wordsworth*, 277.
66. Leslie Stephen, 'De Quincey', in *Hours in a Library*, 1.237–68 (London: Smith, Elder, & Co., 1892), 244.
67. Sara Hutchinson, *The Letters of Sara Hutchinson, 1800–1835*, ed. Kathleen Coburn (London: Routledge, 1954), 36–7; 209.
68. Jordan, *De Quincey to Wordsworth*, 283–90. Chapter 4 provides more details on De Quincey's short-lived editorial career.
69. William Wordsworth, 'Preface' [to *Lyrical Ballads*, 1800], *Lyrical Ballads, and Other Poems. 1797–1800, The Cornell Wordsworth*, 6.746, ed. James Butler and Karen Green (Ithaca: Cornell University Press, 1992). On De Quincey's idiosyncratic retooling of contemporary theories of medicine, see Barry Milligan, 'Brunonianism, Radicalism, and "The Pleasures of Opium"', *Thomas De Quincey: New Theoretical and Critical Directions*, ed. Robert Morrison and Daniel Sanjiv Roberts (London: Routledge, 2008), 45–63. This discussion fits into De Quincey's wider theorising on the body/mind dichotomy and its importance to the analogous issue of eloquence versus rhetoric: both topics are broached in the next two chapters.
70. C 1821, 2.9–10.
71. These essays were first published together after De Quincey's death, under the title *Recollections of the Lakes and the Lake Poets*, in 1862. Edward Sackville-West shortens this to *Recollections of the Lake Poets* for his 1948 edition; John Jordan's 1961 edition instead prefers *Reminiscences of the English Lake Poets*, a title he lifts from De Quincey's articles on Wordsworth, originally titled 'Lake Reminiscences'. David Wright's 1970 edition restores the title from 1862. Whatever their heading, the *Recollections* comprise of a series of articles on Coleridge, Wordsworth and Southey, occasionally supplemented by contextual companion pieces like extracts from the 'Sketches of Life and Manners'. While the *Recollections/Reminiscences* are a posthumous creation, then, they are published so close to one another and mark such a significant watershed in De Quincey's career that this book will refer to this complex of essays through their retrospective title.
72. For other analyses of De Quincey's representation of Wordsworth in the *Recollections*, see Annette Wheeler Cafarelli, 'De Quincey and Wordsworthian Narrative', *Studies in Romanticism* 28, no. 1 (1989): 121–47; Russett, *De Quincey's Romanticism*, 14–52.
73. Wordsworth, 11.52; 11.55; 11.58.
74. Wordsworth's Poetry, 15.230; 15.238.
75. On a personal level, De Quincey appears to have been disappointed by the Wordsworths' disapproval of his marriage, which they regarded as a catastrophic match. 'Mr De Quincey is married', Dorothy remarks in a characteristic note, 'and I fear I may add he is ruined' (*Middle Years*, 2.779).

76. Wordsworth, 11.62.
77. On opium and its reconfiguration of embodied experience, see Chapter 4.
78. Samuel Taylor Coleridge, *Christabel; Kubla Khan, a Vision; The Pains of Sleep* (London: John Murray, 1816), 52.
79. Henry Crabb Robinson, *Books and Writers*, ed. Edith J. Marley (London: J. M. Dent and Sons, 1938), 1.187.
80. A considerable number of letters appear to have been 'systematically destroyed' by Coleridge's heirs in response to De Quincey's articles in *Tait's*. See Earl Leslie Griggs, introduction to *Collected Letters of Samuel Taylor Coleridge* (London: Clarendon, 1971), 1.xxxviii; also see Daniel Sanjiv Roberts, *Revisionary Gleam: De Quincey, Coleridge, and the High Romantic Argument* (Liverpool: Liverpool University Press, 2000), 15–22.
81. This deference, as Roberts notes, is in line with a widespread contemporary tendency to 'grant Wordsworth a pre-eminence of achievement', which has been handed down to present-day readers as 'an interpretative compulsion' to confirm Wordsworth as the crux of canonical British Romanticism, 'the progenitor and source of a largely one-way traffic of influence'. See Roberts, *Revisionary Gleam*, 23.
82. C 1821, 2.13.
83. For a more detailed reading, see Nigel Leask, '"Murdering One's Double": De Quincey's "Confessions of an English Opium-Eater" and S. T. Coleridge's *Biographia Literaria*', *Prose Studies* 13, no. 3 (1990): 78–98.
84. Henry Crabb Robinson, *Books*, 1.58.
85. Roberts, *Revisionary Gleam*, 153. Also see Mark D. Merritt, 'De Quincey's Coleridge and the Dismantling of Romantic Authority', *a/b: Auto/Biography Studies* 20, no. 2 (2005): 195–229.
86. Merritt, 'De Quincey's Coleridge', 197.
87. Coleridge, 10.287; 10.293.
88. De Quincey, 'Note [to Coleridge]', *Recollections of the Lakes and the Lake Poets*, 243.
89. Coleridge, 10.303; 10.318; 10.303.
90. Samuel Taylor Coleridge, *Table Talk*, ed. Carl Woodring (Princeton: Princeton University Press, 1992), 1.581.
91. On the context of the confrontation between the 'Confessions' and the 'Literary Correspondence', see Robert Morrison, 'Opium-Eaters and Magazine Wars: De Quincey and Coleridge in 1821', *Victorian Periodicals Review* 30, no. 1 (1997): 27–40.
92. Wordsworth, *Letters*, 4.1.95.
93. Cited in Jordan, *De Quincey to Wordsworth*, 337; 347.
94. Roberts, *Revisionary Gleam*, 15.
95. Dove Cottage MSS, cited in Jordan, *De Quincey to Wordsworth*, 347.
96. D, 160; 154–5.
97. William Shakespeare, *Macbeth*, 5.3.
98. Samuel Taylor Coleridge, *The Annotated Ancient Mariner*, ed. Martin Gardner (London: Anthony Blond, 1965), 52–3.
99. *Macbeth*, 3.153; 3.150; 3.153.
100. De Quincey's diary attests to his voracious reading of Gothic novels

and poetry, with Lewis and Pilkington singled out as especial favourites. Among Southey's Gothic poems, he read such pieces as 'Ode to Horror' and 'The Idiot'. On De Quincey's own Gothic texts, chief among them 'The Avenger' and *Klosterheim*, see Patrick Bridgwater, *De Quincey's Gothic Masquerade* (Amsterdam: Brill/Rodopi, 2004).
101. D, 160.
102. SGG, 16.
103. Walter Scott, 'Prefatory Memoir of the Life of the Author', *The Novels of Mrs Ann Radcliffe* (London: Hurst, Robinson, & Co., 1824), iv.
104. Scott, 'Memoir', xxxv.
105. SGG, 16.
106. Virginia Woolf, 'Impassioned Prose', *Collected Essays*, ed. L. Woolf (London: Hogarth, 1966), 1.167.
107. Annette Wheeler Cafarelli, *Prose in the Age of Poets: Romanticism and Biographical Narrative from Johnson to De Quincey* (Philadelphia: University of Pennsylvania Press, 1990).
108. John E. Jordan, 'De Quincey on Wordsworth's Theory of Diction', *PMLA* 68, no. 4 (1954), 764.
109. Stephen, 'De Quincey', 1.240–2.
110. SGG, 16.
111. Stephen, 'De Quincey', 1.240; 1.262.
112. BL, 297.
113. BL, 299–300.
114. Thomas Carlyle, *Sartor Resartus: The Life and Opinions of Herr Teufelsdröckh in Three Books*, The Norman and Charlotte Strouse Edition of the Writings of Thomas Carlyle, ed. Mark Engel and Rodger L. Tarr (Berkeley: University of California Press, 2000), 217; 127.
115. LYM, 3.68; 3.71.
116. Coleridge, 10.351.
117. Morrison and Roberts, '"I was Worshipped; I was Sacrificed": A Passage to Thomas De Quincey', *New Theoretical and Critical Directions*, ed. Robert Morrison and Daniel Sanjiv Roberts (London: Routledge, 2009), 14.
118. Charles Macfarlane, *Reminiscences of a Literary Life* (London: Murray, 1917), 81–2.
119. SdP, 15.169.
120. George Gilfillan, *A Gallery of Literary Portraits* (Edinburgh: James Hogg, 1845), 105; 297. De Quincey reviewed Gilfillan's survey in *Tait's* in two instalments, published in 1845 and 1846, seizing on the opportunity to differentiate his work and thought from Godwin, Foster, Hazlitt, Shelley and Keats.
121. J. Hillis Miller, *The Disappearance of God: Five Nineteenth-Century Writers* (Cambridge, MA: Harvard University Press, 1975), 44–5.
122. For Poulet's work on De Quincey, which centres on the links between his work and Baudelaire, who is described as the 'first' 'among the followers of De Quincey', see Georges Poulet, 'Timelessness and Romanticism', *Journal of the History of Ideas* 15, no. 1 (1954): 3–22; esp. 18–22.
123. Robert Maniquis, 'Lonely Empires: Personal and Public Visions of Thomas De Quincey', in *Literary Monographs*, ed. Eric Rothstein

and J. A. Wittreich (Madison: University of Wisconsin Press, 1976), 8.47–127.
124. Bruce E. Graver, 'Wordsworth and the Romantic Art of Translation', *The Wordsworth Circle* 17, no.3 (1986): 169.
125. In his youth, Wordsworth translated from Catullus, Virgil and Horace; later on in life, he translated from Petrarch, Ariosto, Chiabrera, Metastasio, Michelangelo, Tasso, and continued his interest in Virgil. He also translated an anonymous French and Greek poem, a Latin poem by Thomas Warton, and part of a poem by Moschus; and produced imitations of Anacreon, Horace and Juvenal. See Graver, 'Wordsworth and Translation', 169; 174; and William Wordsworth, *Translations of Chaucer and Virgil*, ed. Bruce E. Graver (Ithaca: Cornell University Press, 1998).
126. On Wordsworth's ideology of originality, see Brian Wilkie, 'Wordsworth and the Tradition of the Avant-Garde', *The Journal of English and Germanic Philology* 72, no. 2 (1973): 194–222.
127. William Wordsworth, *Poems, in Two Volumes, and Other Poems, 1800–1807*, ed. Jared Curtis (Ithaca and London: Cornell University Press, 1983), *The Cornell Wordsworth*, 7. 274.
128. Coleridge, 10.309.
129. De Quincey primarily casts his critique of Goethe as an attempt to keep back his pernicious influence from English writing and thinking – see the next chapter for further details. Interestingly, De Quincey's revulsion is either repeated or preceded by Wordsworth, who is recorded to have remarked that he had 'tried to read Goethe, [but] I never could succeed [. . .] there is a profligacy, an inhuman sensuality, in his works which is utterly revolting' (Christopher Wordsworth, *Memoirs of William Wordsworth*, ed. Henry Reed (Boston: Ticknor & Fields, 1851), 2.488). Emerson writes that Wordsworth 'abused Goethe's Wilhelm Meister heartily' whenever afforded an opportunity. He offers the same opinion on Carlyle's translation, which he 'sometimes [thought] insane' as a project. (*English Traits* (Boston: Ticknor & Fields, 1856), 27). For further context, see Catherine Waltraud Proescholdt–Obermann, *Goethe and His British Critics: The Reception of Goethe's Works in British Periodicals, 1779–1855* (Berlin: Peter Lang, 1992).
130. M, 4.170; 4.180.
131. Carlyle, *Carlyle Letters Online*, 11 December 1828 (3.231–6; 4.287–93; 4.1826–8, 432–5). Also see Robert Morrison, '"The 'Bog School'": Carlyle and De Quincey', *Carlyle Studies Annual* (1995): 13–20.
132. Tillar J. Mazzeo, *Plagiarism and Literary Property in the Romantic Period* (Philadelphia: University of Pennsylvania Press, 2007), 112. Also see Robert Macfarlane, '"Romantic" Originality', *Original Copy: Plagiarism and Originality in Nineteenth-Century Literature* (Oxford: Oxford University Press, 2007), 18–49.
133. Coleridge, 10.292.
134. John Wilson et al., *Noctes Ambrosianae* (New York: W. J. Widdleton, 1867), 1.383.
135. Sara Coleridge, 'Letter to Henry Nelson Coleridge', 14–15 September 1834, Harry S. Ransom Center MS. Quoted in Alan D. Vardy,

*Constructing Coleridge: The Posthumous Life of the Author* (London: Palgrave Macmillan, 2010), 30.
136. Hartley Coleridge, 'Letter to Henry Nelson Coleridge', 10 July 1840, Harry S. Ransom Center MS. Quoted in Vardy, *Constructing Coleridge*, 76.
137. 'Note [to Coleridge]', 10.242.
138. Coleridge, 10.291–3.
139. BL, 161–4.
140. Friedrich Wilhelm Joseph von Schelling, *Sämmtliche Werke* (Stuttgart and Augsburg: J. G. Cotta'scher Verlag, 1856), 2.1.196n. The essay in question is Coleridge's 'On the Prometheus of Æschylus', which may be found in his *Literary Remains* (London: William Pickering, 1836), 2.323–59. For a closer analysis, see Paul Hamilton, *Coleridge and German Philosophy: The Poet in the Land of Logic* (London: Bloomsbury, 2007), 103–9. Also see Nicholas Reid, 'Coleridge and Schelling: The Missing Transcendental Deduction', *Studies in Romanticism* 33, no. 3 (1994): 451–79. In Coleridge's work, tautegory describes a totalised symbol: for a detailed delineation of this concept, see Éric Dayre, 'L'impératif tautégorique, de la loi poétique', *Une histoire dissemblable: Le tournant poétique du romantisme anglais 1797–1834* (Paris: Hermann, 2010), 117–254.
141. SdP, 15.178.
142. Plagiarism, 3.118.
143. Coleridge, 10.292.
144. For a closer analysis of the terms involved in such psychologising interpretations of plagiarism, see Tilar J. Mazzeo, 'Coleridge, Plagiarism, and the Psychology of Romantic Habit', *European Romantic Review* 15, no. 2 (2004): 335–41.
145. Coleridge, 10.292; 10.292; 10.322; 10.290. Emphasis mine.
146. Secret Societies, 16.166.
147. Hood, *Prose and Verse*, 87.

Chapter 2

# How to Write English: The Transnationalism of a National Style

### Meeting the Malay Anew

It is symptomatic of the blindness to the role of translation in British Romanticism that not one of the manifold critical readings of the 'Confessions' has hitherto commented on the extent to which De Quincey sets himself up for a lifetime of translation. In his portrait of the Romantic as a young man, he describes himself not as a boy growing into creative masculinity in the Wordsworthian mould, but as a creature condemned to imitation. His account is particularly focused on a self-professed talent for dead languages, to whose study every scholar necessarily arrives late. When he boasts that he was 'very early distinguished for my my classical attainments [. . .] an accomplishment which I have not since met with in any scholar of my times', he flaunts no precocity for creativity or spontaneity. Instead, he demonstrates a capacity for storing and disgorging great amounts of information. In Wales, he serves as a scribe for illiterate farmers; in London, he fancies he might find work as a 'corrector of Greek proofs'; in the Lake District, he moonlights as Wordsworth's editor. Even when he most manifests himself by rebelling against the regimented life dictated by his mother and guardians, he runs from his unstimulating tutor with 'a favourite English poet in one pocket, and a small 12mo volume, containing about nine plays of Euripides, in the other'. De Quincey, that is, locates his voice *in between*; between eras, genres, authors, nations, cultures and languages.

De Quincey most dramatises his talents for mediation as he recalls a curious experience during his time in the Lakes. An exotic element has come knocking, and Britain has need of a translator's aid: opening the door of Dove Cottage to the discombobulating sight of a beturbaned Malay unintelligibly requesting assistance, De Quincey's maid beseeches her master to intercede. The passage in question, a masterclass in Romantic self-performance, bears excerpting at length:

> The servant who opened the door to him was a young girl, born and bred amongst the mountains, who had never seen an Asiatic dress of any sort; his turban therefore confounded her not a little; and as it turned out that his attainments in English were exactly of the same extent as hers in the Malay, there seemed to be an impassable gulf fixed between all communication of ideas, if either party had happened to possess any. In this dilemma, the girl, recollecting the reputed learning of her master (and doubtless giving me credit for a knowledge of all the languages of the earth besides perhaps a few of the lunar ones), came and gave me to understand that there was a sort of demon below [. . .] And a more striking picture there could not be imagined than the beautiful English face of the girl, and its exquisite fairness, together with her erect and independent attitude, contrasted with the sallow and bilious skin of the Malay, enamelled or veneered with mahogany by marine air, his small, fierce, restless eyes, thin lips, slavish gestures and adorations. [. . .] My knowledge of the Oriental tongues is not remarkably extensive, being indeed confined to two words – the Arabic word for barley and the Turkish for opium (*madjoon*), which I have learned from Anastasius; and as I had neither a Malay dictionary nor even Adelung's *Mithridates*, which might have helped me to a few words, I addressed him in some lines from the Iliad, considering that, of such languages as I possessed, Greek, in point of longitude, came geographically nearest to an Oriental one. He worshipped me in a most devout manner, and replied in what I suppose was Malay. In this way I saved my reputation with my neighbours, for the Malay had no means of betraying the secret.[1]

Evidently crafted for purposes of authorial presentation, this vignette has long been used as a testing ground for novel perspectives in De Quincey criticism, and especially for postcolonial critiques, which have seized on the scene as quintessentially orientalist.[2] The parable of the Malay and the Maiden may also serve as a potent entryway into issues of translation. Structured into a series of oppositions – gender, nationality, complexion – and ultimately turning on a total blockage in communication, the episode permits the author of the 'Confessions' to stage himself as a translator tasked with pacifying the frictions between a hapless Englishwoman and her foreign visitor. But for De Quincey's intercession, the encounter would remain unproductive; possibly fatal, even, to his housekeeper's shaky nerves and his guest's delicate constitution. By dint of his brief mediation, however, the meeting yields at least a hint of satisfactory communication. Crucially, this is no more than a hint, further reduced in significance by several examples in the 'Confessions' of encounters disappointingly resistant to translation. For a man who never travelled beyond British and Irish shores (he visits the latter at age fifteen),[3] and for a text that advertises as the 'Confessions of an *English* Opium-Eater', De Quincey is engulfed by an extraordinary range of foreign voices, most of them incomprehensible. There are impenetrable German treatises, inscrutable Arabic characters, unintelligible Italian operagoers, and a set of irate Welshmen, who eject De Quincey from their home upon finding he is a Sassenach.[4] In the 'Confessions', then, De Quincey presents himself as a writer still grasping towards a better understanding of the powers of translation. This project comes to a climax in the mythologised encounter with a traveller from a foreign land. If this fictional event points to a method, however, it is one that its writer does not yet fully comprehend. De Quincey's interpretative intervention is reflexive rather than carefully considered, darkly operating through half-remembered quotes and concluding in mostly mysterious results. Indecision therefore abounds in the allegory of the Malay. What business can a Far Eastern traveller possibly have in Grasmere? What exactly in De Quincey's grab-bag of irrelevant phrases prompts his reverential response? Why, when pressed for a few quick words, does this self-professed linguist manage no more than a few quoted verses? Are we even sure the visitor *is* Malayan? De Quincey, after all, only 'supposes' him so. As an identifier, moreover, 'Malayan' is inscribed with uncertainty and hybridity, the Straits of Malacca long having been known as a meeting place of the most diverse peoples and languages, as the wildly divergent ethnic descriptors attached to the Malay attest. His turban suggests a Sikh; his loose trousers indicate a Turk; his sallow skin, which is somehow also mahogany, might be taken to point to the Far East and the Indian subcontinent; and his response (if a response it is) is elicited by an impromptu quote from the *Iliad*, which is suggestive of a Near Eastern connection by way of Greece and Troy. The Malay, in short, is a sign that is already in internal translation, and the translator that can face up to his challenge must be, too; ready to switch effortlessly between multiple idioms and sources. Significantly, De Quincey keeps this conclusion to himself and to his reader: neither of the two parties in attendance are permitted to note the limits of the impromptu interpreter's modest knowledge. Amid a dearth of appreciation for the workings and benefits of translation, a little learning counts for much, and De Quincey hesitates to surrender those qualities that grant him a foothold in British Romanticism.

Throughout his post-'Confessions' work, De Quincey explores the translational vocation annunciated by the providential visitor from the East, chiefly directing his energies into elucidating its mechanisms and effects. In the course of these attempts at refinement, translation emerges as a clearing station for a variety of antinomies. Having sparked a reorganisation of De Quincey's sense of authorship by offering a figure that bridges the dichotomy of creative production and imitative reproduction, translation goes on to ground a reappraisal of style and thought. In accordance with the chronology of his writings, which first devote attention to the tensions between poetical and prosaic writing before they launch a wide-ranging critique of the conflicts between the noumenal and the phenomenal that divide Romantic philosophy against itself, the present chapter centres on De Quincey's reconstruction of a national literature and style through a novel theory of philology, a career-spanning project that requires multiple passes before a system truly emerges.[5]

### The Pseudo-Philology of English

At the heart of De Quincey's project for a renovated national literature stands a paradox: writing English well requires one *move away* from Britain, if only by hospitably opening one's cottage to whatever drifter happens to come calling. That is, while De Quincey addresses his work to a people united by 'the privilege of a British birth', he maintains that, in order to comprehend its linguistic and cultural specificity and thereby attain to a literature fully attuned to its national characteristics, the British nation must be prepared to suspend its insular spirit. This entails that he commands his compatriots to relinquish a much-cherished trait. Like De Quincey's exemplary maid, dumbfounded to have answered the door to the Malay, the British are described as displaying ignorance of anything beyond their shores. Such egotism has dire consequences for the study of language: absent any external objects of comparison, English speakers feel no need to examine or cultivate their English. '[W]hilst all other nations show their patriotism severally in connexion with their own separate mother tongues',[6] Britain stands alone in having compiled 'no learned grammar of our language [. . .] we have also no sufficient dictionary; and we have no work at all [. . .] on the phrases and idiomatic niceties of our languages'.[7] This situation is 'painful and humiliating to an Englishman', not just because he is alarmed to find his 'venerated mother' lagging behind other nations in its philology, but because in showing themselves 'ever ready, with a dishonourable levity, to undervalue the English language',[8] its speakers lack any basis for identifying the strengths and the weaknesses of their idiom, or any other.

De Quincey's complaints regarding the British unwillingness to harness their native language may seem to mark him out as a prescriptivist; an essentially negative thinker of idiom and nationality, suspicious of neologism and intolerant of imports. And it is true, as Wordsworth, Coleridge and Carlyle knew from direct experience, that he excoriated his contemporaries for various grammatical, lexicographic and orthographic slips, joining forces with an ongoing social standardisation of English grammar and spelling as a sign of bourgeois status but internationalising its stakes.[9] In Britain at least, De Quincey reflects, '[n]o man seems to have reflected that there was a *wrong* and a *right* in the choice of swords, in the choice of phrases, in the mechanism of sentences, or even in the grammar', lamenting that here is 'an anomaly not found perhaps in any literature but ours, – that the most eminent English writers do not write their mother tongue without continual violations of propriety'.[10] Adding to the suspicion of linguistic conservatism, his favoured targets are those errors which originate in deviations from the rightful evolution of language. These counter-historical mistakes, he writes, are aberrations:

> if the evolution of successive meaning has gone on *rightly*, i.e. by simply lapsing through a series of close affinities, there can be no reason for recurring to the primitive meaning of the word: but, if it can be shown that the evolution has been *faulty* [...] then we have a right to reform the word.

A deeper understanding of De Quincey's thoughts on language requires some unpacking. What does he mean when he labels a particular instance of etymological drift faulty? An indication of the standards on which he bases his prescriptive comparisons is to be found in his meditations on linguistic change, in which he notes that a wrong-headed development is best defined either as a break with tradition, which entails an interruption in 'the chain of true affinities',[11] or as an exaggeration of tradition, in that '[g]reat faults [...] may grow out of great virtues in excess'.[12] His complaints about the evolution of language have little to do with anxieties over the disfiguring impact of progress, rather, he targets the preservation of English linguistic identity, whose essence is balance. Both the presumption that change is necessarily for the worse and the opposing view that progress is always advantageous are 'idle misconception[s]':

> No language is stationary. The languages of nations like the English and French, walking in the van of civilisation, having popular institutions, and taking part in the business of the earth with morbid energy, are placed under the action of causes that will not allow them any respite from change. Neologism, in revolutionary times, is not an infirmity of caprice [...] but is a mere necessity of the unresting intellect. New ideas, new aspects of old ideas, new relations of objects to each other, or to man – the subject who contemplates those objects, – absolutely insist on new words. And it would not be a more idle misconception to find a disease in the pains of growth than to fancy a decay of vernacular purity in the multitude of verbal coinages which modern necessities of thought and action are annually calling forth on the banks of the Thames.[13]

When De Quincey writes that 'coinages do not all stand upon the same basis of justification', his concern is with the want of standards by which to judge and steer the growth of a language. Against the permissive attitude displayed by what little lexicographic work has been undertaken in English,[14] he defends the institution of normative categories which are to be enforced by a select group of self-appointed authorities as these steer the language towards its best self. After all, '[w]ithout some preliminary notion, abstractedly, of the precise qualities to be sought for in a language, how are we to know whether the main object of our question is found, or not found, in any given language offered for examination?'[15] Underlying this presumption of linguistic mouldability is the circular doctrine that language derives from the people just as much the people derive from the language. That is, not only does a language reflect the social and cultural circumstances of its speakers; any reconfiguration of a language must also impact on the nation. Language, in short, is 'partly the effect, and partly the cause of the social temperament which distinguishes' a particular people.[16] In insisting on the institution of a normative apparatus, De Quincey targets the conditioning of a national culture: as he frets over the merits of linguistic innovation, he creates his own version of the motif of unacknowledged legislation. His aim is nothing less than the creation, or renovation, of a truly national language through writing.

What does De Quincey refer to, exactly, when he speaks of Britain? That is, what nation does he have in mind when he argues for a transformative interaction between a national style, a national character, and a national language? His definition of nationality participates in the contemporary vogue for defining nationhood through linguistic parameters: he limits the compass of the nation to English-speaking territories. From this expansive zone of reference must be subtracted anything not located in Great Britain: his essay 'How to Write English' refutes at length any suggestion that the United States may ultimately overtake Britain in cultural or political importance, and grows particularly indignant at suggestions of an Irish preponderance in the American population.[17] Within Britain, moreover, it is England that properly constitutes the core of Britishness, with other candidates amongst the four nations relegated to a secondary position. When De Quincey crystallises the tenets of nineteenth-century conservative nationalism in proclaiming that 'one heart, one pride, one glory connects every man by transcendent bond of his English blood',[18] he is not quite performing a breezy equation of England and Britain: in his estimation, fringe nations like Wales simply do not partake in this fabled bond, and appear unable to comprehend exactly what it means to be fully British. Intriguingly, possibly because he evaded his creditors by moving to Glasgow and thence Edinburgh, Scotland is not thus marginalised.[19] Even with this minor concession, De

Quincey emerges as a committed nationalist, if more cosmopolitan than his critics have made him out to be, deploying translation as it relates to questions of linguistics in part to further the cause of an Empire centred on a restrictive equation of Britishness to Englishness.

De Quincey's prescient interest in etymological philology demonstrate his lifelong interest in theories of language.[20] His contributions the *Westmorland Gazette*, which include a piece that argues for the Danish origins of the Lake dialect, confirm he is aware of recent advances in the science.[21] Moreover, he demonstrates an acquaintance with the philosophy of language from which linguistics was beginning to develop by arguing for the interaction of national language and national character.[22] As the Abbé de Condillac puts it in his 1746 response to Locke's 1689 *Essay on the Human Understanding*, influentially translated to English in 1756, 'every language expresses the character of the people that speak it', and they, in turn, 'conform to the character of their language'.[23] The idea that language is best defined as a social phenomenon, implicated in and therefore reflective of the historical unfolding of national identity, powerfully determines the contemporary understanding of language and linguistic change. In his *Biographia*, for instance, Coleridge clarifies his distinction between the fancy and the imagination by situating it in the history of the English language, arguing that the Romantic separation of the two concepts reflects an important shift in the words' underlying evolution, which in turn proceeds from a radical shift in 'general belief' – that is, in the structures of knowledge that subtend British culture. This process of desynonymisation, Coleridge argues, demonstrates that language change must proceed from 'an instinct of growth, a certain, collective, unconscious good sense' that adapts language to the progress of the intellect: in thus adapting to social advances, moreover, language further reinforces the national march of the mind.[24] Crucially, these social modifications to language, in an aside that signals a significant advance on Condillac whose notes on the influence of 'great men'[25] do not yet envisage a policy of active intervention, are to be confirmed or tempered by a cadre of '[m]en of research'.[26] 'It was the schoolmen', Coleridge pointedly observes of the men of letters tasked with linguistic arbitration in medieval times, 'who made the languages of Europe' and the mind of Europe 'what they now are.'[27] Like De Quincey, then, Coleridge proposes a dual theory of linguistic progress, ascribing causative force both to the people at large and to a smallish elite. Unlike De Quincey, however, he is uncomfortable with the tensions between a democratic and a scholarly account of linguistic development, prevaricating on both scores by withholding a precise set of criteria in the reorganisation of English.[28] De Quincey does spell out his methods, presenting the transition from descriptive to prescriptive linguistics as entirely empirical. Both must proceed from a thorough inspection of the English language in its active usage, both historical and current – that is, from the ways in which the language is deployed in actual writing and conversation. It is in the practical use of the language by citizens in the most varied walks of life, and from the most varied periods, that the nature and evolution of the British national identity fully comes forward; and it is here that a policy of watchful intervention finds its tools and targets. 'All languages, it has been remarked', De Quincey notes, adapting Coleridge's theory of desynonymy, 'tend to clear themselves of synonymes [*sic*] – as intellectual culture advances; the superfluous words being taken up and appropriated by new shades and combinations of thought evolved in the progress of society.'

Crucially, 'long before this appropriation is fixed and petrified, as it were, into the acknowledged vocabulary of the language, an insensible *clinamen* (to borrow a Lucretian word) prepares the way for it'.[29] It is by recognising and acting upon this underdefined *clinamen* that the linguist may identify his principles of selection. His role is not to create new ideas, but to nurture those already poised for emergence: his purpose, in short, is to act on the destiny of a language as it manifests in its active use.

It is at this juncture, as he seeks to decide on the nature of a national language and the tools that might permit its creation and reconstruction, that De Quincey brings in the concept of style. Style is here to be understood as the disposition that a language assumes as it is employed in communication; a general temperament that may be further cultivated and exaggerated in specific types of expression. The stylistic qualities assumed by a language as it is used to various ends, moreover, fall into two broad categories, indicated through a range of contrasting terms – all slightly different in scope, but premised on the same basic dichotomy. When the Quinceyan philologist seeks to capture the stylistics specific to a given text, he does so by determining its internal balance of prosaic and poetics traits; its quotient, that is, of matter and manner, of form and content, of rhetoric and eloquence. The practical use of language that ought to inform writers' linguistic policies, then, is to be schematised by studying the interaction of form and meaning; of formal techniques and mimetic content. In summary, '[t]he word *style* has with us a twofold meaning':

> one, the narrow meaning, expressing the mere [. . .] syntax or combination of words into sentences; the other of far wider extent, and expressing all possible relations that can arise between thoughts and words – the total effect of a writer as derived from manner. Style may be viewed as an *organic* thing and

as a *mechanic* thing. [. . .] The science of style as an organ of thought, of style in relation to the ideas and feelings, might be called the *organology* of style. The science of style considered as a machine, in which words act upon words, and through a particular grammar, might be called the *mechanology* of style. It is of little importance by what name these two functions of composition are expressed. But it is of great importance not to confound the functions: that function by which style maintains a commerce with thought, and that by which it chiefly communicates with grammar and with words.[30]

The dual system of style that De Quincey here proposes is purpose-made to anchor a precise taxonomy of national languages. By classifying each idiom according to its propensities for either formal or referential expression, for focusing on either 'words act[ing] upon words' or on the relation of an utterance to the 'ideas and feelings' that it conveys, a spectrum may be established. Such a universal inventory of peoples through the features of their languages is a common ambition amongst eighteenth-century and Romantic linguistics. Condillac, for instance, argues that the entire range of known languages may be schematised. Utilising a scale of gradations between two extremes, 'we might see [languages] assuming different characters according to the extremity to which they approached, and indemnifying themselves for the advantages lost on the side, by this which they acquired on the other'. Condillac defines his double heuristic in terms loosely corresponding to De Quincey's, although he is less interested in dwelling on stylistic differences, preferring instead to attend to the philosophical proclivities that underlie habits of expression. As such, in the French linguist's plan, one limit of language centres on the exercise of 'the fancy, to such a degree, that the people who spoke it must be perpetually blundering'; the other on 'such an exercise of the analytical method, that those to whom it was natural should conduct themselves even in their pleasures, like mathematicians investigating the solution of a problem'.[31]

English, De Quincey argues, is presently immovably positioned on the referential end of the philological spectrum – had he favoured Condillac's phraseology, he might have typified it as analytical. So totemic is the value of prosaic eloquence to English speakers that they regard form as little more than superadded frippery: cute, occasionally enchanting, but expendable. '[A] mere ornamental accident of written composition', in short; 'a trivial embellishment like the mouldings of furniture, the cornices of ceilings, the arabesques of tea-urns.' The issue is not that the British are unaware of form, but that they reject it as parergic to expression. 'Viewing the thoughts as the substantial object in a book, we are apt to regard the manner of presenting these thoughts as a secondary or even trivial concern',[32] or even as a threat to efficient communication that must be exorcised. It is this hostility to form that De Quincey seeks to reverse:

> [o]ur quarrel is [. . .] with that general principle in England which tends in all things to set the matter above the manner, the substance above the external show [. . .] This general tendency operates in many ways but our own immediate purpose is concerned with it only so far as it operates upon Style. In no country upon earth [. . .] is it a more determinate tendency of the national mind to value the matter of a book not only as paramount to the manner, but even as distinct from it, and as capable of a separate insulation.[33]

In 'degrad[ing] the value of the ornamental' and declaring referentiality to be 'the true value that cannot perish', De Quincey notes dolefully, 'we English err greatly'. While the British repudiation of rhetoric hews to the universal law whereby the language adapts to the people, and therefore boasts the minor merit of being 'highly agreeable to the general cast of the national character',[34] an objective evaluation is decidedly in the negative, so much so that it is evident the active usage of English is presently contravention of its destiny. It is plain that things are not well with the language or the people from which it derives. In matters linguistic, political and philosophical, there is presently an overpowering sentiment that the standard shape of thought has grown tiresome. The nation and its writers toil under a crisis that expresses itself as a pervasive lassitude: there is an 'unwilling and mysterious sense' that the exclusive cultivation of referentiality and meaningfulness may well be in contravention of the natural tendencies of the English language and the British nation.[35] The national language tells powerfully on the national psyche: sensing the imbalance in the latter proceeds from an error in the first, De Quincey moves to recommend linguistic tools for a psychic regeneration. Since no help is to be found amongst the British, he turns to outside perspectives.

## Beyond British Prose

Harking to indistinct intimations that a profound sense of lack has eaten into the foundations of English, De Quincey conducts a survey of his outside options. He does so both in order to trace the outline of the void unsettling British culture, and to import any missing elements: in effect, he does for English what he did for himself when he defined his position through the writers in his immediate vicinity. In seizing on a programme of comparison and translation as a potential lifeline, De Quincey reverses the contemporary understanding of language, which infers from the reciprocal relation between language and national character that translation, and most of all literary translation, must be foredoomed to failure.[36] As Condillac puts it, since '[i]t is in the writing of poets, that the character of a language is most strongly painted', one may

> in strict truth affirm, that it is *impossible* to make a good poetical translation: for the reasons which prove that two languages cannot have the same characters, prove likewise that the same thought can be seldom expressed in both with the same beauties.[37]

Similarly, Coleridge admits translation to his linguistic model only as a factor that renders a 'mixed language' like English uniquely prone to confusion, in that 'accidents of translation from original works of different countries' introduce another wellspring of synonymy into the weltering 'conflux of dialects' already present.[38] Against such precedents, De Quincey argues that the specificity of English, and the nature of its issues, can be brought into focus *only* through a programme of judicious importation. 'By this comparison', as he summarises his critical project in a remark imbued with the linguistic exchanges central to its design, 'we shall have the advantage' of undoing our current confusion; 'of doing what the French express by *s'orienter*, the Germans by *sich orientieren*.'[39]

Casting around for plausible compass points, De Quincey alights on 'the five great intellectual nations of modern and ancient history: viz. the Greeks, the Romans, the French, the English, and the Germans',[40] occasionally adding in Hebrew. In a sweeping gesture that sets firm bounds to his apparent hospitality to exotic callers, De Quincey declares that no other languages need apply beyond these six, since only those idioms that derive from a national culture on par with Britain ought to be considered. This disqualifies Italian and Spanish, for instance, which certainly boast a 'literature regularly mounted in all departments', but are respectively judged too indolent and too hysterical. Dutch is deemed bereft of any sort of aesthetic or literary power; fit only for 'filthy purposes upon filthy ditches'.[41] The antiquarian interest in 'Celtic languages' is declared unproductive, as is the modish fascination for 'oriental' languages. Every one of these nations 'has reason to feel interested in the pretensions of its own native language', and has attracted its share of 'eulogists'. However, their intrinsic qualities notwithstanding,

> [w]ithout being strictly barbarous, all these languages are uncultured and rude in a degree corresponding to the narrow social development of the races who speak them. These races are precisely in that state of imperfect expansion, both civilly and intellectually, under which the separation has not fully taken place between poetry and prose. [. . .] Barbarism, in short, through all

degrees, generates its own barbaresque standards of taste, and nowhere so much as in the great field of diction and ornamental composition. A high civilisation is an indispensable condition for developing the full powers of a language; and it is equally a condition for developing the taste which must preside over the appreciation of diction and style.[42]

Though self-evident to speakers of De Quincey's favoured sextet of languages, the dichotomisation between form and reference requires a great deal of work. Nations attain to a two-pronged concept of style only through intense intellectual and social activity in the originating people. Offering a quasi-mathematical summary of the axiom that grounds his philological system, De Quincey notes that

> the difference [. . .] between nation and nation will be in a compound ratio of the complexity and variety of situations into which men are thrown [. . .] on the one hand, and, on the other, of the intellectual activity put forth to seize and apprehend these fleeting relations of things and persons.

As such, when concerned British writers examine blueprints for the restoration of their national language, they ought to eschew 'rude or uncultivated [. . .] people[s], or [. . .] nation[s] subsisting chiefly by hunting, or by agriculture and rural life exclusively, or in any way sequestered and monotonous in their habits'. Instead, those eager to contribute to the rejuvenation of English ought to look to those nations that have attained an index of 'high civilisation'.[43]

The literary feats of '[t]he elder civilisations of Egypt and of [the] Asiatic empires' having been lost to time, the first cultures of verifiably sufficient development to generate a suitably complex understanding of style are those of Greece and Israel.[44] The Greeks are especially important to an audit of the English language in that they laid down the track along which the latter would travel. Like the British after them, they made a concerted effort to purge their language of all traces of form, instead prioritising a purely meaningful expression. And as it does with their British heirs, the Greek rejection of the rhetorical aspects of language proceeds from a high degree of civilisational development. When a nation has sufficiently advanced to grasp that expression may be divided into poetic and prosaic spheres, the former is immediately declared supplementary: form is ill-adapted to the demands of modernity in that it 'shrinks from the strife of business, and could neither arise nor make itself felt in a tumultuous assembly'.[45] The two drivers of (pre-)modernity, an active civil society and a love of speculation, De Quincey reasons, have neither time nor space for the demands of formal productions. Political debate seeks to overwhelm with emotion; scientific disputation desires only to impart naked fact: both are intent on reference and representation to the exclusion of all other concerns. The more the Greek nation grows into its national character, or at least into those aspects that compel its pursuit of civil government and natural philosophy, the more it exorcises poetry from its national style. It is this process that is now affecting British writing, which similarly began to spurn form as Britain developed into a modern state.

De Quincey's historicisation of style as an index of modernity, turning on the principle that the maturation of society causes a diminution of poetic power, implies that those peoples who are yet to establish popular institutions and philosophical schools still maintain their rhetorical talents at full strength, albeit with no differentiation between matter and manner. This is true only of languages wallowing in crude primitivity, however. In those early civilisations that have acquired organisation while eluding urbanisation, the national diction defaults almost entirely to hyper-cultivated form. Just as content-driven prose is the sole branch of style that can effectively sustain urban life, so form-focused poetry is the only form of expression upon which tribal and rural communities can rely for their administration. Since 'in this early stage' of society, all things 'are meant mysteriously, have allegoric values; and week-day man moves amongst glorified objects', all modes of expression are suffused by a language apposite to the communication of mystery, such as can be delivered only by poetry. In thus supercharging the self-referential capacities of language, expression is so unmoored from emotion and fact that it loops around and assumes extra-referential valency: because it presents forms impervious to referential reading, the poetic text forwards interpretation to a confirmation of the transcendent laws and divine decrees required to ensure the cohesion of pre-secular systems of knowledge. In short, whereas prose speaks 'such truth only as ascends from the earth', poetry contains such wisdom 'as descends from heaven, which can never assume an unmetrical form'. Notwithstanding the highly deliberate, constructed nature of its language, then, poetry is the primordial branch of style whence prose must be evolved through intense social activity. By the same token, while prose is presently so ubiquitous as to seem artlessly and spontaneous, a 'thing so well-known to all of us, – most of our "little accounts" from shoemakers, dressmakers, &c., being made out in prose', prosaic expression demands a far greater sense of structure than does poetry: prose, 'strange as it may seem to say so, was something of a discovery'.[46]

True to his comparative methods, De Quincey grounds his critique of Grecian eloquence in a close study of an antique language that has preserved its poetical locution: it is in this acutely rhetorical state that the speech of Israel presents itself to the forensic classicist. Greek and

Hebrew serve to shed light on each other in that they occupy polar ends of the stylistic spectrum; so much so that every one of the national characteristics associated with Greece finds itself contradicted in its Judaean counterpart. In lieu of a popular democracy brimming with debate and disputation, Israel presents a collection of tribes held together by laws considered to originate in the godhead; as a result, instead of prose, poetry reigns supreme. As De Quincey pursues this intercultural comparison, it begins to redound to the discredit of the Hellenes:

> Greece was, in fact, *too* ebullient with intellectual activity – an activity too palestric and purely human – so that the opposite pole of the mind, which points to the mysterious and the spiritual, was, in the agile Greek, too intensely a child of the earth, starved and palsied; whilst in the Hebrew, dull and inert intellectually, but in his spiritual organs awake and sublime, the case was precisely reversed. [. . .] The very languages of these two races repeat the same expression of their intellectual differences, and of the differences in their missions. The Hebrew, meagre and sterile as regards the numerical wealth of its ideas, is infinite as regards their power; the Greek, on the other hand, rich as tropic forests in the polymorphous life, the life of the dividing and distinguishing intellect, is weak only in the supreme region of thought.

Notwithstanding Greek's many gifts, 'the result' of any comparison must be 'immeasurably in favour of the Hebrew'. While Hebrew writers bend their every phrase to the suggestion of eternal truths, their Greek colleagues are so preoccupied with the minor squabbles that upset life in the polis that their texts are inextricably bound to their immediate context.

As a result, the Hellenes consigned themselves to oblivion: their texts are so reliant on realia that they grow more obsolescent with every passing year; as such, their memory will 'perish when any deluge of calamity overtakes the libraries of our planet, or if any great revolution of thought remoulds them'. In their poetic musings on the nature of the divine, by contrast, the Jewish people have hewn for themselves an unconquerable monument: their work is ever 'co-enduring with man's race, and careless of all revolutions in literature or in the composition of society'.

In a marked contrast to the late-Romantic voices that mourn or celebrate the fading of the poet-prophet, De Quincey moves towards a stance that restores poetry to its rightful place among the arts even as it acknowledges the irreversibility of the progress of knowledge. For inspiration, he looks to the Greeks, noting that the latter share with the British both a rejection of poetry and a stubborn refusal to extend their national imaginary beyond territorial frontiers. Their only difference is one of degree: just as the Greeks pursue meaning even more zealously than their British heirs, they are also even more negligent of the exotic. While the English are nonplussed to find foreign elements standing at their thresholds, the Greek concept of the barbarian bespeaks a profound suspicion for 'men who were ἑτερόγλωττοι', a group that comprises 'the whole human race not living in Hellas, or in colonies thrown off from Hellas'. When geographic peninsulation denatures into prideful isolation, a culture dooms itself to expiration. In rejecting the influence of foreign ideas, even if only as an imagined source of competition, Greek consigns itself to ossification; beauteous but essentially lifeless, with no higher aspirations than its own exceedingly narrow standards of prosaic perfection:

> Having no intellectual intercourse with foreign nations, [the Greeks] had virtually no intercourse at all – none which could affect the feelings of the literary class, or generally of those who would be likely to contemplate language as a subject of aesthetic admiration. Each Hellenic author might be compared with others of his compatriot authors in respect to his management of their common language, but not the language itself compared as to structure or capacities with other languages; since these other languages (one and all) were in any practical sense hardly assumed to exist. [. . .] Having no temptation or facilities for holding any intellectual intercourse with those who could not communicate through the channel of the Greek language, it followed that the Greeks had no means or opportunity for comparing their own language with the languages of other nations [. . .] Greece was in the absolute insulation of the phoenix, the unique of birds, that dies without having felt a throb of exultation or a pang of jealousy, because it has exposed its gorgeous plumage and the mysterious solemnities of its beauty only to the dusky recesses of Thebaic deserts.[47]

Absent objects of comparison, languages wither. Writers exhaust themselves in expressing ever more impressively what they already knew, and thereby slowly grow 'monotonous' or 'tautologous'. The remedy for the crisis of confidence that must ultimately plague any language or literature that has condemned itself to tedium is evidently to be 'morbidly impatient of tautology; progress and motion, everlasting motion, [is] a mere necessity of [the] intellect'.[48] All that is needed to bestow on oneself the benefits of life everlasting, then, is to break through insularity by embracing the unfamiliar. In the Greek case, a close observation of a language like Hebrew might have guaranteed its survival to the present day. Inversely, in the Israelite case, a language like Greek, repeatedly described as manly and energetic, might have provoked an intellectual awakening, ensuring the survival of the Jewish state amid its warlike neighbours. The ideal position for any language to occupy on the spectrum of national styles, in short, as Condillac notes, is that of the happy medium: '[t]he most perfect [language] should take possession of the middle, and those who spoke it would be a great people'.[49] If, as De Quincey argues, a perfect middle point is impossible to achieve by drawing on one's own limited resources, any language that wishes to survive its bias towards self-reiteration is called to translate itself into a superior condition. In thus strengthening Condillac's cursory observation that language may serve as a conduit for amelioration, De Quincey makes a significant advance on the endorsements of a mediatory position that were a common feature of eighteenth-century national comparisons, but generally failed to note any possibility of improvement: to enlightened thinkers, superior nations naturally occupy superior positions. In contrast to Condillac, De Quincey insists on the possibility of change through dedicated labour, at least for some languages.

De Quincey introduces a third nation to his schema of ancient peoples to adumbrate the potential for self-amelioration through a policy of linguistic and cultural openness. Relative to the Hellenes and the Israelites, respectively too haughty and too introverted to expand their scope outside national frontiers, the Romans strike an entirely different pose: '[n]ot thus', as De Quincey pithily observes, 'were the Romans situated'.[50] While innately predisposed to rhetoricising, Rome understood the importance of strengthening its language by calquing it on alien examples, developing a much 'subtler conception of style'[51] and thereby reversing the enervation to which lesser nations must succumb. In his description of the bracing effects of translation as illustrated by the case of Latin, De Quincey particularly stresses the example of Cicero, whom he credits with the first serious treatment of translation as well as the first learned discussion of the Roman language. Far from alleging any contradiction in Cicero's combination of patriotism and cosmopolitanism, De Quincey argues that the two require one another. To appreciate Cicero's superficially paradoxical understanding of Latin, one must do as the Romans did – that is, place one's language in a comparative constellation, and map its strengths and weaknesses from an external perspective:

> The Greeks, so profound and immovable was their self-conceit, never in any generation came to regard the Romans with the slightest tremor of jealousy, as though they were or ever could be rivals in literature.[. . .] The Greeks were wrong: the Romans had some things in their literature which a Greek could neither have rivalled nor even understood. They had a peculiar rhetoric [. . .] which [. . .] has no parallel in Grecian literature [. . .] But, if the Greeks did no justice to their Roman pupils, on the other hand, the Roman pupils never ceased to regard the Greeks with veneration, or to acknowledge them for their masters in literature: they had a foreign literature before their eyes challenging continual comparison; and this foreign literature was in a language which also challenged comparison with their own. [. . .] Studying the

Greek so closely, they found by continual collation in what quarter lay the peculiar strength of the Latin. [. . .] Here, viz. in the case of Cicero, we have the first eminent example [. . .] of a man's standing up manfully to support the pretensions of his mother-tongue. [H]ere also we find the first example of a statesman's seriously regarding a language in the light of a foremost jewel amongst the trophies of nationality.[52]

Translation certainly existed before Cicero's Rome, but it barely existed as a sustained practice of the highest cultural relevance; as a mode of writing and speaking that was sufficiently considered a thing onto itself that it merited its own name. 'Outside of Rome', as Berman notes, there was no translation; 'only babbling, pragmatic translations, closed transitive acts, in a word, everything that took place before the Beginning'.[53] In his *Poetics*, Aristotle had briefly entertained the existence of a third mode of art, neither diegetic nor mimetic but focused entirely on 'imitation in and of itself'. Acting on his inborn 'disinterest for a practice that was considered [. . .] at the very least disagreeable', however, he failed to pursue this idea, leaving the 'medium arts' tantalisingly hypothetical.[54] As a result, Cicero finds himself without apposite terms when he first endeavours to report on translation, alternating between various circumlocutions to describe the phenomenon.[55] Even though the 'concept of "translation" [. . .] did not exist until Cicero, in whose philosophical and rhetorical writings we witness [. . .] the birth of this concept (which represents a totally new relationship of man to language)', as Johannes Lohmann writes,[56] once it had been identified and subsequently been granted a name as well as a 'shape, figure, stature' through the efforts of countless writers and speakers, most famous among them Virgil, Horace and Jerome, it came to permeate Roman national identity.[57] 'All of Latin culture', Berman argues, 'became "translative"'; organised around translation, transfer, and exchange: translation is inalienably 'a *res latina, a res romana* (a fundamental element of Latin and Roman culture).' Translation, as De Quincey repeatedly emphasises, in no way threatens the integrity of the nation: while Rome translated with abandon, it did so freely and unanxiously. Its sense of self was not adulterated but fortified by the gains in self-awareness it made by bringing itself into revelatory juxtapositions. In nursing its dependence on translation and eventually, especially in the Christian phase of the late Empire,[58] boldly claiming translation as integral to its national character, Rome baked *translatio* into its foundation, guaranteeing the perpetuation of its government (*imperii*) and thought (*studii*) through the ages.[59]

While demonstrably Latinate in origin, the structure of translation is not without significant precursors. Notwithstanding its deep-seated reluctance to engage with the unfamiliar, Hellas did generate one writer who recognised the advantages of translation. Mindful of the parallels between English and Greek, De Quincey nominates Herodotus as an exemplar for British writers: in his *Histories*, he argues, Herodotus shows himself 'the first respectable artist in prose',[60] in that his work, even if it does not yet fully overcome its author's congenital suspicion of translation, is suffused by a style that bears all the hallmarks of the translational ideal in striving to transform the nation by admixing poetry and prose. This description of Herodotus as the primordial prose-poet derives from an apocryphal account which holds that Herodotus first secured his fame by reciting the *Histories* to a rapt audience of Greeks at the Olympic Games, allegedly around 440 BCE, just as the nation found itself confronting an existential crisis in the guise of the over-ambitious Persians.[61] As De Quincey recounts this legend, if Herodotus makes such an impression on the throning crowds, it is because he creates one of the first texts that activate the mode of impassioned prose. Employed in isolation, prose either drily communicates a series of facts or frantically reports on a speaker's fleeting emotions; similarly, the exclusive use of poetry is fit only for hermetic mysticism. In combining the two, however, and thereby crafting an early, as yet underphilologised and non-translative impassioned prose, Herodotus grants a work of historical reportage the capacity to instil in its auditors a sense of shared history and identity. The *Histories*, that is, have hit on a style that suits their author's aspirations for national renewal. In quasi-instinctively employing impassioned prose, Herodotus signals his desire to join Sparta and Athens, 'the two houses of Grecian blood that typified its ultimate and polar capacities, the most and the least of exorbitations, the utmost that were possible from its equatorial centre' into a unified people. Through his style, which inhabits 'the isthmus between the regions of poetry and [. . .] prose', he mirrors his similarly symbolic geographic position on 'the isthmus of Corinth'[62] which separates Attica and Laconia. Herodotus, in short, creates the nation he seeks to address by inventing a mediatory mode of textuality:

> it is pretty clear that Herodotus stood, and meant to stand, on that isthmus between the regions of poetry and blank unimpassioned prose [. . .] Is it the literary body whom he addresses – a small body everywhere? No, but the public without limitation. Public! but what public? Not the public of Lacedæmon [. . .] not the public of Athens [. . .] No: it is the public of universal Hellas, an august congress representing the total civilisation of the earth.[63]

De Quincey further highlights the relevance of the Herodotean model to late-Romantic Britain in an unfinished essay written in 1853, in the tail end of his career, under the programmatic title 'How to Write English'.

Reprising the familiar thesis that nations are best distinguished from one another by charting the stylistic propensities of their languages, their 'powers' and 'endowments' as they appear in their textual productions, he adds that nations acquire additional specificity through their 'destiny'. The latter term here refers to an ideal future state, to be achieved only when a people have fully awoken to their national character, notably through close study of their own style, and have grown fully intent on actualising that character in history. As for English, De Quincey notes, '[s]ome subtle judges in this field of criticism' – read: De Quincey – 'are of opinion, and ever had that opinion, that amongst the modern languages [. . .] the English had certain peculiar and inappreciable aptitudes for the highest offices of interpretation'.[64] The true nature of English, concealed though it is under centuries of mismanagement, is to translate. As a result, its 'destiny' or 'mission'[65] is to become an international language of culture and communication. The world that takes shape after 1815, not yet global but increasingly 'networked', as Manuel Castells puts it,[66] promises a return of the same propitious circumstances granted to the Greeks of the fifth century BCE and the Romans of the first century BCE: nineteenth-century Britain brings a wide range of peoples into contact and exchange, with so many of them resistant to conducting their own mediation that they cry out for a tertiary lingua franca. Drawing once more on Herodotus' Olympic performance, De Quincey conjectures an event of sufficiently planetary scale to require an intermediary language. This role English, propelled by its imperial destiny, is fated to claim for itself:

> Twenty-five centuries ago, this beautiful little planet on which we live might be said to have assembled and opened her first parliament for representing the grandeur of the human intellect. That particular assembly, I mean, for celebrating the Olympic Games about four centuries and a half before the era of Christ, when Herodotus opened the gates of morning for the undying career of history, by reading to the congregated children of Hellas [. . .] what was the language employed as the instrument of so great a federal act? It was that divine Grecian language [. . .] If now, which is not impossible, any occasion should arise for a modern congress of the leading nations that represent civilisation, [. . .] it would be a matter of mere necessity, and so far hardly implying any expression of homage, that the English language should take the station formerly accorded to the Grecian.[67]

In short, in embracing its translational nature, Britain will become a *translatio* of Herodotean Greece and Ciceronian Rome. The one question remaining is what idioms it ought to import in order to correct its overcultivation of prose.

## Language in the Middle

So how *does* one write English – following the graceless collapse of poetry; amid the changes roiling British society; in recognition of the enervation dragging down the nation; building on antique exemplars? No question could be more pivotal to De Quincey's framing and positioning of his writership. The answer, as Eric Dayre observes, is that one must write English like Herodotus wrote Greek,[68] albeit with the proviso that the Herodotean vision for a new mode of historical writing needs a better developed concept of translation. Herodotus may have intuited the procedure for transforming language into an instrument of national revitalisation, but he had only Greek at his disposal, a proudly insular idiom: in effect, he announced a project to which his language was unequal. Cicero may have deduced that an imperial style requires the weight of *translatio* behind it, but the Roman nation subsequently required several centuries of collective effort to begin grasping its mechanisms. English, by contrast, is a language that originated in translation. Advances in historical linguistics amply demonstrated that English leapt into impossible being from a messy heap of unrelated peoples piled atop one another, and that the language was therefore a collection of disguised acts of translation between the various languages that contributed to its jumbled genetics: a strange hybrid of Anglic and Saxon that combines with Latin and Norman French, and that carries traces of Norse and Brittonic, amongst many other minor influences. Reclaiming Shelley's image of the crucible, used in the *Defence of Poetry* to figure the destructive effects of translation, De Quincey argues that English derives formidable potential for continual regeneration from its status as a language that is in a state of internal translation:

> English is, say the imbecile, a 'bastard' language, a 'hybrid' language, and so forth. [. . .] It is time to have done with these follies. Let us open our eyes to our own advantages. Let us recognise with thankfulness that fortunate inheritance of collateral wealth which, by inoculating our Anglo-Saxon stem with the mixed dialect of Neustria, laid open an avenue mediately through which the whole opulence of Roman, and ultimately of Grecian, thought plays freely through the pulses of our native English. Most fortunately, the Saxon language was yet plastic and unfrozen at the era of the Norman invasion. The language was thrown again into the crucible, and new elements were intermingled with its own when brought into a state of fusion. And this final process it was, making the language at once rich in matter and malleable in form, which created that composite and multiform speech [. . .] with enough remaining of its old forest stamina.[69]

Reflecting on the Latinate origins of translation, Berman notes in an aphoristic aside that '[w]e translators, are and shall remain Roman, even if we must fight against some aspects of Romanness within us; even if, in some way, we must become Greek and Jewish'.[70] In De Quincey's more radical formula, in order that we might remain British, we must become a nation of translators, even if that implies 'we English' must fight against our insularity.

'[T]he very best illustration of all this' – 'all this' comprehending the entirety of the involuted pseudo-philological apparatus outlined above – 'will be found in putting the case of English style into close juxtaposition with the style of the French and Germans, our only very important neighbours', since '[a]s leaders of civilisation, as powers in an intellectual sense, there are but three nations in Europe – England, Germany, France'.[71] Much like Rome prefigures Britain in its stylistic and cultural layout as well as its national destiny, so do Israel and Greece foreshadow France and Germany, albeit with some allowance for their lesser genius. The French national style is considered Hebrew-like in its obsessive focus on formal regulation, if not yet as a means to pursue mystical topics. Similarly, the Germans declare almost exclusively for prose, if they are yet to discover any talent for demagoguery. In thus insisting that an assessment of the present cannot but build on the past, De Quincey is enabled to rearrange his linguistic system, converting a relatively straightforward tripartite structure of opposition (Hebrew–Greek) and imperial synthesis (Latin) into a sextuple architecture riveted together by dedoubled relations of analogy, contrast and reversal – in short, by combining two linguistic triads, he organises his theories into a chiasmus. In the cross-shaped figure that underpins his vision for Romantic translation, French, Greek, German and Hebrew are to be located in the four extreme positions, and English and Latin are to be imagined as the double fulcrum in which these twice two languages meet as they reverse into one another. The reversal that describes the relation between Greek and Hebrew, and that is expanded to the interaction of German and French, is thus held in place by the partial reversal that obtains between the two medium languages of English and Latin, which share an instinctual inclination to translation.

While difficult to parse, the chiastic logic through which De Quincey formalises his theory of translation and national style allows for a highly dynamic layout. In addition, by opting for a chiasm of languages, he also provides a demonstration of the advantages to importing valuable ideas. In their philological application, chiasmi do not come not naturally to British writers: they must be imported from the Greek authors who first harnessed them, or from the German idealists who rescued the figure after centuries of neglect.[72] Through the efforts of such thinkers and writers as Schiller and Jean Paul, in particular, the chiasm was rendered a constructive principle in the fullest sense of the word; 'no longer a merely ornamental or psychological device', as Andrzej Warminski has it, used merely for pleasing effect, but an 'originary form of thought' which demonstrates that seemingly insurmountable polar contrasts need not prevent unified thought, in that 'reversals secure, by the very movement of the inversion of the link that exists between opposite poles [. . .] the agreement of a thing at variance with itself'.[73] One German idealist, Friedrich Hölderlin, even discerned that the idealist chiasmus as it was developed by Schiller in his *Aesthetic Education*, where it operates as a structure that sublates form into meaning, lends itself to a refined theory of translation. Acting on this intuition, Hölderlin reconstructed Schiller's synthetic schema into an early version of De Quincey's chiastic system of translation, albeit focused entirely on the interaction between Greek and German literature. Hölderlin's proposition was, to quote Warminski's summary, that

> there is a (chiasmic) reversal in the relation of [. . .] that which is proper or one's own and that which is foreign, *das Eigene* and *das Fremde*, between the Greeks and us: what is *das Eigene* there is *das Fremde* here, and what is *das Fremde* there is *das Eigene* here. Both the doubleness (of *das Eigene* and *das Fremde*) and the reversal – 'For us, its the reverse (*Bei uns ist's umgekehrt*)' – are explicit.[74]

The following excerpt from an 1801 letter by Hölderlin provides further context:

> [w]e learn nothing with greater difficulty than to use freely what is native [*das Nationelle*]. [. . .] It sounds paradoxical. But I will state it once again, and make it available for your examination and your use: in the development of a culture [*im Fortschritt der Bildung*], the properly national will become ever less of an advantage. For this reason the Greeks have badly mastered sacred pathos, because they were born to it [*angeboren*], while on the other hand they are excellent in their skills of representation from Homer onwards, because this extraordinary man was inspired [*seelenvoll*] enough to capture for his Apollonian realm the Occidental *Junonian sobriety*, and thereby to truly appropriate what is foreign. With us it is the reverse. [. . .] that which is one's own has to be learned just as well as that with is foreign. For this reason the Greeks are indispensable to us.[75]

While unknown to De Quincey, it is evident that he and Hölderlin seek to tackle the same issues, if only because, to quote from Coleridge's apologia for the echoes between his work and Schelling's, both were 'disciplined by the same preparatory philosophy'. While strikingly similar, however, Hölderlin's understanding of translation diverges from De Quincey's in several respects. Firstly, the former specifies the translation zone to the distance between German and Greek, whereas De Quincey logs the transfers between no less than four languages and nods at several more. Second, while Hölderlin and De Quincey both trace the contours of the national character by attending to linguistic expression, and while they establish analogous conceptual cuts (the former's 'sacred pathos' maps onto the latter's 'poetry'; 'representation' onto 'prose'), the former associates poetry with Greek. Third, while both argue that a transfusion of alien matter may reanimate the national body literary, Hölderlin sharpens this paradox by noting that nations are naturally at their most proficient when they imitate foreign habits. Finally, and most importantly, while both men seek to repeat the Herodotean (or Homeric, *pace* Hölderlin) experiment by making their work and thence their culture translative, De Quincey is adamant that it is Britain, alone amongst modern nations, that can truly make interpretation into its destiny. He therefore places English at the heart of his chiastic involutions, whereas Hölderlin leaves void this focal point, merely charting the exchanges between the two idioms that he seeks to compare. The central position De Quincey assigns to English does not mean that the latter is to become a babelic synthesis: this would imply that translation is a teleological process, which runs counter to its chiastic structuration. Chiasmi, as Gasché remarks, gesture at a totality of comprehension that they are designedly powerless to deliver in that they continually forward writer and reader to an infinite ping-pong of reversals: in a word, they are dialogic, not dialectic.[76] De Quincey defines English as he defines himself; as a hyper-mobile thing that sits at the centre of the traffic between languages, armed with a fantastic variety of interests yet endowed with a definite but slender core identity, only ever briefly flashing up amidst fervid exchanges. Bucking the assumption that this reduced identity must consign the nation to an interstitial and marginal existence, he aims to construct an aesthetic ideology of translation, in which English is solely granted the privilege of what Levinas calls the 'pleasure of contact at the heart of the chiasm'.[77]

In De Quincey's chiasmic configuration of translation, '[w]e English', in obeisance to our mongrel pedigree which divides into a Romance and a Germanic section, 'occupy a middle position between the French and the Germans'.[78] Just as his (auto)biographic writings are preoccupied with determining the precise nature of his authorship, which stands astride the categories of production and reproduction, his reflections on style project this conundrum onto a national language that is preordained to inhabit a median position. The central question, then, as Gasché phrases it, is 'if a work' (or a writer, or a language) 'deliberately situates itself between figures, themes, or motifs that could and normally would authoritatively confer unity, what, then is its status?

Indeed, what sort of unity does an in-between establish?'[79] De Quincey begins to answer this question by investigating the exact nature of 'our relation [. . .] to the Germans', observing that the structural function of Germany is to represent Britain to itself in instructively hyperbolic form. It is in this 'Brobdingnagian and exaggerating mirror' that British readers find repeated back to them '[o]ur own popular style, and (what is worse) the *tendency* of our own', inflated to breaking point in a uniquely 'German extreme'.[80] German writers and speakers, that is, are so monomaniacally intent on perfecting prose that they have irradiated even those meagre remnants of poetry that yet survive in English. As such, '[a] chapter upon German Rhetoric would be in the same ludicrous predicament as Van Troil's chapter on the snakes of Iceland, which delivers its business in one summary sentence, announcing that – snakes in Iceland there are none'.[81] The upshot of the German escalation of prose is that the dissatisfaction presently afflicting British authors manifests overwhelmingly in German writing, which strikes even those inured to the foibles of English as 'an object of legitimate astonishment', in that '[w]hatever is bad in our ideal of prose style [. . .] we see there carried to the most outrageous excess [. . .] with a zealotry of extravagance that really seems like wilful burlesque'.[82] The German exaggeration of British proclivities extends even to the British predisposition to splendid isolation in that Germany does not simply resist foreign imports but advocates purging its language of alien elements. Germany, in short, has walled itself in:

> This independence of alien resources has sometimes been even practically adopted as the basis of a dictionary, and officially patronised by adoption in the public *bureaus*. Some thirty years ago the Prussian government was said to have introduced into the public service a dictionary which rejected all words not purely vernacular. Such a word, for instance, as *philosophie* was not admissible; the indigenous word *weltweisheit* was held to be not only sufficient, which it really is, but exclusively legitimate. Yet, with all this scrupulosity and purism of veneration for his native language [. . .] the true German has no sense of grace or deformity in the management of his language. Style, diction, the construction of sentences, are ideas perfectly without meaning to the German writer. If a whole book were made up of a single sentence, all collateral or subordinate ideas being packed into it as parenthetical intercalations, – if this single sentence should even cover an acre of ground, – the true German would see in all that no want of art, would recognise no opportunities thrown away for the display of beauty.

France has spared itself from Germanic errors; so much so that the position of German may be summarised as 'the reverse'[83] or 'the counterpole to the French style'. This also implies that French has an orientation that runs counter to the natural bent of English. Imagine, then, 'the astonishment of an English author [...] with no previous knowledge of French literature' let loose in a French library. From its stacks, he would dig up volumes shaped to stylistic norms wildly at odds with their own, in that the monopoly of eloquence, 'which in English books is all but universal[,] absolutely has not an existence in the French'. The inverse also holds. '[T]o make a Frenchman sensible' that prose might possess anything of merit, 'you must appeal to some *translated* model.' The French nation, then, has resisted the advent of prose which the progress of the intellect ordinarily demands. Reflecting on the 'cause of this national immunity from a fault so common everywhere else, and so natural when we look into the producing occasions', De Quincey hypothesises that the French national character provides a corrective headwind. Uniquely amongst European peoples, they have managed to combine a high degree of civilisation with an unrelenting delight in sociable conversation rather than self-important soliloquy. As a result, '[w]hereas now, amongst us English' and Germans 'the too general tendency of our sentences [is] towards hyperbolic length', the French have trimmed their sentences to suit their inborn desire for rapid dialogue:

> The secret lies here; beyond all nations, by constitutional vivacity, the French are a nation of talkers, and the model of their sentences is moulded by that fact. [...] 'De Monologue', as Madame de Staël, in her broken English, described this mode of display when speaking of Coleridge, is so far from being tolerated in France as an accomplishment that it is not even understood as a disease. [...] In France, therefore, from the intense adaptation of the national mind to real colloquial intercourse, for which reciprocation is indispensable, the form of sentence in use is adjusted to that primary condition; brief, terse, simple; shaped to avoid misunderstanding, and to meet the impatience of those who are waiting for their turn. [...] an Englishman in such a situation has no urgent motive for turning his thoughts to any other object than the prevailing one of the moment, viz. how best to convey his meaning.[84]

Its rhetorical proficiency notwithstanding, French is not beyond reproach. As in German and English, 'the very advantages of a language, those which are most vaunted' easily 'become defects' when they grow into an inflexible canon.[85] Too vigorously pursued, wit grows stale and 'monotonous', deforming trouvailles into clichés, 'solemnity' into 'flippancy', and a '*style soutenu*' into a '*style coupé*'.[86] While poetry should move those who wield and witness it to ponder on ineffable mysteries, as biblical scribes did in Hebrew verses, in French hands, the deliberate deployment of form is perverted into hollow artifice. The very power of the French language as a language for 'social intercourse', De Quincey argues, 'is built on its impotence for purposes of passion, grandeur and native simplicity.'[87] English, then, must partake of *both* a prosaic and a poetic, both a German and a French, influence to cancel out each language's weaknesses through their counterparts' strengths: the judicious admixture of poetry and prose that De Quincey names impassioned prose is always also a translational style.

## Impassioned Prose as Idealist Translation

Germany and France are both burdened by considerable defects: between them, De Quincey appears most likely to counsel an emulation of the latter. And yet he limits his own efforts almost entirely to *German* sources, ignoring his own postulates as well as the tendency in contemporary journals to favour translations of French books over their German counterparts. Part of the explanation for this mismatch may be found in De Quincey's desire to associate himself with the intellectual set, in which German literature and metaphysics enjoyed a markedly higher profile. Unwilling to confess to such pragmatic motives, he also offers a theoretical motive for his teutophilia. Having placed translation on the novel structural footing of chiasmus, his initial concern is to fine-tune this model: French writing, however excellent in other respects, is devoid of inspiring instances of chiastic structuration. De Quincey offers this argument in one of his first published forays into translation, published under his 'Grasmeriensis Teutonizans' handle. The article prefaces two translated short stories by Jean Paul Richter with a lengthy disclaimer detailing why German, not French, is the superior choice in the early phases of a translational project. Presented as a letter 'to a young man whose education has been neglected', allegedly penned on 18 October 1821 by the 'author of the English Opium-Eater' and published in December in the same journal that two months previously carried his 'Confessions', the essay exhorts its fictional respondent, named only as F., to read beyond British borders so as to ensure the continual renewal of his language, literature and nation. Crucially, such adventures should not be wasted on French fare, which is so beset by a spirit of insularity that it might seduce British readers into completely shutting themselves in. In the best tradition of scholarship on translation, De Quincey phrases his argument through horticultural metaphors:

> I suppose, F., you know that the golden pippin is now almost, if not quite, extinct in England: and why? Clearly from want of some exotic, but congenial inoculation. So it is with literatures of whatsoever land: unless crossed by some other of different breed, they all tend to superannuation. Thence comes it that the French literature is now in the last stage of phthisis – dotage – palsy, or whatever image will best express the most abject state of senile [. . .]

imbecility. [. . .] Now whence comes this poverty of the French literature? Manifestly hence, that it is too intensely steeped in French manners to admit of any influences from without: it has rejected all alliance with exotic literature; and like some royal families, or like a particular valley in this county, from intermarrying too exclusively in their own narrow circle, it is now on its last legs; and will soon go out like a farthing rushlight.[88]

This passage hits on a productive, if not entirely adroitly handled,[89] figure through which to imagine translation. Taking literally the capacity of nations for bodying themselves forth in language and literature, De Quincey tropes the impact of translation as a physical modification to the national body linguistic and literary. *Inoculation* here refers to grafting – or, to spell out the organising metaphor, to a process whereby a self-sterilising stock is perpetuated by the superaddition of a foreign element, base and scion joining forces to ensure survival. Crucially, this trope grows unstable when the precise nature of the text that fruits from the combination of base and graft is queried. Does a German inoculation ensure the preservation of an otherwise impotent native strain, or does it really reduce the latter to a slavish delivery system of nutrients? Indeed, how can categorical distinctions between native and foreign at all be maintained? In its earliest iterations, De Quincey's philosophy of translation finds it difficult to resolve such questions. Before long, however, he describes the process of translative inoculation as a process that delivers an external impulse to qualities that were always already latent in the native constitution, allowing a continued distinction between languages. In thus employing *inoculation* in a positive sense, De Quincey revises an earlier and more critically famous use of the term. In the 'Confessions', he characterises his ingestion of opium as a courageous experiment in vaccination, akin to patently lethal (but mercifully fictitious) tests undertaken by 'a French surgeon [who] inoculated himself lately with cancer, an English one twenty years ago with plague, and a third, I know not of what nation, with hydrophobia'.[90] A few paragraphs later, he recycles the image to describe his drug-fuelled nightmares, which deal in chimeric amalgamations of humans and animals, as 'horrid inoculation[s] upon each other of incompatible natures'.[91] Inoculation is used here in a context in which hybridity can still disclose 'a world of troubles'.[92] Written into being in 1821, the allegoric Malay still appears as the presiding deity of terrifying vistas of freakish fusion, rather than the herald of a new kind of literature. Even at the short distance of few months, however, De Quincey rewinds the term's etymology, returning the medical reading to an older and more positive sense. This striking revaluation flags his conversion from a fearful attitude to the outside world, which is to be imported in controlled quantities to arm against future invasions, into a stance which actively encourages an influx of alien elements. The sole reservation that De Quincey adds to his advocacy for the importation of foreign grafts is that they be harvested from literatures in the blush of youth, lest the British root stock be further degraded by ailing transplants. Since immature languages tend to civilisational underdevelopment, moreover, the burden must especially fall on those advanced languages who have secured for themselves a state of regained juvenility. Having the 'horrid example' of French self-debilitation 'before our eyes', German is the only sensible candidate. Moreover, the point in studying German texts is not to translate as Coleridge did; to ransack them for random narratives, figures or forms. The focus should fall on its recent achievement (in 'the last twenty years') of a chiastic structure that enforces a beneficial suspension of insularity: it is this vital energy that De Quincey seeks to harness, in that '[n]ot the tropics, not the ocean, not life itself, is such a type of variety, of infinite forms, or of creative power, as the German literature, in its recent motions'.[93] If the question is posed:

> What should we English do? Why, evidently, we should cultivate an intercourse with that literature of Europe which has most of a juvenile constitution. Now that is beyond all doubt the German. I do not so much insist on the present excellence of the German literature [. . .]: what weighs most with me is the promise and assurance of future excellence held out by the originality and masculine strength of thought which has moulded the German mind since the time of Kant. [. . .] Come therefore, dear F. [. . .], and I will engraft such German youth and vigour on thy English trunk that henceforwards thou shalt bear excellent fruit.[94]

In recommending an energising injection of German matter to British writers exhausted by their long diet of prose, and in cautioning against the stultifying effects of French, De Quincey formalises the lines of transnational influence through which British Romanticism shaped itself. That is, he echoes a common tendency amongst his nearest colleagues to credit German writers with supporting their remaking of British literature while withholding such praise from their French counterparts.[95] An association with French thought was a dangerous thing immediately following the Revolution; moreover, in literary terms, a more significant objection was that French artists had little to offer to budding Romantics, as they had largely remained in the classicist mould, and would continue to do so until well into the 1830s.[96] De Quincey accordingly pits French tastes against the all-important Romantic virtue of a well-integrated imagination: in France, '[o]ne advantage', its close attention to all things rhetorical, 'is sadly counterbalanced by [. . .] penury of thinking from radical inaptitude in the thinking faculty to connect itself with [. . .] the imagination'.[97] France, in short, has no texts of interest because it has no Romantic texts.

The situation is very different for Germany, which does sport a handful of writers who have rejuvenated their language and literature. 'I have three favourites', De Quincey impresses on his narratee, 'and those are Kant, Schiller, and John Paul Richter. But setting Kant aside, as hardly belonging to the literature in the true meaning of that word, I have, you see, two.'[98] In keeping with De Quincey's low opinion, Goethe is absent from this list. Even though his *Sorrows* had sparked a sensation, and had been translated into English no less than twelve times between 1784 and 1792,[99] he is rejected in that his prose fails to meet local needs: Britain, after all, has a superabundance of the stuff about. As a result, De Quincey alleges in his review of *Wilhelm Meister*, those who insist on translating Goethe always come to grief. Once more drawing on horticultural and medical imagery, he argues that 'the dulness of the works which were translated [. . .] triumphantly repelled the contagion before it could spread'. Even amid such 'tyrannic' attempts to foist him upon hapless readers, a British Goethe was always to be 'a languishing plant'. Indeed, his work has latterly 'been drooping [. . .] we are disposed to think that it is – if not *agonizant* – yet in what is medically termed the crisis'.[100]

Slightly less marketable in Britain than Goethe but sufficiently esteemed to have sparked four translations of *Die Räuber* between 1792 and 1801, Schiller is pelted with plaudits.[101] As with Goethe, De Quincey's approbation reflects both his own enthusiasm and a wider trend. When Coleridge first read *The Robbers* in 1794, he wrote to Southey to express his astonishment that nothing in British literature could touch it: 'My God! Southey! who is this Schiller? This convulser of the heart? [. . .] Why have we ever called Milton sublime?' A teenage Hazlitt was similarly bewildered. *The Robbers*, he writes,

> stunned me like a blow, and I have not recovered enough from it to describe how it was. [. . .] Five-and-twenty years have passed since I first read the translation [. . .], but they have not blotted the impression from my mind.[102]

Capitalising on the British appetite for Schillerian fare, Coleridge hastened to translate the *Wallenstein* trilogy upon its completion in 1799. In the process, he took such licence with the original that he produced a uniquely English version, causing significant confusion among contemporary readers which text was the original.[103] In so successfully adapting a foreign source to local tastes that the translation almost displaces its source, Coleridge embarked on precisely the course of action De Quincey recommends in his 1821 letter to British readers stunned to find themselves faced with something irreducibly exotic but thrillingly valuable – that is, to go forth and translate.

De Quincey's most outspoken exhortation for a transplantation of German excellence occurs in 1842, in an entry for the *Encyclopaedia Britannica* that promises to treat of Schiller's life and work, but shunts any such discussion to the sidelines of a meditation on translation. De Quincey's lemma paints the literary field from which Schiller emerges as 'an absolute wilderness, unreclaimed and without promise of natural vegetation'. If contemporary German writers are fatally insular, eighteenth-century Germany is burdened by the inverse problem: its dishevelment stems from a misdirected policy of hospitality. While intellectuals are interested in outside influences, far from letting their language flow through an engrafted medium, the fashion arose to have the language conform entirely to outside influences, inevitably twisting it into outlandish shapes. As a result, the local literature resembled an untilled field in which invasive exotics smothered all native growth:

> the authors of Germany wrote a macaronic jargon, in which French and Latin made up a considerable proportion of every sentence: nay, it happened often that foreign words were inflected with German forms; and the whole result was such as to remind the reader of the medical examination in the Malade Imaginaire of Molière.

Amid this overgrowth of unfamiliar elements, a handful of visionary authors finally began to exhume the original stock. These rare creatures 'had no demoniac genius [. . .] but [. . .] some taste, and, what [is] better, [. . .] some sensibility'. Instead of broadcasting their genius, they humbly styled themselves mediators; moreover, they moved their country of reference in matters from taste to more sympathetic climes, and began to cultivate a more sensible method of combinatory translation than the traumatic transplantation previously in vogue. In short, a new generation of authors emerged who premised their writing on a poetics of judicious transfer. De Quincey seizes on these innovators as precedents for his own project, reinforcing this international connection by noting that all such German proto-translators acted on a fundamental kinship between Germany and Britain, sensing that Britain might save Germany from frenchification. The forerunner to this movement, identified by De Quincey as the Swiss philologist Jakob Bodmer, accordingly

> lived among the Alps; and his reading lay among the alpine sublimities of Milton and Shakspeare [*sic*]. [. . .] He was taught by the Alps to crave for something nobler and deeper. [. . .] He translated passages of English literature. He inoculated with his own sympathies the more fervent mind of the youthful Klopstock, who visited him in Switzerland. And it soon became

evident that Germany was not dead, but sleeping; and once again, legibly for any eye, the pulses of life began to play freely through the vast organisation of central Europe.

If De Quincey here cedes one of his greatest claims to literary eminence, resigning his title as the first writer to have perceived that modern *translatio* ought to structure itself as *inoculatio*, he does so to reinforce the chiastic scheme on which his theory of translation reposes. In arguing that the German pre-Romantics inoculated their language with British matter, De Quincey also suggests that those British Romantics who seek to transfuse German vigour into their work do little more than reverse a process that has been undertaken before, and will presumably be infinitely repeated.

So what, at long last, having established the full background to De Quincey's admiration for Germany above France, for certain German authors above others, and for Schiller in particular, does he mean for his own poetics when he posits that German inoculation attains its consummation in Schiller, 'by and through [whom] it was, as its main organ, that this great revolutionary impulse expressed itself'?[104] De Quincey is correct in noting that Schiller evinces an interest in translation in taking the unusual step of actively managing his interpreters. He acquiesces to Coleridge's request for an authenticated draft of *Wallenstein*, for instance; and he actively negotiates with publishing houses for the rights to translate the same play.[105] These activities hint at little more than a better than average pragmatic understanding, however – an impression that is hardly lifted by running through Schiller's scattered comments on the topic, which barely rise above the commonplace that '[a] bad translation is the worst thing conceivable, and a good translation takes time'.[106] De Quincey's interest in Schiller does not derive from the latter's practice or theory of translation; indeed, even the contents of his writings are rejected, in that they are 'indefensible' as 'coherent work[s] of art'.[107] Rather, Schiller's genius resides in the structures that his texts enact: it is these deeper principles that require urgent transposition into English. In his article for the *Encyclopaedia*, De Quincey does not indicate what these vaunted structures encompass, or from what texts they might be distilled. He does, however, offer a hint in his fragmentary 'Notes from the Pocket-Book of a Late Opium-Eater' (1823–4). Having held forth on a favourite subject, the indeterminate sense of absence presently vexing British literature, he remarks on the remarkable coincidence between his own views and 'a passage in an interesting work of Schiller's [. . .] (*on the Aesthetic Education of Men*, in a series of letters: vid. letter the 6th.)'.[108] Since no English translation of the *Ästhetische Erziehung* had been published in the two decades after its first publication, De Quincey proceeds to supply a few extracts from Letters Six through Nine (the next sampler, a part of the fifteenth letter, would come in 1831, courtesy of Carlyle).[109] Summarised through De Quincey's pseudo-philological apparatus of terms and concepts, Schiller's diagnosis of modern life is that it is marked by a profound discontent pivoting on the monopoly of prose. In an analysis that resonates with De Quincey's, Schiller argues that disaffection is inherent in civilisational development, in that developing languages cannot but list ever more towards an unadorned communication of facts. As a result, modern man, sensible that he has lost a capacity for beautifully crafted expression, 'with the monotonous whirling of the wheel that he turns everlastingly in his ear [. . .] never develops the harmony of his being'. When Schiller turns to prescribe a remedy, gearing up to assess if 'the totality of our nature, which art has destroyed, might not be re-established by a higher art', his interpreter cuts him short, as 'this, as leading to a discussion beyond the limits of my own, I omit'.[110] Perhaps because the programme for literary reinvigoration that Schiller is poised to deliver veers so close to his own proposals, De Quincey suppresses the former's observation that those artists who would release their country from its 'tottering' and 'rotting' condition must first transform themselves, enacting the change they wish to see by growing into a 'foreign shape':

> The artist is indeed the child [*Sohn*] of his age; but woe to him if he is at the same its ward, or worse still, its minion [*Zögling*]! Let some beneficent deity snatch the suckling betimes from his mother's breast, nourish him with the milk of a better age, and suffer him to come to maturity under a distant Grecian sky. Then, when he has become a man, let him return, a stranger [*eine fremde Gestalt*], to his own century; not, however, to gladden it by his appearance, but rather, terrible like Agamemnon's son, to cleanse and to purify it. His theme he will, indeed, take from the present; but his form he will borrow from a nobler time.

The Romantic artist, Schiller here argues, receives his transformative powers from a dual parentage. He is the child of his own nation and the adoptee of another, the 'son of his own age' and the 'son of Agamemnon', impelled like Orestes to restore the laws of old; combining a modern talent for exacting representation with an antique sensibility for exquisite design. Significantly, Schiller does not note that his allegory of dedoubled heritage ought to involve a dual linguistic filiation: he imagines the ideal artist not so much as an accomplished bilingual divided between German and Greek, but as a talent stylist nimbly navigating between an older formal and a newer thematic drive in writing. The Romantic author must honour both these forces, combining them in a third drive; a derived *Spieltrieb* that recalls Coleridge's *tertium aliquid*. The sole objective of this play drive is to ensure that neither of the two primary drives chokes the other: since a strict fusion or synthesis is impossible, the only way a synthesis can be attained is by organising 'a reciprocal action [*Wechselwirkung*] between the two drives'. Truly artful writing, that is, seeks to ensure that the pendulum of creation and reception forever swings between the extremes of matter and manner by organising a constant mediation between the two:

> Once you postulate a primary, and therefore necessary, antagonism between these two drives, there is, of course, no other means of maintaining unity in man than by unconditionally *subordinating* the sensuous drive to the rational. From this, however, only uniformity can result, never harmony, and man goes on for ever being divided. Subordination there must, of course, be; but it must be reciprocal. [...] Both principles are, therefore, at once subordinated to each other and co-ordinated with each other, that is to say, they stand in reciprocal relation to one another: without form no matter; and without matter no form.[111]

From its deliberations on the difficulties of a truly combinatory Romantic style, this passage extrapolates the structure that will permit an ideal distribution of information, through which prose and poetry may finally be 'at once subordinated to each other and co-ordinated with each other'. The compressed chiasm that concludes this excerpt stands at the heart of Schiller's entire treatise – 'without form no matter; and without matter no form'. It is this structure of reversal that animates De Quincey's career-spanning attempt to craft a new mode of authorship and writing: his contribution to idealist debate, however, is that he refocuses its interminable debates over the nature of third terms and drives to questions of language and national identity.

Even the great Schiller, pre-eminent among German authors, is infinitely outmatched by another German idealist. De Quincey professes to admire Schiller for 'the memory of the man', for the moral fibre that he displayed throughout his life; however, his worship he reserves for a man of ferocious genius, who boasts an unparalleled grasp of the double vision required of modern writing. 'The characteristic distinction of Paul Richter amongst German authors, I will venture amongst modern authors generally', De Quincey notes, 'is [a] two-headed power [...] or rather, [...] this power is not two-headed, but a one-headed Janus with two faces [...] composing out of their union a third metal *sui generis*'. The text most suffused with such duality is the 1804 *Vorschule der Ästhetik*. Truly,

> on this poor earth of ours, I am acquainted with no book of such unintermitting and brilliant wit as his *Vorschule der Ästhetik* [...] [which is] absolutely

so surcharged with quicksilver, that I expect to see it leap off the table as often as it is laid there.[112]

The *Preparatory School of Aesthetics*, as its title is generally rendered in English,[113] remoulds Schiller's *Aesthetic Education* into a poetics in which the challenges of modern experience might be productively salvaged. The book accordingly starts on a familiar note. Outlining an ideal past localised to Attic Greece in which writing struck a perfect balance of the material and the meaningful, Jean Paul describes current literature as a shabby affair. '[P]oetry was the object of the people among the Greeks, as the people were the object of poetry', he sighs, sketching out a super-efficient chiastic communication that has now disappeared, in that 'today we sing from one study across the hall to another about what is most interesting in each'. Modern literature has been sundered into two factions: the traditionalist 'poetic nihilists' live only for ideas; by contrast, the insurgent 'poetic materialists', sensing that an exclusive focus on contents leaves man's capacities underused by half, overload their texts with a glut of forms, 'throwing, as it were, a whole universe between man and his god'. True literature, however, Jean Paul insists, providing his own spin on a familiar argument, requires for its author a materialist nihilist, or a nihilist materialist; or, better yet, both if by turns. Since a combinatory Attic style can no longer sustain itself, the sole method by which the rift between matter and manner can be sutured is to stage a hypermobile form of writing, in which perspectives incessantly reverse into one another:

> If the nihilist transparently dissolves the particular into the general and the materialist petrifies and ossifies the general into the particular, living poetry must comprehend and achieve a union of the two in which every individual can find himself and in whose generality [. . .] each will find only his own particularity. In short, poetry should become like the moon, which by nights follows one wanderer in the woods from peak to peak and at the same time another from wave to wave and thus attends each, while it simply describes its great arc across heaven and yet ultimately draws it across the earth and around the wanderers also.

Nursing his own arboreal metaphor, Jean Paul describes the stylistically perfected text as one that 'reconciles – indeed weds – helpless life with ethereal sense, as the edge of still water the real tree and its reflection seems to grow from a single root towards two heavens'. Like Schiller, Richter argues that those texts that seek to be fully attuned to the dichotomies of modern experience must operate *between* styles, epochs and nations. To De Quincey's gratification, the multinational aspect receives considerable emphasis in Jean Paul's hybridisation of style. If the Athenians struck the 'golden mean' in all things, it is because they hit the mid-point between prose and poetry just as proficiently as they 'hit the mean between Norman and Arab'. Converting his notes on the treelike nature of an amphibolic style into an actionable binary of nationality, Richter runs through a list of the most admirable modern and recent writers, each time foregrounding their ability to mix native and foreign strengths:

> Lessing [. . .] where does he, with his thought belong? [. . .] he let the rays of every other system pass into his own solid system, as the brilliant diamond, despite its hardness and density, allows the passage of every ray of light, and even holds sunlight fast. The ordinary philosopher resembles cork – flexible, light, porous, but incapable of transmitting or receiving light. [. . .] Are there not spiritual hybrids, first of periods, then of countries? [. . .] As a mediator between countries we can cite Lichtenberg, whose prose is an intellectual link between England and Germany. Pope is an alley crossing between London and Paris. Voltaire binds the two cities from the opposite direction on a higher level. Schiller is, if not the chord, still the dominant note between British and German poetry.

Jean Paul's provocative description of literary visionariness as 'border genius' is far more elaborate than Schiller's abstract spiel on the benefits of duplicate citizenship. And yet here, too, there is no clear concept of interlinguistic translation. Even though the *Vorschule* rebukes the German people for their insularity, issues of linguistic difference barely attract attention: Richter's literary philosophy is centred on distinctions in national character, not on the labours required to organise the interlingual communication that he admires; as such, while De Quincey equates specific languages with distinct subtypes of style, Jean Paul's understanding of language remains vague.

It takes a Cicero to understand a Herodotus; it takes a Coleridge to appreciate a Schelling: Jean Paul, too, De Quincey suggests, fully comes into his own only as he passes through British hands. The *Vorschule* itself wryly hints at the inability of its intended readers to appreciate its value, noting that '[t]he German, especially in the nineteenth century, is in a position to be impartial towards all nations except for his own misunderstood nation'.[114] De Quincey promptly inflates this complaint, claiming that Jean Paul is reputed to be 'the most difficult of all German authors'. Having established these credentials, he uses them to magnify his own: 'it has often been said to me, as an Englishman, "What! can you read John Paul?" – meaning, can you read such difficult German?' If a British gentleman-scholar can digest a text that baffles its primary readership, it is because, De Quincey argues, Richter's difficulty proceeds less from his texts' learned diction than their incessant shifts between a formal and a referential logic. '[T]he nimbleness of his transitions often makes him elliptical', De Quincey observes; 'the fineness and evanescent brilliancy of his oblique glances and surface-skimming allusions, often fling but half a meaning on the mind; and one is puzzled to make out its complement.'[115] In being read by English eyes, the text finds this complement: not only is the *Vorschule* a work *on* translation, it is also written in expectation *of* its translation.

And yet De Quincey does not directly translate the acclaimed *Vorschule*.[116] There is a commercial argument for this strange failure to import the one text that might stave off British ruination: excepting academic translations of Kant's *Critiques*, monograph-length translated treatises of philosophy and criticism are rare in the early nineteenth century, and while summaries offer an alternative, as in the case of De Quincey's translation of Lessing's *Laokoon*, it is difficult to imagine a compression of a book as extravagantly textured as Richter's. The economic constraints on translated texts do not pre-empt indirect strategies of importation, however. The 'Richter' letter, along with a few further articles on style and language, therefore largely opt to enact rather than theorise Jean Paul's philosophy of style. It is precisely as De Quincey translates into English a German philosophy of dedoubled writing that he renders explicit its potential as a translational structure. When De Quincey asks '[w]hat then is that I claim', his response is to offer not theory but performance, unbridling his writing in spectacular fashion to demonstrate the explosive capacities of a national style returned to its native powers following its passage through a foreign medium. What follows is a vignette of impassioned prose in which a profusion of images set to poetical rhythm mix with a prosaic layout; the whole showing the frantic work of restatement through which the textual tissue is woven together:

> What is it then I claim? – Briefly, an activity of understanding, so restless and indefatigable that all attempts to illustrate, or express it adequately by images borrowed from the natural world, from the motions of beasts, birds, insects, &c. from the leaps of tigers or leopards, from the gambolling and tumbling of kittens, the antics of monkeys, or the running of antelopes and ostriches, &c., are baffled, confounded, and made ridiculous by the enormous and overmastering superiority of impression left by the thing illustrated. [. . .] the wild, giddy, fantastic, capricious, incalculable, springing, vaulting, tumbling, dancing, waltzing, caprioling, pirouetting, sky-rocketing of the chamois, the harlequin, the Vestris, the storm-loving raven – the raven? no, the lark (for often he ascends 'singing up to heaven's gates', but like the lark he dwells upon the earth), in short, of the Proteus, the Ariel, the Mercury, the monster – John Paul [. . .] To say the truth, John Paul's intellect – his faculty of catching at a glance all the relations of objects, both the grand, the lovely, the

ludicrous, and the fantastic – is painfully and almost morbidly active: there is no respite, no repose allowed; no, not for a moment.[117]

Ostentatious as this passage may seem, De Quincey is pained to emphasise that it is not foreign. In transfusing Richter into his work, he has found himself awakened to talents that were always already latent in the native constitution of the English language: Jean Paul serves to bring Britain back to its golden age of thought; that is, to the Restoration and to the exemplary work of Jeremy Taylor and Sir Thomas Browne. In Taylor and Browne, De Quincey recognises the earliest British precedents for his ideal of an impassioned prose that is alternates between poetic and prosaic registers, predating his German idol by over a century:

> In them first, and perhaps (if we except occasional passages in the German John Paul Richter) in them only, are the two opposite forces of eloquent passion and rhetorical fancy brought into an exquisite equilibrium, – approaching, receding, – attracting, repelling, – blending, separating, – chasing and chased, as in a fugue, – and again lost in a delightful interfusion, so as to create a middle species of composition, more various and stimulating to the understanding than pure eloquence, more gratifying to the affections than naked rhetoric. [Taylor is characterised by] everlasting strife and fluctuation between his rhetoric and his eloquence, which maintain their alternations with force and inevitable recurrence, like the systole and diastole, the contraction and expansion, of some living organ.

The 'middle species of composition' is here described through a rapid-fire sequence of binaries culminating in the embracing figure of the fugue, a polyphonic composition in which chase (*fugare*) and flight (*fugere*) constantly reverse, each point generating an equal and opposite counterpoint. The texture created by these oscillations is punctuated by brief moments of exhilarating equilibrium as one melodic stream transitions into the next, much as De Quincey marks his restatements by commas, dashes and question marks. On De Quincey's account, in short, Taylor and Browne created a poetic prose or prosaic poetry, uniquely capable of both 'great passion and high thinking'. When they passed away in the late seventeenth century, however, their style 'disappeared from literature altogether.' When Jean Paul is grafted onto British stock, momentarily represented by De Quincey, the result is a resurrection of the best that British writing has to offer. This is the central claim of De Quincey's defence of translation: if translation energises writing, it is because it reinvigorates energies already extant.

The Richter essay presents the apogee of De Quincey's construction of a translational style, demonstrating the dependence of impassioned prose on an underlying structure of interfusing idioms pseudo-philologically equated to distinct styles. What remains unclear, however, is why De

Quincey is so insistent on the need for a new theory of style, other than to position his work. The following chapter attends to the void that De Quincey alleges has invaded modern thought. It argues that he deploys translation as Schiller and Jean Paul were poised to do; in order to resolve a question vexing many in the wake of Kant's separation of the noumenal and the phenomenal. In playing off styles and languages, he offers a British translator's take on German idealism, demonstrating how literature might productively rejoin what modern life has torn asunder. The following sections examine just what philosophy De Quincey aims to articulate through his style.

## Notes

1. C 1821, 2.13–14; 2.17–18; 2.20; 2.28; 2.56–7.
2. The analysis of this curious scene has become something of a rite of passage for Romanticists of a postcolonial persuasion. An early example is Daniel Sanjiv Roberts, 'Exorcising the Malay: Dreams and the Unconscious in Coleridge and De Quincey', *The Wordsworth Circle* 24, no. 2 (1993): 91–6. An interesting take is offered by Rzepka, who connects De Quincey's 'Asiatic' anxieties with his fraught relationship with Wordsworth: see Charles Rzepka, 'De Quincey and the Malay: Dove Cottage Idolatry', *The Wordsworth Circle* 24, no. 3 (1993): 180–5.
3. Frederick Burwick notes that De Quincey may have visited Germany in 1825 and 1831. In 1823, he includes in his letters a resolution to visit Germany in order to 'revive his creativity and give him proper access to the German works which he craved'; in 1825, he explains his lapse in rent payments by claiming that 'I was called over to Germany.' See Burwick, *Knowledge and Power* (London: Palgrave Macmillan, 2001), 69.
4. C 1821, 2.21.
5. Part of the problem in deciding what essays to include in an overview of De Quincey's theories of style is that he regards language, translation, criticism, epistemology and rhetoric as concepts that require and rely on each other; as such, many of his essays, even those ostensibly unrelated to questions of style, include brief remarks on the importance of expression to thought and communication. This caveat notwithstanding, his main articles on the topic are arguably 'Jean Paul Frederick Richter' (1821); 'English Dictionaries', 'On Languages', 'On the Knocking at the Gate in Macbeth', 'Letters to a Young Man Whose Education has been Neglected' (all 1823); 'Elements of Rhetoric' (1828); 'The English Language' (1839); 'Style' (1840–1); 'Schiller' (1842); 'Conversation' (1847); 'On the Present Stage of the English Language' (1850); and 'How to Write English' (1853). Some of these have previously been gathered in collections aiming to provide insight into De Quincey's theories of style and rhetoric; for instance, *Selected Essays on Rhetoric*, ed. Frederick Burwick (Carbondale: Southern Illinois University Press, 1967).
6. TEL, 11.328.

7. ER, 6.185.
8. TEL, 11.32627; 11.328.
9. See Janet Sorensen, *The Grammar of Empire in Eighteenth-Century British Writing* (Cambridge: Cambridge University Press, 2000), esp. ch. 2: 63–103.
10. ER, 6.185.
11. English Dictionaries, 155. Emphasis mine.
12. S, 12.5.
13. SEL, 17.56.
14. At the time of De Quincey's writing, the two main English dictionaries are Charles Richardson's *New Dictionary of the English Dictionary* (1836) and its highly influential precursor, Samuel Johnson's *Dictionary of the English Language* (1755). In 'The English Language', De Quincey takes note of several further grammars and dictionaries, including Webster, but omits Richardson (TEL, 11.326–7). For further comments, see J. Mark Smith, 'De Quincey, Dictionaries, and Casuistry', *ELH* 84, no. 3 (2017): 689–713.
15. TEL, 11.328
16. SEL, 17.63.
17. HWE, 18.52.
18. EMC, 16.424. It should be noted that De Quincey also complicates his nationalism: see Charles Rzepka, 'Bang-up! Theatricality and the "Diphrelatic Art" in De Quincey's English Mail-Coach', in *Selected Studies in Romantic and American Literature, History, and Culture: Inventions and Interventions* (Farnham: Ashgate, 2010), 63–80.
19. A discussion of De Quincey's negotiation of Britishness and Englishness may be found in Anne Frey, 'De Quincey's Imperial Systems', *Studies in Romanticism* 44, no. 1 (2005): 51–2.
20. De Quincey, of course, hardly stands alone among the British Romantics in investing etymological philology with such philosophical authority. Following the example of John Horne Tooke's theory of etymology, outlined in his Ἔπεα Πτερόεντα, *or the Diversions of Purley*, whose first edition was published in 1786, Coleridge took to etymological thought (see H. J. Jackson, 'Coleridge, Etymology and Etymologic', *Journal of the History of Ideas* 44, no. 1 (1983): 75–88). The Grimms commenced work on their *Deutsches Wörterbuch*, which marks the high point of nineteenth-century philology and etymology, in 1838, and began publishing the dictionary in 1852.
21. Danish Origin of the Lake-country Dialect, 292–8.
22. This is a simplification of a more involved debate: while the assumption that there existed national characters with distinct effects on cognition was so commonplace as to require almost no added justification, several thinkers struggled with the question of priority. See Richard Marggraf Turley, *The Politics of Language in Romantic Literature* (Basingstoke: Palgrave Macmillan, 2002), 1–32; further examples, relating specifically to De Quincey's theory of language, may be found in René Wellek, 'De Quincey's Status in the History of Ideas', *Philological Quarterly* 23 (1944): 264–8.
23. Étienne Bonnot de Condillac, *An Essay on the Origin of Human*

*Knowledge: Being a Supplement to Mr Locke's Essay on the Human Understanding*, trans. [Thomas] Nugent (London: J. Nourse, 1756), 284; 291–2. The entire chapter ('Of the Character of Languages', 283–300) is a relevant source for De Quincey's theories on style and language.
24. BL, 82.
25. Condillac, *Essay*, 292.
26. BL, 86.
27. Samuel Taylor Coleridge, *Specimens of the Table Talk* (London: John Murray, 1836), 55.
28. Roberts, *Revisionary Gleam*, 140.
29. LYM, 3.91.
30. S, 12.24.
31. Condillac, *Essay*, 295–6; 296.
32. SEL, 17.67; 17.65–6.
33. S, 12.6.
34. SEL, 17.66; 17.63; 17.65.
35. S, 12.7.
36. This is a point entirely ignored by Wellek in his point-by-point evisceration of De Quincey as a profoundly unoriginal thinker in matters of language and linguistic evolution. See Wellek, 'History of Ideas', 264–7.
37. Condillac, *Essay*, 298. Emphasis mine.
38. BL, 83.
39. S, 12.18.
40. SEL, 17.57.
41. Logic of Political Economy, 68.
42. SEL, 17.58.
43. TEL, 11.331.
44. SEL, 17.58.
45. ER, 6.161.
46. S, 12.32; 12.37; 12.32.
47. SEL, 17.59; 17.61; 17.60–1.
48. ER, 6.186.
49. Condillac, *Dissertation*, 284.
50. SEL, 17.61.
51. S, 12.46.
52. SEL, 17.61–2.
53. Berman, *Donne*, 10.
54. Lieven D'hulst, 'La traduction: un genre littéraire à l'époque romantique?', *Revue d'histoire littéraire de la France* 97, no. 3 (1997): 391.
55. For example, *vertere, convertere, aliquid (Latine) exprimere, verbum e verbo, ad verbum exprimere, (Graece, Latine) reddere, verbum pro verbo reddere*. See Johannes Lohmann, *Philosophie und Sprachwissenschaft* (Berlin: Duncker and Humblot, 1965), 85.
56. Lohmann, *Sprachwissenschaft*, 85.
57. Berman, *Donne*, 10. Also see Rener's observation that '[i]n late Roman times, Virgil's three works, the *Bucolics*, the *Georgics*, and the *Aneid*, were regarded as "translations" of three Greek poets, Theocritus, Hesiod, and Homer, in that order'. See Frederick M. Rener, *Translatio:*

*Language and translation from Cicero to Tytler* (Amsterdam: Rodopi, 1989).
58. See Berman, *Donne*, 8; 10, n11.
59. For a history of the concept of *translatio*, see Rener, *Translatio*, and Enrico Fenzi, 'Translatio studii e translatio imperii: Appunti per un percorso', *Interfaces: A Journal of Medieval European Literatures* 1 (2015): 170–208.
60. S, 12.32.
61. The story of Herodotus's Olympic recitation appears primarily based on a short passage in Lucian's *Herodotus, or Aetion*. A contemporary account, along with a rejection of the anecdote as entirely fictitious, may be found in [Friedrich Christoph] Dahlmann, *Life of Herodotus Drawn out from His Book*, trans. G. V. Cox (London: John W. Parker, [1823] 1845), 8–27.
62. HWE, 18.50. For a closer consideration of Herodotus's Panhellenist ambitions, and the dangers of reading this project into him, see Michael A. Flower, 'From Simonides to Isocrates: The Fifth-Century Origins of Fourth-Century Panhellenism', *Classical Antiquity* 19, no. 1 (2000): 69–76.
63. S, 12.33–4.
64. HWE, 18.48–9; 18.51.
65. See TEL, 11.325 and SEL, 17.60–1.
66. See Manuel Castells, *Economy, Society, and Culture: The Rise of the Network Society*, vol. 1 of *The Information Age* (Oxford: Blackwell, 1996).
67. HWE, 18.50.
68. Eric Dayre, *L'absolu comparé: littérature et traduction: une séquence moderne: Coleridge, De Quincey, Baudelaire, Rimbaud* (Paris: Hermann, 2009), 76–7.
69. TEL, 11.325–6.
70. Berman, *Donne*, 10–11.
71. S, 12.18.
72. For a refreshingly lucid (and instructively illustrated) primer on the chiasmus in German idealism, particularly in the work of Schiller, see Elizabeth M. Wilkinson and L. A. Willoughby, Appendices to *On the Aesthetic Education of Man in a Series of Letters: English and German Facing* by Friedrich Schiller (Oxford: Clarendon, 1982), 348–51. Also see Rodolphe Gasché, 'Reading Chiasms', *Of Minimal Things: Studies on the Notion of Relation* (Stanford: Stanford University Press, 1999), 263–84.
73. Gasché, 'Reading Chiasms', xvii.
74. Hölderlin's development of chiasmus in his work on translation and national character has been incisively analysed by Andrzej Warminski (*Readings in Interpretation: Hölderlin, Hegel, Heidegger* (Minneapolis: University of Minnesota Press, 1987), 29). Even though Gasché addresses the chiasmus in a chapter which reflects on de Man's theory of *Übersetzung* (literally, translation, but more properly in this context, figurative speech), he does not explore the chiastic nature of translation. See *The Wild Card of Reading: On Paul de Man* (Cambridge, MA: Harvard University Press, 1998), esp. 28–9.
75. Friedrich Hölderlin, 'Brief Nr. 237: An Casimir Ulrich Böhlendorff, 4

December 1801', *Sämtliche Werke und Briefe in drei Bänden* (Frankfurt am Main: Deutscher Klassiker Verlag, 1992–4), 3.460.
76. See Gasché, *Wild Card*, 28–9.
77. Quoted in Gasché, 'Reading Chiasmi', xvii.
78. SEL, 17.65.
79. See Gasché, *Wild Card*, 28–9.
80. S, 12.23.
81. ER, 6.181. De Quincey, incidentally, misattributes this observation, which features not in Uno von (not *Van*) Troil's *Letters on Iceland* (translated to English in 1780), but in Niels Horrebow, *The Natural History of Iceland* (London: Linde, 1758), 91.
82. S, 12.21–2.
83. SEL, 17.64–5; 17.64.
84. S, 12.23; 12.18; 12.20; 12.18–19.
85. TEL, 11.330.
86. S, 12.26.
87. TEL, 11.332.
88. R, 3.18–19. The Golden Pippin is first documented in the early seventeenth century, and was particularly popular in the eighteenth century.
89. De Quincey appears unaware that while most varieties of apple are self-sterilising, and therefore require inoculating in order to be propagated, some types of pippin do not require grafting at all, and may be cultivated from seed. The Golden Pippin is, in fact, self-fertilising. De Quincey also betrays a less than perfect command of horticulture when he suggests that grafts lead to a fruit that bears traits of the stock as well as the scion: only the latter will be carried forward.
90. C 1821, 2.57. Variolation had been imported to Britain from France in 1721, and formalised by Edward Jenner in 1796. 'Hydrophobia' here presumably refers to rabies, the first vaccine for which is introduced in 1885. A plague vaccine was first used in 1890. Both these vaccines would have been self-evidently fatal in 1821; an inoculation with cancer cells, at least one following Jenner's methods, would generally have been without effect, though perhaps it was suspected to be equally lethal.
91. EMC, 16.422.
92. C 1821, 2.57.
93. AB, 10.162.
94. R, 3.19–20.
95. One issue in compounding a reliable survey of external influences is the discrepancy between qualitative and quantitative data. That is, while contemporary journals contain a far greater proportion of direct and indirect translations from French sources, and rarely grant German writing a significant presence, they tend to ascribe a greater and far more positive impact to the latter, often signalling misgivings regarding French politics and morals. See Chapter 4 for a further consideration of this question.
96. Hutchinson, 62–94.
97. S, 12.26.
98. R, 3.20.
99. See Max J. Herzberg, 'Wordsworth and German Literature', *PMLA* 40, no. 2 (1925): 311.

100. M, 4.170.
101. See Peter Mortensen, 'Robbing *The Robbers*: Schiller, Xenophobia, and the Politics of British Romantic Translation', *Literature and History* 11, no. 1 (2002): 43. Also see Herzberg, 'Wordsworth and German Literature': 312; and L. A. Willoughby, 'English Translations and Adaptations of Schiller's *The Robbers*', *Modern Language Review* 27 (1921): 297–315.
102. William Hazlitt, *Lectures on the Dramatic Literature of the Age of Elizabeth* (New York: Wiley and Putnam, [1820] 1845), 216.
103. While Schiller sent Coleridge a draft of the play, he neglected to inform him of the drastic changes the manuscript underwent before its publication in Germany. This has given rise to a persistent myth that Schiller revised the German text after having read Coleridge's version. Coleridge's contemporaries considered his translation an extraordinary achievement; so much so that later, more literal retranslations of Schiller's final version were judged wanting. Hazlitt called it 'admirable and almost literal.' (Hazlitt, *Lectures*, 216) Modern critics and editors are less forgiving: see Joyce Crick, 'Coleridge's "Wallenstein": Two Legends', *The Modern Language Review* 83, no. 1 (1988): 76–86.
104. Schiller, 13.274; 13.277; 13.275–6; 13.276.
105. Crick, 'Two Legends', 77–8.
106. Friedrich Schiller, *Briefwechsel zwischen Schiller und Körner* (Stuttgart: J. G. Cotta, n.d. [1892–6]), 4 October 1792.
107. Schiller, 13.276.
108. Notes from the Pocket-Book of a Late Opium-Eater, *The London Magazine* 10 (1824), 27.
109. Wilkinson and Willoughby, *Aesthetic Education*, 338.
110. Pocket-Book, 27.
111. Friedrich Schiller, *On the Aesthetic Education of Man in a Series of Letters: English and German Facing*, ed. Elizabeth M. Wilkinson and L. A. Willoughby (Oxford: Clarendon, 1982), 25; 56–7; 85n1; 85–7. Further adding to the increasingly complex picture of echoes and mutually reinforcing influences, Schiller credits this observation to Fichte's 1794 *Fundaments of the Theory of Knowledge*.
112. R, 3.20; 3.21–2; 3.23.
113. The more literal, if perhaps somewhat undignified, translation of *Vorschule* is nursery school. Its only English translation is *Horn of Oberon: Jean Paul Richter's School for Aesthetics*, trans. Margaret Hale (Detroit: Wayne State University Press [1804; 2nd edn 1813] 1973). Selections have also been published in David Simpson (ed.), *The Origins of Modern Critical Thought: German Aesthetic and Literary Criticism from Lessing to Hegel* (Cambridge: Cambridge University Press, 1988), 291–318.
114. Richter, *School*, 18; 58; 27; 43; 46; 33–4; 56.
115. R, 3.24.
116. For an overview of the texts that De Quincey translated from Jean Paul's oeuvre, see Frederick Burwick, 'The Dream-Visions of Jean Paul and Thomas De Quincey', *Comparative Literature* 20, no. 1 (1968): 2; 2n4.
117. R, 3.23. Vestris refers to Auguste Vestris, a French ballet dancer (1760–1842).

# Chapter 3

# Translating (against) Kant: A Translator's Idealism

## Translating Kant

De Quincey first half-publicly comes forward as an interpreter during his eighteenth-month editorship of the *Westmorland Gazette*, which he anonymously holds from July 1818 to November 1819.¹ Founded by the Tory Lowther brothers in May 1818 as a response to the *Kendal Chronicle* which had come out in support of the local Whig candidate, the *Gazette* mixes news and propaganda in order to stage what De Quincey terms, in his second editorial for the paper, an 'adequate counteraction'.² His vision for the journal is clear. '[I]n contribution to more powerful efforts from the resident gentry', he announces, 'this Paper will henceforward call the attention of the public, from time to time, to a dispassionate examination [. . .] of the leading political questions which concern our time and nation.' Also projected to be featured in the journal's pages are 'upon an average, perhaps, two and three columns [. . .] occupied by miscellaneous articles extracted from the *Literary Gazette*'. In an editorial published on 17 April 1819, addressed to 'the higher class of readers', he further promises that future issues will include a greater selection of intellectual fare 'which will give to the *[Westmorland Gazette]* an interest and a character scarcely claimed by any English Journal even exclusively devoted to literature'. To outdo its metropolitan competitors in matters of culture, he envisages four new types of article:

I. With Statistical Tables – British and Continental. – II. With Original Essays. – III. With a Horilegium collected from the most unfrequented parts of European literature (especially English). – IV. And chiefly with translations from the best parts of German Literature, and more rarely from the German Philosophy.

In defending his innovations, De Quincey claims that this new material boasts an 'extraordinary interest' amongst the public. Moreover, his fourth category of writing, which focuses on translated German literature and philosophy, is sure to trigger nothing short of a cultural renaissance in the journal's subscribers. While he concedes that '[i]n poetry and the finer [...] parts of literature, the merit of the German is generally overrated', in many other subspecies, it ranks as 'the most opulent in Europe', making it eminently suited for transfusion. Several years before he was to reiterate his recommendations for a transfer of German genius in much more detailed fashion, De Quincey promptly subjoins a call for a nationwide programme of translation. The latter particularly ought to focus on crafting a theory of language and style that might inspire translators to make better choices, since at present 'the English nation have as yet imported noting but the coarsest part of the ore'. There has been too much admiration for writers 'immeasurably below the English': Goethe's limping prose comes in for a perfunctory kicking, as do Wieland and Bürger. No qualified German authors are named at this early juncture; instead, cancelling his promise to focus on exemplary literature, De Quincey moves to philosophy, since '[i]t is in this department of intellectual power [...] that Germany is eminent'. Amongst these superior sages, one is singled out: the *Gazette* announces it will shortly be delighting its readers with translations of the work of Immanuel Kant. De Quincey pledges a piece on Kant's 1755 *Universal Theory and Natural History of the Heavens*, along with 'a letter to a friend on the study of Transcendental Philosophy; with some account of the English expounders' and '[a]n analysis of Two Essays by Wolf and Kant on the introduction of mathematical conceptions into philosophy'.

Sensing that his intended readership, 'the Yeomanry of Westmorland and the Artizans of this town', may be less enamoured of Teutonic stodge, De Quincey ensures his readership and proprietors that they 'need not however fear that [they] will be oppressed by German metaphysics'. The editor is cognisant of the need to adapt German abstraction to British pragmatism, and, more importantly, to integrate German insights into a project for the betterment of Britain – 'to give something of *unity* to the four different departments of his journal by directing them all into a common service ministerial to the purposes of a wise and enlightened patriotism'.[3] As part of this project of adaptation, De Quincey somewhat speciously claims Kant for the conservative readership he addresses through the *Gazette*.[4] When criticism of De Quincey's eccentric editorial programme comes flying from quarters ideologically opposed to the *Gazette*'s politics, he further strengthens this appropriation of Kant's writings to the Tory cause. A few weeks after proclaiming the Britain-bracing effects of German thought, he is stung into a repeat performance when his chief adversary, the Whiggish *Chronicle*, attacks De Quincey's editorship by mocking his enthusiasm for Kant. In a hatchet piece, the *Chronicle* incongruously casts Kant as at once an airy mystic and an arid logician; briefly, as an extraordinarily dull and irrelevant creature. 'It is amusing to remark the inconsistencies and contradictions into which the *Kendal Chronicle* suffers itself to be betrayed by it's [*sic*] enmity to the *Gazette*', De Quincey thunders in his rebuttal. Previously defending the inclusion of Kantian matter chiefly on the grounds of his alleged politics, he now inflates him into a thinker of universal significance, claiming that in slighting the pretensions of so outstanding a genius, his rival has embarrassed itself:

> The Editor of the *Gazette* had expressed his veneration for the great restorer (and, as he may justly be called, with reference to some branches, the great founder) of philosophy in the eighteenth century. Forthwith the *Chronicle* addresses itself to the task of disparaging him. [. . .] if ever it could be affirmed of any man that he had agitated and almost convulsed the nation to which he spoke, emphatically might this be affirmed of Immanuel Kant: since the time of Luther no one man has had so extensive – not so many at any time so deep – an influence upon the course of human thought [. . .] Great indeed is the strength of Kant: to other philosophers he stands in the relation of the Titans in Heathen Mythology to ordinary men; or one of the earliest Patriarchs of the human race in physical powers to his post-diluvian descendants.[5]

For all its bluster, there is a strange hiatus in De Quincey's defence of the Kantian revolution. It is difficult to divine from his account just what Kant has actually accomplished. Much to the aggravation of such later readers as Wellek, De Quincey often favours hyperbolic claims regarding the boons of German metaphysics over specifications of its exact contents or benefits. What he does slowly clarify, however, is that he is drawn to Kant's philosophy not for its doctrines but for its structures. As De Quincey sees it, the crux of the Kantian revolution is its institution of a rigorous separation of all aspects of experience and cognition into binaries, generally summarised to revolve around an irreducible polarity between the phenomenal and the noumenal. De Quincey mainly seizes on Kant for the translative structure that lies behind this foundational distinction: in constructing a new tradition in German thought, Kant explicitly aims to combine the apparently irreconcilable traditions of French and British thought, thus mending the rift between Cartesian rationalism and Lockean empiricism that had long divided European philosophy. It is this ambition of transnational mediation that also informs one of Kant's earlier works, his 1764 *Observations on the Feeling of the Beautiful and the Sublime*, translated by De Quincey in 1824, in which he credits the

German nation with possessing 'a mixed temper composed of the English and the French, but partaking much more of the first'. Much like the ideal speaker conjectured by Condillac, the ideal German is to occupy 'a happy equilibrium of sensibility to the Sublime and the Beautiful, and if he does not rival the Englishman in the first nor the Frenchman in the second, yet he surpasses either separately in so far as he combines them both'.[6] It is this translative structure that De Quincey hopes to lift from Kant. To his increasing exasperation, however, the latter's unwillingness to act on the translational structures implicit to his thought by examining how diverging idioms might be reconciled in furtherance of a practical recombination of the phenomenal and the noumenal means that De Quincey is never to find it in the German's writings.

Following his resignation of the editorship of the *Gazette* in 1819, De Quincey comes to justify his interest in philosophy less by orchestrating political battles by proxy than by pointing to Kant's untold gifts. If it is true that German literature in the style of Jean Paul will trigger the re-emergence of a British poetic-prosaic mode currently in abeyance, the importation of German thought on the model of Kant may similarly be predicted to reanimate a mode of tertiary thinking. In engrafting Kant onto the native body philosophic, then, De Quincey again seeks to lend an impetus to tendencies that are already latent in the British constitution. As a result, only those ideas which have demonstrably already evolved among English speakers, however inchoately, are candidates for a fortifying transfusion, since 'no complex or very important truth was ever yet transferred in full developement from one mind to another'. That is, to revisit a favourite figure, a base must have asserted itself as a natural excrescence of the national mind before the foreign adjuvant can be introduced:

> truth of that character is not a piece of furniture to be shifted; it is a seed which must be sown, and pass through the several stages of growth. No doctrine of importance can be transferred in a matured shape into any man's understanding from without: it must arise by an act of genesis within the understanding itself.

By way of example, De Quincey draws on the distinction between the fancy and the imagination. This one pivotal dichotomy, he suggests, British Romantic writers, chief among them Wordsworth, have managed to push through to its transformative implications without much external assistance. Other such foundational polarities, however, like the stylistic disjunction of poetry and prose, do require translational intercession. This also holds for the philosophical separation of the transcendent and transcendental, the noumenal and the phenomenal, or the spiritual and the material: while analogous to ideas already surmised by home-grown thinkers, they are as yet insufficiently developed.

As with his translations of Jean Paul, De Quincey's translations of Kant never quite transpire, at least not in the form or through the platform he initially envisages. The *Gazette* publishes three pieces, the latter two of which serve to introduce Kant's cosmogony to British readers: 'Immanuel Kant and John Gottfried Herder', 'Immanuel Kant and Dr Herschel', and 'The Planet Mars'. Further essays which attempt to make good on the advertisements trumpeted by the *Gazette* are to be found scattered across the various periodicals De Quincey favours with his writing in the course of his career, particularly *Blackwood's*, *Tait's* and the *London*. The two articles that most realise his avowed ambition to anglicise Kant are his 'Letters to a Young Man Whose Education has been Neglected' (1823) and 'The Age of the Earth' (1833). The former is a collection of pseudo-epistolary essays which advocate a constant study of German thought.[7] The latter promises '[f]or the benefit of our readers, [to] digest[] the sum of what [Kant] has said into a brief memoir', but actually offers a nearly exact rendition of Kant's 1754 original.[8] In addition to the quotes and comments that pepper several of his essays on style and philosophy, a full inventory of De Quincey's engagement with Kant requires the addition of a handful of other pieces which translate (sections of) the *Observations on the Feeling of the Beautiful and the Sublime* (1764; 1824), *Dreams of a Spirit-Seer* (1766; 1824), 'Idea of a Universal History on a Cosmopolitan Plan' (1784; 1824), 'Perpetual Peace: A Philosophical Sketch' (1795; 1830), and 'On the Common Saying' (1795; 1830).[9] Most of these articles are the first known English versions of the essays concerned; taken together, they attest to an abiding interest in Kantian thought, as well as a programme for its promulgation. They also demonstrate De Quincey's sense of the commercial constraints on translation: while he argues that his selections are based on local needs, it is clear that he especially translates those brief and pragmatic pieces that will fit the periodical format.

De Quincey's avowed adoration of Kant is a feature he shares with many of his contemporaries. Few of them embark on exhaustively reading his work, however, generally declaring themselves content with receiving his ideas in heavily summarised form. This lack of direct engagement with German philosophy, and even with German literature, calls into question a significant portion of present-day Romanticist scholarship. While much criticism on the British Romantics productively frames its readings through German connections, and while 'Kant was and still is thought to exert the major influence of German idealist philosophy on British romanticism',[10] the actual extent of this influence is difficult to divine.[11] Even amid the welter of studies on Kant's influence in England, much remains indistinct.[12] Not even the recent surge of periodical studies, which has complicated the critical map of Romanticism in many respects, has shed much light on this question, as the treatment of German literature in contemporary magazines is often disappointingly 'patchy'.[13] Kathleen Wheeler has even argued that 'we cannot assert that Kant's influence was either necessary or decisive for the change from Augustan and Enlightenment attitudes to Romantic ones'.[14] Notwithstanding the difficulties of weighing influence, however, the actual impact of particular literatures and authors arguably matters less than their *perceived* importance. While leading journals are either, like the *Edinburgh Review*, more interested in French texts, or, like *Blackwood's*, hesitant to convert their professed admiration of German writing into actual translations, a quantifiably larger presence of French texts matters little if literary culture studiously dissembles any such connection, and instead defines itself through an imagined Germanic affiliation. Especially in the earlier phases of the movement, British Romantic authors largely understood their work to be treading paths first laid down by German authors: even the *Edinburgh* repeatedly scorns French writers their 'frippery, triviality, bombast, and lack of sublimity'[15] while praising their German counterparts. In appointing himself out as a purveyor of choice for all things German, then, De Quincey seeks to serve as a legislator of British Romanticism's sense of itself, however ideologically determined that identity is.

Joining De Quincey's efforts to adapt German thought to British preferences are a handful of other translator-scholars: few achieve his reputation for pre-eminence in German letters, however. Following *Sartor Resartus*, Carlyle largely abandons his flirtation with German idealism, and other potential translators-in-chief, like Henry Crabb Robinson, Thomas Wirgman or Frederic Nitsch either avoid the public eye or are too specialised in their output.[16] Coleridge cuts a notable exception in professing himself a Kantian and framing his own work as a transfusion of transcendental philosophy. As the previous chapters explored, however, he is also apt to conceal his debts. By contrast to all would-be competitors, De Quincey fully markets himself as a connoisseur of German letters: if his scandalous love of opium is designed to appeal to the casual reader of the 'Confessions', his repeated assertions of metaphysical knowledge derived through dedicated study of 'the writings of Kant, Fichte, Schelling, &c.' serve to secure his reputation amongst his colleagues. One central ambition of the 'Confessions' is to fuse these two identities by connecting the author's opium habit to his philosophical pursuits: 'I now took only 1000 drops of laudanum per day', De

Quincey will record, suggestively adding that 'I read Kant again, and again I understood him, or fancied that I did.' In the same vein, when he projects a picture of his ideal self, he invites readers to imagine an author scribbling away at night; a flask of 'ruby-coloured laudanum' close and 'a book of German Metaphysics placed by its side'.[17]

While it has been alleged that De Quincey pursues his forays into German letters 'to the bewilderment of the Lakeland farming population',[18] he is careful to wear his learning lightly. 'De Quincey (unlike Coleridge)', Leask observes, 'was never obscurantist in his writing.'[19] He frames his early translations through a superior ability for explication; for communicating difficult information by adapting it to the language, style and ideas already present in the receiving audience. Part of this performance is to insist on his difference from Coleridge, who was famously asked by Byron to 'explain his explanation' as he 'explain[ed] Metaphysics to the nation'.[20] More importantly, in presenting himself as a skilled teacher, he also clarifies the impact of his work. Kant is recurrently painted as an academic who 'had no talent for communicating luminously'.[21] Yes, 'Kant and his colossal scheme of thinking' constitute 'a work of great labour and difficulty', but 'to *communicate* it with effect to a nation, whose intense habits of business make it intolerant of all the profounder studies, a work of even greater'.[22] The *Critiques* and their accompanying texts, moreover, are so alien in their proposals that they demand a reinvention of the language into which they are rendered. English alternatives for Kantian jargon do exist, but they cannot assist in the growth of a British varietal of transcendental thought unless the English language is retrained. '[Y]ou will often hear such challenges thrown as this (or others involving the same error)', De Quincey advises those requesting a rough-and-ready transplantation of Kantian matter; '"Now, if there be any sense in this Mr Kant's writings, let us have it in good old mother English."' This sort of provocation must be refused, since the demand to translate at speed is really a demand to neuter Kant into a harmless tautology of British prejudices:

> the way to deal with this fellow is as follows: My good sir, I shall do what you ask: but, before I do it, I beg that you will oblige me by, 1. Translating this mathematics into the language of chemistry 2. By translating this chemistry into the language of mathematics: 3. Both into the language of cookery: and, finally, solve me the Cambridge problem: 'Given the captain's name, and the year of our lord, to determine the longitude of the ship.' This is the way to deal with such fellows. The terminology of Kant then is not a rebaptism of ideas already existing in the universal consciousness: it is, in part, an enlargement of the understanding by new territory (of which I have spoken); and, in part, a better regulation of its old territory.[23]

Echoing Coleridge's remark that the British appreciation of Kant has been deformed by near-universal reliance on the vacuous observations of 'Reviewers and Frenchmen',[24] De Quincey identifies as the chief culprit for the desolate state of British transcendentalism a national underdevelopment of linguistic skills. 'For many years [Kant's] philosophy was accessible only to those who read German', he writes, noting that this was 'an accomplishment exceedingly rare down to the era of Waterloo'.[25] Even if this monolingualism were resolved, however, a deeper uncongeniality would remain. 'Metaphysics are pretty generally out of the reach of nation made up of practical men of business',[26] he comments, invoking the trope of the shopkeeper nation to characterise the British intellectual disposition and the consequent difficulties in adapting Kant to 'a country where the structure and tendency of society impress upon the whole activities of the nation a direction almost exclusively practical'.[27] 'It is not for its *abstruseness* that we shrink from the Transcendental Philosophy', then,

> but for that taken in connexion with its visionariness, and its disjunction from all the practical uses in life. In an age which, if ever any did, idolatrizes the tangible and the material – the shadowy (but not therefore unreal or baseless) texture of metaphysics is certainly called into a very disadvantageous comparison.[28]

In short, least of all in Britain, 'mere skill in the treatment of language could not avail to popularise a philosophy so essentially obscure'. Still, De Quincey reflects, 'a judicious version might have availed to disarm this philosophy of all that is likely that is likely to prove offensive at first sight'.[29] Many have chosen the easy way out, 'to fall in with the national infirmity, to profess a total ignorance even of the German language' and 'to treat a great scheme of philosophic truth [. . .] as a momentary candidate for half an hour's jesting and buffoonery'.[30] Precious few have coveted the arduous office of defending the Kantian legacy, and none of these aspiring translators have as yet 'succeeded in throwing a moonlight radiance upon his philosophy'. De Quincey, of course, heralds himself as the one exception: 'I do myself really profess to understand the dark words.'[31]

Looking to reinforce his claims to exceptional gifts of communication, De Quincey frames his comments on the lacklustre British response to transcendental thought through detailed catalogues of his incompetent competitors. The section on 'The English Notices of Kant' which rounds off the 'Letters to a Young Man' launches into a tirade against all notable opposing parties. Amongst the buffoonish clique 'who originally introduced the Kantean philosophy to the notice of the English public', he takes especial umbrage at two popularisers of German extraction, Anthony Florian Madinger Willich and Frederic Augustus Nitsch.[32] Nitsch is a figure of particular importance in the early mediation of Kant, greatly influencing Coleridge and Wirgman.[33] The latter attests that

> I first studied [Kant] under Frederic Augustus Nitsch, who originally imported the seeds of transcendental philosophy from its native country, to plant them in our soil [. . .] I trust that a sufficient number have taken root to maintain the growth of this vigorous and flourishing plant, till the time shall come when by its general cultivation England may be unable to enrich other nations with the most perfect specimens of its produce.[34]

De Quincey is less positively disposed. 'It is difficult to say', he notes of Willich and Nitsch, 'which wrote the more absurd book.' The former has produced 'a mere piece of book-making';[35] the latter is pronounced that most odious species of commentator, eternally adamant 'never to deliver any doctrine expect in the master's words; [. . .] and not even to venture upon the experiment of a new illustration drawn from their own funds'.[36] Further hopeful explicators are handled according to the same scheme: their translations are stamped as too literal, and their commentaries are judged hopelessly daft.[37] 'For take notice of this', he writes in 1830, in a *soi-disant* letter to the editor of *Blackwood's*;

> that every thing yet published on the subject of Kant, in the English language, errs by one of two defects. Either it is mere nonsense, in a degree possible only to utter and determined ignorance of the German language; or it is so close a translation of the *ipsissima verba* of Kant, as to offer no sort of assistance to an uninitiated student [. . .] nor a single attempt at anticipating and smoothing the difficulties likely to arise in the effort to grasp so subtle an idea, nor an atom of illustration wrought out *proprio marte*.[38]

Even such figures as Thomas Brown, Dugald Stewart and de Staël attract De Quincey's opprobrium. Each of these writers has made the fatal error of 'drawing their information from imbecile French books'. The only exception that De Quincey will allow, even if he does sneak in a parenthetic kick, is Coleridge, 'having – or professing to have – [] direct acquaintance with the original works'. Brown, who relied on Charles de Villers[39] as his source, is judged to have spawned something 'entirely childish'. Stewart took his Kant through de Gérando, who has no 'ability to penetrate below the surface of the Kantean system'.[40] De Staël produced a book that made Kant 'tolerably easy to apprehend – but unfortunately at the expense of all definite purpose, applicability, or philosophic meaning'.[41] Coleridge, the sole contestant with the wherewithal to give a wide berth to French sources, has 'too little talent for teaching or communicating any sort of knowledge'. Finally, finding to his indignation that an 1828 article in the *Edinburgh Review* holds up Wirgman as Britain's most incisive Kantian on account of his contributions to the *Encyclopaedia Londinensis*, De Quincey mounts a furious countercharge. The *Edinburgh* praised 'Mr T Urgmann' as an enlightened peddler who 'composed while he went about with silver-plate and scissars to his customers'.[42] De Quincey retorts that

> [a] grosser mis-statement cannot be; Mr *Wirgman*, (not *Urrgmann*,) the person here alluded to, a very respectable blockhead, is *not* a journeyman, but a master tradesman, with a town and country house, – think of *that* in the first place; secondly, he has no sort of connexion with mechanic institutes, or any new lights of any description [. . .] thirdly, he is not a person whom any party needs to be proud of, – having done nothing but degrade and misrepresent Kant by the heap of stupidities which he has fathered upon him, and the absolute Babylonian gibberish in which he has delivered them.[43]

One may not 'agree with this all too hasty execution of Kant's expounders', Wellek drily comments on De Quincey's scathing overview, but 'one can grant the justice of the general remark, that Kant lacked any commentator in England who would combine thorough knowledge with an original mind and the abilities of a populariser'.[44] The question, of course, is whether De Quincey does meet this challenge, and whether popularisation best describes his aims in translating Kant. A notable shift may be observed in his stance towards the practicability of crafting a popular Kant from the later 1820s onwards, climaxing in the stark observation that '[p]opular the Transcendental Philosophy cannot be. That is not its destiny.'[45] Of course, a national translation requires explication, and '[o]n some future day, it is very possible, that I may trouble you with a short exposition of the Transcendental Philosophy, so framed that [. . .] it shall convey, for the first time, to merely English ears, a real account of what that philosophy is'.[46] Just not now, and, as it transpires, not ever: for his primary audience, De Quincey prefers those men and women of letters who cut a figure similar to his own. While he innovates on his German forerunners by designing a stylistic system that acknowledges the irrepressibly linguistic nature of communication, De Quincey tends to refuse to address those not in his social group, much as he increasingly limits the compass of his sense of Britishness to England alone.

In keeping with his ambition to accommodate learned readers suspicious of philosophy, De Quincey's translations are highly selective. In addition to choosing texts not yet, or not recently, translated to English, De Quincey prefers material certain to find favour with his preferred journals' typical audiences of educated middle-class readers, with minor changes to suit a publication's ideological profile. As such, he mostly chooses works touching on 'Civil Polity, for example, Natural Theology, Political Economy – these are parts of knowledge which furnish an arena, not less to the subtleties of the speculative, than to the good sense of the practical.'[47] While he tries to connect Kant to British theories of political economy, and occasionally remarks on Kant's compelling work on religious philosophy, only the first of these fields, touching on 'Civil Polity', really features significantly in his translations of Kant. In addition, De Quincey particularly excerpts from the political work those sections that will garner broad appeal. Only his rendering of Kant's 'Idea of a Universal History' offers nearly unadulterated access to the original; by contrast, the translation of Kant's *Observations* slashes the original by as much as two thirds, preserving only the section in which the philosopher holds forth on national temperaments as they relate to propensities for particular subspecies of aesthetics. No mention is made of this abridgement, except to offer the essay under the heading of 'Kant on National Character, in Relation to the Sense of the Sublime and Beautiful'. The 'Abstract of Swedenborgianism', which unlocks Kant's *Dream of a Spirit-Seer*, deletes a vast amount of Kant's philosophical reflections, opening the text on an abrupt ' – [b]ut now to my hero'.[48] In 'Kant in his Miscellaneous Essays', the translator provides a lengthy preface on the merits of transcendental thought and translates two essays which 'I purpose to lay before your readers, not in a full version, but in a critical abstract.' The first such essay, Kant's 'On the Common Saying', is truncated to a quarter its original size, mostly taken from the '*second* section; because this treats a question of politics in a high degree interesting to ourselves'. The second, a translation of *Perpetual Peace*, foreshortens the 'six articles upon which a perpetual peace can be founded' to their title and a few sentences and whittles down the following eighty pages of German prolixity to a single English page.[49] These data points only begin to describe De Quincey's methods in translation: the true crux of his efforts emerges from a nearer consideration of the structural and stylistic changes he makes.

## The Metaphysics of Stylistics

As De Quincey chips away at Kant's sprawling oeuvre, dissonant notes of criticism begin to creep in amongst the professions of undying adoration. In 'Kant on National Character', the translation of the fourth section of the *Observations*, the interpreter annotatively upbraids the philosopher for his praise of French poetry, observing that '[t]o the judicious reader it needs not be said how strikingly in opposition to facts is Kant's judgment on the French taste in the Fine Arts'.[50] Another note chides Kant for his claim that '[t]he negroes of Africa have from nature no feeling which transcends the childish level'. Brought up an abolitionist, and keenly aware he is writing for the similarly inclined *London*, De Quincey protests that 'common sense demands that we should receive evidence to the intellectual pretensions of the Blacks from the unprejudiced judges who have lived amongst them'.[51] In portraying Kant as a philosopher who declines to engage in empirical observation, these comments participate in the common charge that metaphysical philosophy is an armchair discipline with little bearing on practical matters. While his sympathetic translation of 'On the Common Saying' suggests De Quincey knows such accusations to be facile, and while his engagement with Kant's nebular theory demonstrates his appreciation of the latter's capacity for formulating accurate hypotheses through inductive reason alone, De Quincey continues this line of attack in his 1830 *Blackwood's* piece on 'Kant in his Miscellaneous Essays'. Having first tarred Kant as 'an enemy to Christianity', a common accusation born of the royal order Kant receives in 1794 to cease his investigations into religious matters, he lays into him for another instance of his disdain for close observation. Explaining his motives for focusing on the second section of 'The Common Saying', in which Kant theorises on constitutional jurisprudence, X. Y. Z. notes his outrage at Kant's description of the Glorious Revolution. Much as he does in his observations on culturally stunted Africans, the 'transcendental pedant' betrays an unwillingness to travel beyond his preferred dwelling, a Königsberg-based 'transcendental closet'. The translator addresses his countrymen, and especially the conservative subset that read *Blackwood's*, as follows:

> it must excite the burning indignation of Englishmen to find Kant roundly and broadly denying the existence of any [] right [to depose a tyrant] [. . .]; and, too, with a special regard to the particular case of England. [An] unwilling side-glance at the knout as the appropriate instrument of reply [] must come over every body, friend or foe, who reads Kant's attack on the English nation for their political Revolution of 1688–9. A great people solemnly effect a change in the government [. . .] Forth stalks a transcendental pedant, and addresses them thus: [. . .] 'just step into my closet, and I shall shew you, in one volume octavo, that such conduct as yours merited capital punishment.'[52]

As in De Quincey's fraught interaction with Wordsworth, what began as worship is complicated by a string of distancing manoeuvres. In converting diffidence into difference, De Quincey further aligns himself with Carlyle and Coleridge, both of whom commence their mediation of German thought in admiration of Kant only to find their hopes crushed. Coleridge volunteers a mild sense of disenchantment, noting that Kant's metaphysics evince a number of lacunae. 'The few passages that remained obscure to me, after due efforts of thought [. . .] and the apparent contradictions which occur', he notes, 'I soon found were hints and insinuations referring to ideas, which KANT either did not think it prudent to avow, or which he considered as consistently left behind in a pure analysis.'[53] Less tolerant of anticlimaxes than Coleridge, Carlyle remarks that

> Kant's philosophy has a gigantic appearance at a distance, enveloped in clouds and darkness, shadowed forth in types and symbols of unknown and fantastic derivation. There is an apparatus, and a flourishing of drums and trumpets, and a tumultuous *Marktschreyerei* [vocal publicity], as if all the earth were going to renew its youth; and the *Esoterics* are equally allured by all this pomp and circumstance, and repelled by the hollowness and airy nothingness of the ware which presented to them. [. . .] I wish I fully understood the philosophy of Kant! Is it a chapter in the history of human folly or the brightest in the history of human wisdom? Or of both mixed? And in what degree?[54]

For his own part, when De Quincey disparages Kant, he directs his annoyance at the philosopher's 'want of reading', a charge that resonates with his critique of the 'transcendental pedant' as a shut-in fearful of unfamiliar experiences.[55] Not only, he alleges, does the philosopher refuse 'to take the common-sense course of reading [another] nation's account of its proceedings' when he sits in judgement of such events as the Glorious Revolution; his reluctance to consider outside sources is almost absolute. De Quincey constructs this disinclination to read widely as the mirror to the charge of plagiarism through which he separates from Coleridge. That is, if the plagiarist is too much possessed by his pathologically voracious reading to risk an original notion, the writing non-reader is too shiftless to anchor his originality in previous work. In a word, Kant is lazy; not out of stupidity, but because the force of his intellect permits a retirement from a careful consideration of outside ideas:

> One fact, which struck me [. . .] after a long familiarity with Kant's writings, is this, that in all probability Kant never read a book in his life. [. . .] What! none? No, none at all; no book whatsoever. [. . .] Kant's power of thought gave him a ready means of evading the labour of reading the book. Taking the elementary principles of the writer, as stated by himself or another, and supposing that he thought it worth his pains, he would then [. . .] supply [himself] all that was wanting [. . .] it was his duty to have examined the writings of others who had trod the same ground; as in this way only he could ascertain the amount of his coincidences with former philosophers.[56]

While Kant himself is engaged in adapting French rationalism to British empiricism through the intermediary of German philosophy, then, he greatly underestimates the power of judicious importation. There is a translation-shaped hole in the Kantian revolution; one that De Quincey is poised to fill.

Activating once more the interaction of style and thought, De Quincey argues that the ramifications of Kant's contempt for reading are most distinct in the notoriously ponderous manner in which he expounds his ideas. While it is something of a commonplace to complain of the sage's needlessly complex prose, De Quincey claims that it is far from a superficial gripe.[57] Drawing on his distinction between texts of knowledge and books of power,[58] he alleges that the little reading that Kant deigned to do as he superficially researched his treatises and lectures was entirely focused on the latter. The philosopher, that is, almost entirely neglected his country's extraordinary literature, instead preferring to read publications on the model of

> a dictionary, a grammar, a spelling-book, an almanack, a pharmacopoeia, a parliamentary report, a system of farriery, a treatise on billiards, the court calendar [. . .] books of voyages and travels, and generally all books in which the matter to be communicated is to paramount to the manner or form of its communication.[59]

By refusing the regulating influence of books of power, whose capacity for poetical power depends on its careful management of the economy of matter and manner, and by consequently regarding as his only duty an exhaustingly exacting communication of facts without the relief of form, Kant has elected to communicate in a torrential non-style, completely focused on a logorrhoeic explosion of barely structured information. In his *Critique of Judgment*, Kant defends this preference by dividing language into two spheres – the familiar dichotomy of meaning and form, or prose and poetry – and subsequently claiming that the only way to rescue communication from ceaseless conflict between these two is to bracket the latter as a 'a treacherous art' that is 'worthy of no respect'.[60] In keeping with the national infirmity that cripples British and German writers alike, Kant considers form to be parergic to sense, if even more radically than his countrymen. As such, if German writing is bad, Kant's is catastrophic. 'In reality Kant was a bad writer', De Quincey writes; 'something of a brute', in that Kant 'wrote his own language most uncouthly, some would even say *barbarously* [. . .] without composition or digestion'.[61] He is paraded as an egregious example of unreformed writing; 'a monster of vicious diction, so far as regards the construction of his sentences',[62] 'a great man, but [...] obtuse and deaf as an antediluvian boulder with regard to language and its capacities.'⁶³

Still persuaded that '[s]uch is the value of his philosophy [...] that within no long interval we shall certainly see him naturalised amongst ourselves', yet also noting that 'it is the prevailing character of his style, that we insist on as the most formidable barrier to the study of his writings',⁶⁴ De Quincey argues that a translation of Kant needs must encompass a stylistic overhaul. Parodying the type of sentence engendered by Kant's prosaic circumlocutions, and opposing it to the rectification to be applied through a poeticising translation, he asks the reader to appreciate the labours required to bring Kant to frictionless communication. Kant presents a formidable challenge, such as may only be overcome by an equally formidable interpreter:

> [h]ow [...] I ask, could that man have had any sense for the graces of style, [...] for the arts of preparation, of recapitulation, of peroration, together with the whole world of refinements which belong to a beautiful and impressive diction? – how, I demand, could he have had any organ for the perception of all this, who in his own case, and in those works which he most of all designed as the classical monuments of his own power, shews uniformly that, in a question of manner, he knows of no higher a purpose that a man can, or ought to have, than in any way whatsoever, no matter how clumsily, disordinately, ungracefully – no matter with what perplexity or confusion, tautology or circumlocution, to deliver himself of a meaning? One or two of these smaller essays of Kant, therefore, with all their defects, that is, [...] with the absolute defect of a bad style, and bad in that way which least allows of a remedy being applied in any faithful translation, I purpose to lay before your readers, not in a full version, but in a critical abstract.⁶⁵

So what, then, if Kant disposes of his sentences 'upon the model of [...] an old family coach [...] Everything to be crammed [...] into the front pockets, side pockets, or rear pockets, of the one original sentence'?⁶⁶ What if Kant 'might naturally have written a book from beginning to end in one vast hyperbolical sentence?'⁶⁷ What, indeed, is finally the point of a polished style; of heaping criticism on Kant and the German nation for their interminable paragraphs? De Quincey intersperses his essays on style with dark comments on the dangers of a monoculture of prose, alleging it leeches the native vigour, but fails to provide a more definite reason. It is as he lays out his objections to Kant's monomaniacal focus on meaning that De Quincey begins to name the dangers of constraining style to half its natural ambit. The most evident benefit of a superior style is a more efficient communication of ideas in that it augments their intelligibility and their appeal:

> Light to *see* the road, power to *advance* along it – such being amongst the promises and proper functions of style, it is a capital error, under the idea of

its ministeriality, to undervalue the great organ of the advancing intellect – an organ which is equally important considered as a tool for the culture and *popularisation* of truth.

Style accomplishes far more, however; so much, in fact, that those critics err comparatively little who disbelieve a better-balanced play of meaning and form enhances a text's attractiveness and persuasiveness. In undervaluing those two applications of style, 'we simply underrate the enormous services that are or might be rendered by style to the interest of truth and human thinking'. There is a 'third case', however, which if ignored 'go[es] near to abolish a mode of existence'. It is this neglect of a third case, which pivots on the philosophical potential of style, that anchors De Quincey's criticism of Kant. As long as form is conceived as Kant does, 'as a thing separable from the thought; in fact, as the *dress* of the thoughts – a robe that may be laid aside at pleasure', this philosophical force of style will remain obscure. When form is brought into contact with content, however, the text grows resonant with 'metaphysical relations'.[68] While Kant, having granted his thought a solid foundation by recognising the dichotomisation of modern life, subsequently refused any reintegration of his antinomies, impassioned prose demonstrates that the separation of subject and object may be sutured after all. The prose poet does not describe the method of this synthesis theoretically, as is Kant's and his idealist critics' custom; instead, he *enacts* the idea of a total style. Tracing the chiasmus on which he builds his translational restyling and rethinking of Kant, De Quincey proposes to reconceive Kant's polarities:

> The human body is not the dress or apparel of the human spirit: far more mysterious is the mode of their union. Call the two elements A and B; then it is impossible to point out A as existing aloof from B, or *vice versa*. A exists in and through B; B exists in and through A. No profound observer can have failed to observe this illustrated in the capacities of style. Imagery is sometimes not the merely alien apparelling of a thought, and of a nature to be detached from the thought, but is the coefficient that, being superadded to something else, absolutely *makes* the thought as a third and separate existence.

In pruning his sentences down to the barest minimum of form, not even the great Kant can ever truly comprehend what his thought is ultimately about. He condemns his thought to an endless exercise in tautology, in which only a yearning for pure meaning endlessly reasserts itself. Perceiving the same handicap, Carlyle remarks that even if the great disadvantage with philosophers like Hume is their 'materialism', Kant presents the other extreme. 'If I read Kant', Carlyle reflects, 'I arrived at precisely opposite conclusions, that all the world was spirit namely, that there was nothing material at all anywhere.' While Carlyle is unable to furnish a remedy, resolving 'to have nothing more to do with metaphysics at all',[69] De Quincey claims that a structural solution emerges when philosophy takes its irrepressible textuality as its starting point. Consider, he writes, 'the word transcendental, as used in the critical philosophy', which Kant never fully explained because he failed to control for the parameter of language. Nimbly analogising between linguistic, stylistic and philosophical questions, he notes that

> [w]henever Kant undertakes to render into popular language the secrets of metaphysics, one inevitably thinks of Bardolph's attempt to analyse and justify the word accommodation; – 'Accommodation – that is, when a man is (as they say) accommodated; or when a man is being whereby he may be thought to be accommodated, which is an excellent thing.' There are sometimes Eleusinian mysteries, sealed by nature herself, the mighty mother, as *aporreta*, things essentially ineffable and unutterable in vulgar ears. Long, for instance, he laboured, but vainly he laboured, to render intelligible the scholastic idea of the transcendental. This should have been easy to deal with [. . .] and yet did Kant, throughout his long life, fail to satisfy any one man who was not previously and independently in possession of the idea. Difficulties of this nature should seem as little related to artifice of style and diction as geometrical difficulties; and yet it is certain that, by throwing the stress and emphasis of the perplexity upon the exact verbal nodus of the problem, a better structure of his sentences would have guided Kant to a readier apprehension of the real shape which the difficulty assumed to the ordinary student.[70]

Style, then, is a thing pursued not so much for the benefit of the reader, although the reader does profit from it, but for the writer. By the same token, in rearranging Kant's obstinately disorderly writing, De Quincey conducts his translations less in order to communicate new information to interested parties, although they do offer valuable education, than to push transcendental thinking to its idealist conclusion. In translating, De Quincey is philosophising. Neither style nor translation are ancillary to thought, then: they are to be cultivated for their own sake, and deliver a distinct aesthetic ideology when they are; centred on a steady progress towards a moment of total identity, in which form fully corresponds with meaning, languages coalesce into each other, and De Quincey finally comprehends himself.

Having gestured at a practical solution to the reconstitution of an integrated world, De Quincey is enabled to perform a more aggressive critique of Kant. As with Wordsworth and Coleridge, such acts of assassination require careful preparation. Following an early laudatory stage, in which De Quincey praises Kant as 'the very tree of knowledge in the midst of this Eden'[71] that is German philosophy, and a transitional phase of growing scepticism, he devotes the rest of his career to denouncing his proposals. His 1834 biographic essay on Coleridge is a watershed in this regard, in that it evolves from criticising smallish issues of content and large problems of style to lambasting Kant's entire philosophical edifice. In denying the problems he has created by sternly separating subjective and objective reality without charting any communicating path between the two, De Quincey alleges, the German thinker has done grievous damage. Thus turned against itself, the modern mind may be compared to a digestive organ that begins to dissolve itself:

> he had no instinct of creation or restoration within his Apollyon mind; for he had no love, no faith, no self-distrust, no humility, no childlike docility; all which qualities belonged essentially to Coleridge's mind [. . .] As the stomach has been known, by means of its own potent secretion [. . .] sometimes to attack itself and its own organic structure, so, and with the same preternatural extension of instinct did Kant carry forward his destroying functions.[72]

This passage imputes Coleridge with the powers required to guide into its rightful channels the universal acid that is Kant's antinomic thought. Coleridge had himself grown impatient with Kant, increasingly preferring the company of his idealist critics, and like De Quincey, he singles out the foreclosure of artful access to the objective as his particular objection, since 'I could never believe it was possible for him to have meant no more by his *Noumenon,* or THING IN ITSELF, than his mere words express.'[73] De Quincey's tribute to Coleridge is not performed gratis, however: in the following paragraphs, he notes that Coleridge's opium habit disqualifies him for a career in adaptive translation. The stylistic adaptation of Kant requires a playful reorganisation of the latter's malformed writing which De Quincey is solely qualified to organise.

What, however, is the philosophical vision to which De Quincey's advertised compositional rearrangements finally gesture? Critical assessments have somewhat incongruously taken his separation from Kant either as proof of a conversion to idealism, or as a materialist epiphany. That is, De Quincey has been seen to be affrighted by the void of religious meaning that lurks behind Kant's proposals – or to be frustrated by the excess of spirit with which Kant injects his system. On the former reading, he is horrified to see subjective reality unmoored from any objective ground: 'the idea that space and time, causation, even logic itself might all be properties of human consciousness with no basis in external reality', Grevel Lindop argues, 'was one which he found terrifying to confront'.[74] On the latter reading, proposed by David L. Clark and Paul Youngquist, De Quincey rejects the philosopher's neglect of the physical and the bodily.[75] These mutually exclusive interpretations inevitably run into trouble. Materialist readers must contend with De Quincey's occasional proclamations of a sincerely held faith. 'Man's nature has something of infinity within itself', he writes in response to the *Critiques*, 'which requires a corresponding infinity in its objects.'[76] Yet a fully spiritualist reading falters in the face of what Wellek describes as 'a fundamental insincerity'. Contrasting the wilful Brit's development of a translative idealism with orthodox German idealism, Wellek notes that a representative poet like Kleist 'drew similar excessively sceptic conclusions' as did De Quincey. The former, however,

> was in the deepest core of his being hurt by the point of [Kant's] idea [. . .] How much more intense, how much more sincere, sound his complaints compared to De Quincey's. We feel in his narration that he never did seriously believe in these limitations.[77]

De Quincey's alleged inconsistencies and insincerities grow more tractable upon noting that he develops a brand of idealism that veers closer to much later developments in literary theory than it does to Kant's immediate philosophical heirs. Having once pined for 'a life dedicated and set apart to philosophy', conducted in emulation of Kant, who was once 'a pole-star to my hopes, and [. . .] the luminous guide to my future life',[78] his disillusionment in Kant's revealed powers trigger a move away from philosophy strictly defined. The 'Confessions' offer perhaps the most dramatic demonstration. Proclaiming himself a 'philosopher' in his opening statement, the physical and intellectual predicament that he falls prey to midway through the narrative is as much the result of his laudanum habit as it is of over-indulging in Kantian metaphysics. Both these substances hold out promises of order restored and insights unlocked; upon being disappointed by both, De Quincey foreswears both. Just like opium visits upon him a host of physiological and psychological ailments, '[i]ntellectual philosophy' had 'become insupportable to me', and 'I shrunk from them with a sense of powerless and infantine feebleness that gave me an anguish the greater from remembering the time when I grappled with them to my own hourly delight.'[79] There is a tradition of failure amongst many Romantics revolving around similar moments of creative crisis. Through the 'Confessions', De Quincey inscribes himself in this lineage of exploded hopes; moreover, in situating its origins in a regimen of opium and Kant, he assures he is seen at once to subvert and to intellectualise the habitual diagnosis that the poet's vision has waned due to his estrangement from the imagination. If De Quincey is to be believed, the key issue is not that Kant robbed him of the capacity to live and write organically, but that having identified the fundamental structures of modern thought, Kant decided to withdraw. '[M]an was an abject animal', De Quincey observes some fifteen years after the 'Confessions',

> if the limitations which Kant assigned to the motions of his speculative reason were as absolute and hopeless as, under *his* scheme of the the understanding and *his* genesis of its powers, too evidently they were. I belonged to a reptile race if the wings by which we had sometimes *seemed* to mount, and the buoyancy which had *seemed* to support our flight, were indeed the fantastic delusions which he represented them.

If Kant is to be saved from himself, he must not only become more poetical: he must also be made more literary and more translative. '[T]truth and value there certainly *is* in one part of the Kantian philosophy; and that part is its foundation', but the subsequent operationalisation of the foundational revelation that reality is constituted by a material and a spiritual sphere requires one abandon Kant – much as a fully developed understanding of language and authorship requires its abnegation. Form and meaning may have been irrevocably dissociated, but a position may still be available through which their reconciliation may be imagined, however briefly: Kant's philosophy can only be repaired through a life lived *between* – between authorship and translatorship, poetry and prose, creation and imitation; in short, between philosophy and literature.

In testimony of his own deeply felt paralysis, De Quincey increasingly paints Kant as a dangerous force. Antedating his anti-Kantianism to his early twenties, he remarks that

> [t]he philosophy of Kant [...] already, in 1805, I had found to be a philosophy of destruction, and scarcely, in any one chapter, so much as *tending* to a philosophy of reconstruction. It destroys by wholesale, and it substitutes nothing.[80]

The spoliation with which such passages charge Kant ultimately revolves around his irradiation of a spiritualist idealism or a materialist scepticism; De Quincey's chief target, however, is Kant's infuriating inability to extend the programme of translation on which his philosophical design is based. As such, when De Quincey proclaims that his stylistic experiments ought to coalesce in a 'philosophy of reconstruction', he does not defend a reactionary turn to a pre-Kantian obscurantism. Instead, he proposes to build on its foundations by staging a renaissance of border-crossing on a scale not seen since the days of Herodotus and Cicero. His response to the great question that Kant poses in dividing the world into objective and subjective realities, then, is not to adopt the monomaniacal approach that characterises the conventional solution offered by idealist philosophy, which typically organises itself around either a sublation of antinomies into pure spirit or a collapse of all subjects into pure matter. Instead, he decides to be indecisive, or at any rate to alternate swiftly between decisions. Much as impassioned prose strives to merge poetry and prose while knowing that the two extremes can only ever be combined by means of a chiastic pattern of oscillation and reversal, De Quincey's writing receives its motive force from an ideal which it can only ever fleetingly glean, and to which it must endlessly recommit itself. These, of course, are all highly theoretical remarks. The question remains: How does De Quincey's critique of Kant's style impact on a practice of translation?

## The Last Days of Immanuel Kant

In keeping with De Quincey's translational alternative to Kantian metaphysics, the text which has been argued to offer his most sustained criticism of Kant is a translation, albeit not of one of the philosopher's writings. In 1827, signing as the Opium-Eater, he publishes 'The Last Days of Kant' in *Blackwood's* as the third and final instalment in his short-lived 'Gallery of the German Prose Classics' series, which had previously featured a two-part translation of Lessing's *Laocoon*. The 'Last Days' article renders accessible to British readers in heavily compressed fashion a monograph by Ehregott Andreas Wasianski, first published in 1804 as part of a larger series of book-length recollections written by Kant's closest friends and associates following the philosopher's death. A modestly sized book, Wasianski's original is over double the length of its English adaptation. De Quincey hints at this difference in his title, which contracts the years of material promised in the German title, *Immanuel Kant in seinen letzten Lebensjahren*, into a mere handful of days.

While much shorter and less elaborate than his other work on the philosopher, 'The Last Days' is one of De Quincey's most-read essays on Kant; something of a touchstone text in biographies of the philosopher, even. An intriguing and symptomatic aspect of its reception is its misclassification as an original composition,[81] to the point that it has sparked tertiary translations of its own, including into German.[82] This confusion does not flow from any double-dealing on De Quincey's part. Two paragraphs into his introduction, he explicitly positions his essay as a translation of Wasianski, 'checked and supported by the collateral testimonies of Jachmann, Rink, Borowski, and other biographers'.[83] He reaffirms this frame in his article's full title, displayed under his foreword: 'The Last Days of Kant: From the German of

Wasianski, Jachmann, Borowski, and Others.'[84] As if to render the text's status blindingly obvious, De Quincey ensures that even the body of his article disclaims his authorship. Much like the interpreter's prefatory remarks are spatially removed from the translated text, De Quincey's occasional comments are delivered in small-print footnotes which highlight Wasianski's authority in identifying him as 'the author' of the text. While these annotations repeatedly censure the German progenitor for various oversights – 'Mr Wasianski is wrong', 'the author should have added', and so on – the translator is demonstratively careful not to interfere in the source text, staging gestures reminiscent of the loudly vocalised internal debates that had featured in the *Cintra* episode.[85] He dithers over the precise date intended by the author, slotting in an absurdly long note to excuse the alteration: 'Mr. Wasianski says – *late* in the summer: but, as he elsewhere describes the same expression [...] a day which was confessedly *before* the longest day [...], I have translated accordingly.' In another note, he confesses he has removed a trivial detail, and in noting its absence paradoxically re-enters it into the record. De Quincey, in short, deploys a well-developed paratextual apparatus in order to mark himself out as a translator.

As his reduction of Wasianski's original suggests, De Quincey intervenes more than his notes might suggest, albeit rarely to insert his own observations. Here as elsewhere, his methodology of translation is relatively exact in the reproduction of contents: his alterations centre on problems of style. Since the original offers a prototypically German sprawl of independent anecdotes, spread out over several years with nary an indication of their precise chronology and no semblance of structure other than a meandering drift towards Kant's death, De Quincey enforces a strict dating system, along with a segmentation of the text into eight sections, each concerned with a distinct period and theme. This involves a significant redistribution of the original matter, the occasional insertion of dates and structural phrases, and a frequent deletion of inconsequential details. De Quincey's most sizeable omissions tend to focus on excursuses that detract from the narrative arc, often targeting those episodes in which Wasianski expatiates on his closeness to Kant. Amongst these cuts, the most telling concern Wasianski's prologue. The original preface expends considerable effort on presenting an apology for the insensitivity of reporting on the private life of so august a personality as Kant, especially since the life under examination is now over. Such genteel touches are unceremoniously pruned; instead, De Quincey offers a breezy preface in which he 'make[s] no apology to the reader for detaining him upon a short sketch of Kant's life and domestic habits'. By way of apology, the Opium-Eater offers the thesis that the lives of truly great philosophers ought to parabolically stand in for their works, and that a narrative of Kant's life should therefore offer the public at large, incognisant of his language and unappreciative of the virtues of speculative thought, a philosophical allegory. Much as the man's philosophy is characterised by austerity and rigour, so, too, De Quincey argues, is the man himself; his life exemplary 'not so much for its incidents, as for the purity and philosophic dignity of its daily tenor'.[86] Against this declaration, the translated narrative turns out to focus less on biographic matter than it does on thanatographic information; on a description of the philosopher's death. In the English translation, Kant is presented as a person of interest not so much for his life as for his life's *end*, which ought to demonstrate the nobility of mind acquired by living one's life in pursuit of wisdom.

That, at least, is what a thanatography ought to do. In refocusing Kant's *Letzte Jahre* onto the philosopher's last days, all the while juxtaposing the great thinker's final moments with his philosophy, however, De Quincey's translation readies itself to pass a devastating verdict on transcendentalism through its founder's inglorious demise. This critical energy may also be read into Wasianski's original. While ostensibly written by a close friend concerned to safeguard Kant's legacy, the latter's portrayal includes several anecdotes that appear tailored to explode the mythological image of Kant as a thinker whose life and thought accorded to perfection. Wasianski seems out to defy the received notion that a biography of Kant must be entirely uneventful in that the philosopher, as Heine observes, 'neither had a life nor a history. He lived a mechanically ordered, almost abstract, bachelor life in a quiet out-of-the-way lane in Königsberg.'[87] This is a stereotype constructed for Kant as much as it is constructed by Kant, who had commanded all would-be enlightened thinkers to marshal their mental faculties so as to counterbalance their emotions, 'to master [their] morbid feelings by sheer resolution'. This includes the curbing of any grossly physical urges, including the lowly impulsion to 'stupefy[] oneself by the excessive use of food and drink'.[88] A gluttonous, inebriated, addicted body is to be condemned as irrational, and therefore inherently unphilosophic. 'It is obvious', Kant writes, 'that putting oneself in such a state violates a duty to oneself.' In occupying a body that masters the mind, the individual is debased, akin to 'a mere animal, not to be treated as a human being', in that it has passed into an irrecoverable subjugation of the mind to a deregulated body; a 'condition in which [it] no longer has clear eyes for *measuring*'.[89] In stark contrast to Kant's performances of an austerely disembodied life, however, Wasianski offers his readers an elderly mind increasingly brought to indignity by an insurgent body. His subject initially comes forward in his habitual trappings – as a man whose life is conditioned by his thought. The biographer particularly dilates on Kant's obsessive self-regulation, which extends even to such animal functions of the body as respiration (to be nasal), and perspiration (to be avoided). Any perturbation of this regimen demands an immediate remedy. Should the body assert itself by an outbreak of sweat, Kant, '[r]etiring to some shady place [. . .] stood still and motionless', forcing his body into thermostatic obedience, 'with the air and attitude of a person listening, or in suspense – until the impulse to sweat had passed'.[90] As such, 'if only a trace of perspiration had sullied him, he mentioned the case with great emphasis, as if an adverse event had befallen him'. Work and relaxation are to cleave to a strict routine, to be followed punctiliously every single day; food and drink, necessary yet inherently suspect, are to be taken 'once a day', at dinners orchestrated to provide a maximum of sustenance and sociability in the briefest time. Addictive substances are to be regarded with particular suspicion. One pipe of tobacco is permissible in the morning for its energising effects, as is one glass of wine at dinner for its social lubrication; the commoner's drink of beer, however, Kant regards as deeply dangerous. 'Of this liquor he was the most vocal enemy', Wasianski records, in that

> [w]hen someone had died in the best years of his life, Kant would say – 'He has probably been drinking beer.' If the conversation turned to the indisposition of another, the question would not be distant, 'Does he drink beer in the evening?' According to the answer to this question, he would draw the patient's horoscope.[91]

This, at least, is Kant prior to his old age: as the philosopher enters his final decade, he begins to eat and drink in excess, craving luxurious substances like coffee, wine and cheese. Ventriloquising the stern warnings against low pleasures Kant uttered earlier in life, the biographer claims that these sudden yearnings demonstrate a drooping self-government: his abandonment of dietary strictures prove and aggravate his mental and physical dissolution. Previously living a rational existence, in which the mind so regulated the body as to ward off any ailments, Kant is reduced to a body:

> The most important day in Kant's life up to this moment was 8 October 1803. On this day, for the first time in his entire life, Kant became truly ill. [. . .] In the last months of his life, Kant's appetite had become irregular, or rather, depraved. He no longer took pleasure in food, but was seized by a violent desire for bread and butter, which he tore into morsels and dredged through grated English cheese and enjoyed greedily. [. . .] This was especially the case on 7 October, on the day before his illness, when he enjoyed with abandon this injurious dish between every dish he spurned. I and another

friend dining with him advised against his frequent enjoyment of fatty, heavy, and dry foods. [. . .] He insisted that the cheese had never harmed him, and never could. The evil result, which could have been mathematically deduced, occurred. A restless night preceded a sad day. Until 9 in the morning all was as it always was; but around this time Kant [. . .] suddenly sank senseless to the ground. [. . .] I hurried down to his house, and found Kant lying in bed, unconscious, speechless, and senseless [*mit gebrochenem Auge*].[92]

'Twas cheddar killed the philosopher, if Wasianski's tyromantic narrative is to be believed. Few readers have been comfortable to do so: in his biography of Kant, Manfred Kuehn brackets Wasianski's contribution in arguing that his 'anecdotes about Kant's scurrilous habits indicate nothing about his philosophy or about his *true personality*'.[93] For all the potential for embarrassment, however, the *Letzte Jahre* has the backing of Kant's own writings: Wasianski's tale, as Clark observes, 'is not conjured out of thin air; in many significant ways it recalls Kant's own account of his psychic and bodily life'.[94] In his late essays, Kant recorded his mounting misgivings about the application of his thought to lived experience, rhetorically asking 'why do I curtail the enjoyment of life I am used to just to stay alive? Why do I prolong a feeble life to an extraordinary age by self-denial?' While he maintains that philosophy, in enforcing a strict 'regimen' of habits and thereby furnishing a natural '*stimulant* to the mind [. . .] [which] keeps the vital force from running down', he notes with some anxiety that 'metaphysicians are incapacitated sooner than scholars in other fields or in applied philosophy'.[95] Even when the biographer observes Kant in advanced decrepitude of mind and body, then, recording his loss of memory and sight; even when he mercilessly logs how Kant, in his very final moments, 'pushed away the bedclothes and exposed his body', he appears to do so out of a documentary interest. Indeed, while the incidents recorded by Wasianski seemingly mark him out as highly critical, his biography is so devoid of irony that it appears an honest record of Kant's old age.

When De Quincey transposes Wasianski to English, it becomes impossible to read the text as anything but a highly charged satire. No longer parsable as a sentimental document suffused with misdirected earnestness, it now appears a parody of a man whose unquiet death demonstrates the dangers of remaining purblind to the material aspects of life and language. After decades of suppression, Kant's physical form asserts itself through an escalating series of moves irrecoverable by his rationalism; a process of bodily rebellion that culminates in the greatest crime that may be visited upon a great mind – sheer senility. This analysis of 'Last Days' as a thanatographic pastiche has long been dominant, largely as a consequence of the text's association with

De Quincey, in spite of his repeated attempts to disclaim authorship. Even without the opium-eater's signature, however, 'Last Days' would always have seemed parodic: as he translates, De Quincey plays up the materialist reading that subtly infiltrates Wasianski's account. The English version preserves especially those scenes that detail the extent of Kant's eccentric behaviours and childlike cravings, subtly exaggerating those episodes that might hold critical potential. The German reference to Kant's attempts at controlling his perspiration, 'until the impulse for transpiration had passed',[96] thus transforms into 'until his usual *aridity* was restored'. Similarly, the cheese incident is granted greater emphasis when the interpreter interjects that it is clearly this event that 'ushered in [the] closing stage' of Kant's life.[97] There are several further such touches: for instance, the vivid if somewhat trivial sketch of the philosopher's bedtime habits, and particularly his love of swaddling himself in his sheets, snugly 'wrapped up and cocooned',[98] is recast into an allegory of mental solipsism when it is rendered as 'swathed like a mummy, or (as I used to tell him) self-involved like the silk-worm in its cocoon'. In keeping with his complaints regarding the philosopher's style and thought, De Quincey most expands those episodes which detail the jarring physicality of Kant's old age. Much of the work in this regard is accomplished by an extensive apparatus of footnotes, allowing an apparent preservation of Wasianski's original even as the translator asserts his own reading. Pushing forward the philosophical implications of the philosopher's dread of perspiration, and offsetting any accusations of tendentiousness by attributing the observation to another writer, De Quincey thus comments that Kant was 'drier than dust in both body and mind [. . .] a more meagre, arid, parched anatomy of a man, has not appeared upon this earth'. He also draws attention to Kant's yearning for coffee, noting on the authority of Jachmann's biography that the philosopher was always 'extravagantly fond of coffee', but previously managed to control his urges 'under a notion that it was very unwholesome'. Significantly, the footnotes repeatedly intimate the opium-eater cannot condone such self-regulation: Kant's abstemiousness may have proceeded from 'a sense of duty', but his dietetics 'rest[ed] probably upon erroneous grounds'. Wasianski's hand-wringing over the lethality of cheesy comestibles is therefore declared absurd: 'Mr W.', one note sighs, 'falls into the ordinary mistake of confounding the cause and the occasion.'[99] Kant's digestive troubles, which he endeavours to alleviate with 'a few medicinal applications, against which he had previously proselytised [*geeifert*]: a few drops of rum on a lump of sugar, naphtha, magnesium oxide, glucose',[100] invites a prescription of laudanum. 'For Kant's particular complaint, as described by other biographers', the

Opium-Eater opines, 'a quarter of a grain of opium, every twelve hours, would have been the best remedy, perhaps a perfect remedy.'[101] As he is only too aware, this counsel is in flagrant contradiction of Kant, who had branded the ingestion of drugs a 'base act, since they make the user silent, reticent, and withdrawn by the dreamy euphoria they induce'.[102] In recommending laudanum, then, the translator assumes a philosophical position, albeit one disguised as medical advice: just as opium upsets and reorders the Opium-Eater's life, all that would have been required for Kant's unsatisfactory old age to regain its dignity was a recalibration of his system of thought; an extension towards the bodily aspects of experience and expression. This is not to say that the translator here recommends one prostrate oneself completely before the impulsions of the body. Opium, as De Quincey well understands, is a psychosomatic compound. Its action, as he discovers in 'The Pleasures of Opium', is to upend any assumption that mind and body may be hierarchised. Its doctrine, as he learns in 'The Pains of Opium', is that the ideal state experienced in drug-induced highs cannot sustain life if it is achieved by short-circuiting the dialectic exchanges though which idealist thought ought to be actualised.

## A Frightful Co-Existence

The question is what mode of reading, writing and thinking is most appropriate to De Quincey's translations, whose authorial status sits between creation and derivation. The 'Last Days of Immanuel Kant' derives from a German source, which the translator unhesitatingly acknowledges as the rightful originator – and yet the text also indelibly bears the stamp of its translator. Who, then, is the reader reading in reading De Quincey translating? Or, to phrase the quandary in pragmatic terms, can 'The Last Days' fully be considered a part of De Quincey's oeuvre? These questions, which revolve around the perplexities attendant upon the status of the Romantic translator, came to a head in 2000; in a brief yet vigorous discussion between Paul Youngquist and Charles Rzepka in the letters section of the *Publications of the Modern Language Association*. In an article that sparks a letter from Rzepka, Youngquist creatively misreads De Quincey's 'The Last Days' as a pseudo-translation; as an essay, that is, which inscribes itself in a tradition of original texts that merely disguise themselves as translations.[103] Having firmly situated the text in De Quincey's oeuvre, which he argues is permeated by an 'antipathy for things Kantian', Youngquist contends that 'The Last Days' is an elaborate satire of the transcendental failure to account for the embodiedness of the mind. This interpretation, of course, relies heavily on an accurate identification of authorship. When Rzepka responds to Youngquist by pointing out the latter's underestimation of Wasianski's significance, he therefore adds that De Quincey's 'faithful adherence to Wasianski' really 'invalidates much of Youngquist's argument'. Reacting in turn to Rzepka, Youngquist flatly rejects the notion that the former's revelation of misidentification amounts to a falsification, arguing that the denial of De Quincey's authorship reflects 'a larger institutional issue', whereby some critics employ 'bibliographic criticism' in order to 'protect [. . .] traditional beliefs and practices against unmannerly encroachments'. Aligning his own, self-avowedly counter-bibliographic criticism with De Quincey's counter-Kantian thought, he claims that the philological cabal that oppose his mode of criticism exhibit 'exactly the attitude Kant's philosophy takes to the unruly life of the body'.[104] The inverse might also be argued: Youngquist's claim that De Quincey seeks to critique a lacking conception of materiality itself requires a Kantian erasure of the text's material history.

The Rzepka/Youngquist dispute on the De Quincey/Wasianski interface neatly retraces the space of paradox in which De Quincey positions his translatorial authorship. Translation divides against itself, precariously straddling the irreconcilable categories of imitation and invention. It is true that a translation is no more than a reproduction; composed and read as strictly ancillary, as a more or less transparent window into a chronologically prior and qualitatively superior original. Yet it is *also* true that a translation is an entirely new text, both in that one idiom is substituted for another, and in that the text is relocated to a new context, in which previously unavailable readings are unlocked. On the former, strictly reproductive reading, the translator must irrevocably surrender his rights to ownership: in keeping with this demand for self-erasure, De Quincey submits to the precedence of Wasianski, limiting his appropriation to a few necessary emendations which are flagged as such. This strategy is evident even to readers with little eye for German origins: Youngquist muses that the 'antipathy for things Kantian rings less clear in "Last Days" than elsewhere'.[105] On the latter, creative reading, by contrast, the translation displaces the original: the author dies at the moment of his translation, and the original text dies with him, both of them reincarnated in the translator and the translation. 'Mr W' still figures in De Quincey's text, but he only does so as a narrative voice. Moreover, in assertively publishing the text under his 'opium-eater' sobriquet rather than opting for the usual course of suppressing any identifying details regarding the translator, De Quincey may be seen to insist that 'Last Days' be read through his broader oeuvre. In the Kantian view, these two angles on translation cannot logically hold at the same time: a translation cannot be *both* derivative and originary; much as a text cannot simultaneously be read semantically *and* formally, a system of thought cannot be both materialist *and* spiritual, and we find it difficult to consider ourselves at once mind *and* body. The two perspectives can, however, be pursued sequentially, with the reader exploring each in a possibly infinite series of readings and rereadings. It is this spiralling pattern of oscillation that De Quincey recommends to readers looking to distil a philosophical method from his comments.

In an 1852 article on William Hamilton, a Scottish philosopher who rewrote Kant's dichotomisation of knowing into an epistemology of infinitude, De Quincey offers the most elaborate overview of his poetics yet. A magisterial demonstration of the philosophical potential of impassioned prose, the essay offers a meditation on the difficulties attendant on describing just what post-Kantian thought entails. De Quincey renders tangible his predicament by noting his impotence to deliver a précis of the character he ought to be dissecting. 'Here is a man', he intones, who has discovered a method to rectify Kant's failings: whereas the latter 'contented himself with cleansing the general field' but 'built nothing', 'Sir William' really '*has been* a discoverer.' Acting the part of a reader exhorting the essayist to deliver his explication, he continues:

> [m]ake us understand in what direction his studies have moved: towards what capital objects; with what immediate results [. . .] what evidence or presumption of having impressed lasting change upon some great aspects of intellectual philosophy.

This, however, is an essay of power, not of knowledge. No encyclopaedic information is forthcoming. Instead, the text is ever seen to be beginning, constantly interrupting itself to discourse on the manifold practical problems that conspire against it. Above all, the essayist is tormented by the impossibility of capturing a life performative of a philosophy that evades theorisation. Chronology, summary, fantasy, eulogy: all are defeated by Sir William, whose name designates not a recordable complex of actions and ideas but a hiatus; a locus that must remain a blind spot to conventional life writing. Hamilton is 'not merely a screw that is loose' but

> a link that is missing, and no use advertising for it now. [. . .] the human mind does really yearn and sicken after intellectual modes of solution applied to any intellectual intricacy or nodus. Art must thaw the dilemma which art has frozen together [. . .] My own personal embarrassment on this occasion, in effecting a transit or in evading a transit, was of a nature hardly paralleled in literature.

The problem with forcing this one dark interpreter into the light is that Hamilton evades articulating his ideas in a language that is tractable to those who operate to Kantian methods. The few insights he has published are recondite meditations on the Aristotelian syllogism, a rhetorical figure that constructs a combined claim out of two apparently unrelated propositions by deducing a shared middle term. De Quincey recognises in such excursuses a hint of a structure that might actuate a poetics of the medium, but no more than a hint: 'what the public misses chiefly, and still looks for with hope from the hands of Sir William Hamilton, is a *comprehensive* treatise on every part of Logic' which should address how 'two ideas *can* be associated or dissociated by the mediation of a third'. While De Quincey does not know whether 'Sir W. H. will ever raise an edifice of so much labour and fatigue', he notes that a three-part *Critique* must be an intolerable prospect to a thinker of the Hamiltonian persuasion: whatever his system of thought will be, it manifestly cannot be expressed through endless disputations on the current and ideal structure of human thoughts. The great Hamilton 'was not properly a philosopher – nor would [. . .] have called himself such', at least not in the mould established by Kant and his disciples; as such, it is to his manner of *being* that De Quincey attends.

Even if '[*l*]*ively* seems a strange epithet for the characterising of a "Logic"', this adjective may well best describe Hamilton, who writes his work by living it. His lived philosophy defies the Kantian suspicion of the corporeal in that he cultivates both his intellectual faculties and his physical strength. The latter resides in his feats as a polyhistor and polyglot of impressive 'combining powers'; the former in 'his extraordinary muscular strength [. . .] Sir William's powers [. . .] as an athlete, were indeed unusually great'.[106] While De Quincey, too, comes forward as eminently physical in his autobiographical writings, his embodied life is always precarious; assailed by an impressive range of maladies and ever teetering on the verge of collapse. Such performative frailty suits his modest vocation: 'a more worthless body than his own the author is free to confess cannot be', he writes, noting that 'he should almost be ashamed to bequeath his wretched structure to any respectable dog'.[107] While a 'person worse qualified than myself for recording the extent of [Hamilton's] athletic powers cannot be imagined', De Quincey does profess to understand his reasons for foregrounding his bodily life. He is on surer footing in describing Hamilton's intellectual exploits, which revolve around his voracious reading, and inspire a disquisition on the importance of readership and translatorship:

> But what ultimate value attached to this hyperbolical acquisition? If one wrote an epitaph for his eminence, one might be tempted into saying, 'Here

lies a man that, in the act of dying, committed a robbery, absconding from his poor fellow-creatures with a valuable polyglot dictionary.' Assuredly, any man who puts his treasures into a form which must perish in a company with himself is no profound benefactor to his species. Not thus did Sir William proceed, as I soon learned after I made his acquaintance; and the results of this reading are now sown and rooted at Paris, not less than at Berlin; are blossoming on the Rhine; and are bearing fruit on the Danube.

Much like he constructs Wordsworth, Coleridge, Carlyle and Kant as his counters, De Quincey's biofictional rhapsody on Hamilton creates out of the Scotch idealist a figuration for himself. Hamilton models what De Quincey, too, endeavours to be: a British idealist who seized on the English instincts already present in Kant and corrects his errors by superadding a British sense of balance. The equation is inaccurate only in that Hamilton neglects to carry his lived philosophy into his writing, whence it might spark a mode of writing that would furnish a practical demonstration of the metaphysical potential of polyglotism. The Hamiltonian shape names the fulcrum that will render fully operational an idealist counter-Kantian chiasmus: he inhabits the position that De Quincey seeks to occupy through his translatorship and his impassioned prose.

So what, then, is a writer to do when ordered by his imperious readers to chronicle the life of a man who defies description? De Quincey proposes a mode of writing that emulates his subject's wilful mode of being – a poetics of composition, that is, which strives to find the common ground between the physical and intellectual dimensions of language; not by imposing predetermined rules, but by chasing the living flux of language. The essayist is out to 'autoschediase', as he terms it; a word apparently of his own coinage, based on a Greek term for acting with little forethought or preparation. To autoschediase 'or improvise', he writes, 'is sometimes in effect to be forced into a consciousness of creative energies that would else have slumbered through life'. It is by allowing the writing to preserve its improvisational gestures that Hamilton appears in the text; a lively system of philosophy that only occasionally flits into the reader's ken, in the quieter interstices between longer paragraphs or in half-remembered recollections of his intrusion at the breakfast table, where De Quincey can only 'presume that at such times Sir William Hamilton, being thoroughly social, would keep us company. From the circumstances given, I infer a probability.' Much as the translator only fully identifiably emerges in footnoted comments, and much as a fully poetic prose is only ever gleaned as the text's switches registers, Hamilton emerges in flashes from the ruck and tumble of the words that seek to describe him. '[A]ll great executants on the organ' have been confronted with the paradox of musical improvisation, which inspires 'sudden felicities of impassioned combinations' but makes it impossible 'to arrest [...] those flying arabesques of loveliest melody, which the magnetic inspiration of the moment has availed to excite'.

In further explication of the amphibolic structures that underpin his impassioned rhapsody on Hamilton, De Quincey stages a sequence of examples illustrative of the dilemmas that his dynamic method renders cognisable. Each of these self-contained vignettes is premised on a Kantian antinomy carried to the highest pitch: two incommensurable perspectives are made to face off, whereupon the philosopher feels compelled to opt for either a materialist or a rationalist reading, yet cannot in good conscience decide between the two. Instead of dispelling the resulting discomfort by dissolving the material into the rational, as Schiller and Carlyle recommend, the truly conscientious idealist revels in the dissonance, even if this entails remaining caught in the 'scandal of an irreconcilable schism'. The most elaborate instance of De Quincey's proposed response to philosophical quandaries comes courtesy of an old favourite amongst logicians, the paradox of Achilles and the tortoise. In allegorising the collision between rationalist and empiricist cognition, whereby the former operates to the infinite divisibility of time and space and the latter rejects such fruitless theorising, the chase between demigod and reptile hints at 'great metaphysical problems, and elementary perplexities, such as never cease to awaken and to interest the human mind', especially the sort of human mind that happens to dwell in a Quinceyan frame, who 'when a schoolboy, invented several' more such problems. In a winding passage which the essay chooses to shunt off into a concluding footnote, De Quincey offers his reading of the allegory by reframing it through a range of concepts which serve to rearticulate the central polarity: Achilles and the tortoise, hypothesis and experience, physical reality and metaphysical law, reason and nature – in short, two opposed modes of being that cannot both hold and yet demonstrably both exist:

> It is precisely *because* Achilles will in practice go ahead of the tortoise, when, conformably to a known speculative argument, he ought *not* to go ahead – it is precisely this fact, so surely to be anticipated from all our experience, when confronted with this principle so peremptorily denying the possibility of such a fact – exactly this antinomy it is, – the *will be*, as a physical reality, ranged against the *cannot be*, as apparently a metaphysical law – this downright certainty as matched against this downright impossibility, – [...] which constitutes our aporia, that is, our resourcelessness. [...] There was, therefore, war in the human mind, and the scandal of an irreconcilable schism. Two oracles within the human mind fought against each other. But, in such circumstances, to reaffirm or to exalt either oracle is simply to reinforce and strengthen the

feud. [...] The conflict depends upon the parity of the conflicting forces [...] The antinomy it is – the frightful co-existence of the *to be* and the *not to be* – this it is that agitates and distresses you. But how is that antinomy, – a secret word of two horns, which we may represent for the moment under the figure of two syllables, – lessened or reconciled by repeating one of these syllables [...] leaving the secret consciousness to repeat the other?[108]

Much as this essay captures the wilful Hamilton by oscillating between styles, De Quincey recommends conditioning thought to ceaselessly alter its preferred option. The purpose of this dialogic structuration is not to accomplish an infinite deconstructive deferral, but to gesture at a moment when an altogether new species of thought will surely emerge. At present, this tertiary mode can only be gleaned at those junctures where two epistemes playfully backflip into another. Such 'revolving forms of alternate repulsion, where flight turns suddenly into pursuit, and pursuit into flight' is a process entirely 'natural [...] to the morbid activity of men', even as it is often cut short by writers, readers and philosophers dispirited by the prospect of fatiguingly see-sawing between perspectives. In spite of the labours required to render it operative, however, a dedoubled system of thought

> *is* or *can* be grand when it reverses or comes round upon its mediating point, or point of reaction. [...] You depress your hands, and, behold! the system disappears; you raise them, it reappears. [...] Clap your hands like an Arabian girl, and all comes back. [...] To and fro; it is and it is not – is not and is. Ah, mighty heaven, that such a mockery should cover the whole vision of life! It is and it is not; and on to the day of your death you will still have to learn what is the truth. The eternal now through the dreadful loom is the overflowing future poured back into the capacious reservoir of the past. All the active element lies in that infinitesimal *now*.[109]

Of course, the true blind spot in De Quincey's richly textured portraits of Hamilton, or Kant, Wordsworth, Coleridge and a gallery of others is De Quincey himself. It is precisely 'in that infinitesimal *now*', arising as lucid interlude betwixt imitation and creation, that De Quincey may be seen to thread the loom of his writing. Faced with an antinomic text, which a translation that fully inhabits its mode must always be, readers will be tempted to perform a pragmatic reduction of the avenues of interpretation, but this De Quincey cannot allow: the antinomic principle of composition revels in the frightful co-existence of contradictory perspectives, encouraging an interpretation work in acknowledgment of a double filiation. One figure for translation, discussed in the next section, bears particular traces of this antinomic poetics.

## Spectres of Coleridge

In *Les Paradis Artificiels*, Baudelaire arrestingly observes that De Quincey most speaks as himself when he speaks as a revenant. He explains this label in a passage of impassioned prose in which he interlaces figurative and literal readings of his curious figure: read through its etymology, a revenant designates a restless peripatetic; read through its denotation, the word refers to a partial demise or a deficient resurrection. De Quincey speaks in two voices, both of which defy a straightforward ascription of identity in that they are structured around movement or incomplete transfer. To explain the involuted structure to which he is obliquely adverting, Baudelaire provides two illustrative images with evident intertextual resonances, an old mariner and a returning traveller. Through this doubly personified instance of movement and transfer, Thomas morphs into a master trope for translative writing:

> Browsing again and again these singular pages, I could not help but dream of the different metaphors harnessed by poets to paint the man returned from the battles of life; say, the ancient mariner [*le vieux marin*], his back hunched, his face embroidered with a tangled lacework of wrinkles, warming his heroic body at his hearth, escaped from a thousand adventures; or the traveller who returns in the evening to the countryside he began to cross at dawn, and who remembers with tenderness and sadness a thousand fancies which possessed his brain while voyaging through those lands now vaporised into horizons. This is what I would generally be happy to call the tone of a revenant; an accent that is not supernatural, but almost alien to humanity, one half earthly and one half extraterrestrial.[110]

Baudelaire's astute summary of De Quincey's authorship through images of transfer, culminating in the figure of a revenant structured into halves, invites further inspection of De Quincey's spectral figures as they image his translative poetics, chief among them the dark interpreter previously invoked in this book's introductory chapter.

The closing movement of the 'Suspiria de Profundis' summons the reader to an excursion to the sublime Brocken, the highest mountain in the German Harz range, where a 'very striking phenomenon has been continually described by writers, both German and English, for the last fifty years'.[111] The authors in question include Goethe, Hogg and Coleridge; the phenomenon they describe is 'the famous Spectre of the Brocken', a haloed apparition known to haunt the mountain at dawn, so dependably startling hikers as to spark a minor stampede of ghost hunters from the 1750s to the 1850s.[112] Those interested in a description of this picturesque occurrence are referred to David Brewster's 1832

*Letters on Natural Magic*, which in its sixth chapter reproduces the following testimony:

> One of the best accounts of the spectre of the Brocken is that which is given by M. Haue, who saw it on the 23rd of May, 1797. [...] The sun rose about four o'clock in the morning through a serene atmosphere. In the south-west [...] a brisk west wind carried before it the transparent vapours, which had not yet been condensed into thick heavy clouds. About a quarter past four he went towards the inn, and looked round to see whether the atmosphere would afford him a free prospect towards the south-west, when he observed at a very great distance [...] a human figure of a monstrous size. His hat, having been almost carried away by a violent gust of wind, he suddenly raised his hand to his head, to protect his hat, and the colossal figure did the same. He immediately made another movement by bending his body, an action which was repeated by the spectral figure.

While Brewster's *Letters* features an expansive list of Gothic and fantastic examples, including 'aërial spectres seen in Cumberland', the proliferation of details in the description of these occurrences indicate his intention is not to publish a compendium of thrilling episodes: his purpose is to demonstrate the powers of empiricism.[113] Brewster considers samples of natural magic only to have them on explode on contact with natural philosophy; with 'scientific comment'.[114] Arguing that superstitious explanations of extraordinary happenings pivoting on conjectured demons and 'divine agency' will no longer pass muster now that 'science has reduced them to the level of natural phenomena', he punctures the mysteries of the Brocken, noting that it is produced by a simple combination of an angled light source, a suitably large object, and an atmospheric canvass. Brocken spectres are refractions: they are

> shadows of the observer projected on dense vapour or thin fleecy clouds, which have the power of reflecting much light. They are seen most frequently at sunrise, because it is at that time that the vapours and clouds necessary for their production are most likely to be generated; and they can be seen only when the sun is throwing his rays horizontally, because the shadow of the observer would otherwise be thrown either up in the air, or down upon the ground.[115]

Brewster here operates in standard empiricist fashion, following a model influentially laid down by Hume in his 1748 *Enquiry Concerning Human Understanding*. As the latter indicates in its chapter on the interpretation of miraculous events, the purpose of empiricist experimentation and education is to combat those whom Hume labels, in a turn of phrase taken from Bacon, 'the writers of natural magic [...] who seem to have an unconquerable appetite for falsehood and fable'. When alleged wonders are reproduced before truly philosophical eyes, a conflict of explanatory frames ensues which must always be decided in favour of the sciences. There is, as demonstrated by Brewster in his mercilessly scientific commentary on the Brocken, 'a contest of two opposite experiences of which the one destroys the other, as far as its force goes'.[116]

In a characteristically ambivalent gesture that hints at a translator's unwillingness to have one perspective irrecoverably destroyed by its counter, De Quincey offsets his reference to Brewster's empiricist manual by offering a very different type of text. Casting around for a literary source that might prove more vivid than the empiricist account, he lands on a poem by Coleridge, first published in 1828 but likely composed earlier. 'Constancy to an Ideal Object' is now generally read as a cryptic meditation on the poet's unrequited love for Sara Hutchinson – De Quincey, however, favours a different interpretation. Coleridge, he claims, composed the poem in memory of his ascension of the Brocken 'on the Whitsunday of 1799' in hopes of witnessing a ghostly apparition and, following the trip's failure, of its recuperation. The poet recounts the adventure in a lyric on 'Brocken's sovran heights' as well as a letter to his wife in which he writes of travelling to 'the foot of the Great Brocken [. . .] those who go there may see their own Ghosts walking up & down'. Significantly, neither text makes mention of ghostly sightings: the sublime refuses to manifest, and a dispirited Coleridge can report no grander personal experience than the toll exacted by German landscapes on English feet. 'My toe', he complains, 'was shockingly swoln, m[y feet] bladdered, and my whole frame seemed going to pieces with fatigu[e].'[117] Even if Coleridge 'failed to see the phantom', as De Quincey encapsulates the poet's disappointment, he did manage to import the occurrence to Britain, where it is 'a much rarer phenomenon'.[118] In his *Aids to Reflection*, Coleridge claims 'I have myself seen it twice' in Britain, adding that its occurrence in the Vale of Clwyd has been scientifically attested 'in the first or second Volume of the Manchester Philosophical Transactions'.[119] As De Quincey reads 'Constancy', then, it is a poem that is implicitly a product of translation. Moreover, it is also a poem that embodies the structures of translation in that it allegorises how a philosophical problem may be transposed into literary writing. De Quincey's *Suspiria* reproduces the text's final lines:

> And art thou nothing? Such thou art, as when
> The woodman winding westward up the glen
> At wintry dawn, where o'er the sheep-track's maze
> The viewless snow-mist weaves a glist'ning haze,
> Sees full before him, gliding without tread,
> An image with a glory round its head;

The enamoured rustic worships its fair hues,
Nor knows he makes the shadow, he pursues![120]

While Brewster so structures the scene at the Brocken as to orchestrate a Humean clash of epistemologies, Coleridge shudders at such violent collisions. In one of his first published references to the Brocken, dated a few years before 'Constancy', he employs the spectre so as to demonstrate that the two dominant attitudes to literary genius – one sophisticated and critically cogent, the other hopelessly naïve – allow of no mechanisms through which their contest might be decided. Literary talent, that is, meets with the same dichotomy of reactions invited by spectral mirages; as problems of culture rather than nature, however, literary questions resist empiricist resolution. 'The Beholder either recognises [genius] as a projected Form of his own Being, that moves before him with a Glory round its head, or recoils from it as from a Spectre', and never can the two meet.[121] In much similar fashion, in an 1811 lecture on *The Tempest*, Coleridge posits a strict division between 'two classes' of readers; one characterised by intellectual 'feeling and understanding', another 'merely' sentimental. 'Between the two', he argues, 'no medium could be endured.'[122] By way of explanation, he offers a spectral allegory:

> In the plays of Shakespeare every man sees himself without knowing that he sees himself, as in the phenomena of nature, in the mist of the mountain, a traveller beholds his own figure, but the glory round the head distinguishes it from a mere vulgar copy; or as a man traversing the Brocken in the north of Germany at sunrise, when the glorious beams are shot askance the mountain; he sees before him a figure of gigantic proportions and of such elevated dignity, that he only knows it to be himself by the similarity of action.[123]

The structure that Coleridge here hints at is that of a permanent parabasis; a design much different from the 'willing suspension of disbelief for the moment' which he hypothesised in 1817 as a conceit through which enlightened readers might continue to enjoy without compunction 'persons and characters supernatural, or at least romantic' by temporarily bracketing their powers of reason.[124] This conservative reading of irony is substituted for a subversive programme of play in the Brocken poem, where supernatural phenomena are no longer to be enjoyed against one's better knowledge: instead, the ode preserves intact the dignity of both the pre-empiricist and the post-empiricist experiences. Even though the interpretation of the spectre by the rustic contrasts sharply with the educated perspective of the outside observer, here embodied by the lyrical speaker, the former is not undone by the latter. The woodsman is permitted to bask in naïvety even as his views contrast with those of the natural philosopher: his voice is at once subordinate to and coordinate with the latter; framed by the voice of reason, but not thereby defeated. It is this tense dual structure that Coleridge marshals to explain the nature of an 'ideal object', whose disposition is such, his poem demonstrates, that it cannot be captured through any one discourse alone. The object envisaged by an idealist critique of the Kantian circumscription of art and thought can only be experienced practically; by constructing and decoding emblematic scenes in which figures are mediated by different perspectives.

When De Quincey summons the Spectre of the Brocken by speaking the names of the scientist Brewster and the poet Coleridge, he is aiming for an idealist architecture that outdoes even 'Constancy' in that it is designed to house double the two perspectives that Coleridge manages. The section on the 'Apparition of the Brocken' is constructed as a chiasmus – that is, as a sequence of four self-contained perspectives whose reading necessitates travelling between each of the extreme positions in a logical square. The essay opens on a protracted authorial address to the reader on the nature of the Brocken Spectre; then shifts into a supernatural register; next becomes a personal account of the author's memories and dreams, startlingly projected onto the reader by its use of the second person; and ends in a fragment detailing a gruesome murder not published until 1891.[125] A closer consideration of the four vectors that interleave to construe the spectre will help to clarify why De Quincey builds the Brocken and the Interpreter into the chief figures for his philosophy of style. The first part of the essay is clearly conceived as an imitation of Brewster: hence its recurrent references to minutiae included in the *Letters*, chiefly relating to dates and measurements, and hence its insistence on dispelling through careful experimentation the myths that cling to the ominous manifestation. The reader, who within the fictional design of the text is confronted by a strange vision as they navigate the Brocken, is invited to 'test the nature of this mysterious apparition' through 'two or three experiments'. As expected, these demonstrate that the figure is really 'but a reflex of yourself'. However, in contrast to the empiricist blueprint modelled by Brewster, this conclusion does not herald a victory of modern science over popular naïvety. Explaining his motives for recommending optical tests, the narrator curiously reasons that one ought to do so because the superstitious reading may well be correct, and '[w]hat we fear, and with some reason, is, that as he lived so many ages with foul Pagan sorcerers, and witnessed so many centuries of dark idolatries, his heart may have been corrupted'. Paradoxically, the pre-enlightened angle grows even more prominent when the narrator proposes further scientific tests. The first such experiment involves crossing oneself, a gesture redolent with religious associations that are not quite dispelled by the order to 'observe whether he repeats it'. The second trial veers fully occult in recommending an impromptu prayer: 'Look now! the apparition [. . .] also bends his knee, he also raises his right hand to God.' By way of a third test, De Quincey dismisses the stalemate between positivism and prerationalism by prescribing a ritual rooted in personal recollection, decodable to readers of the 'Suspiria' as a reference to the trauma of his sister's death. In memory of this tragic event, he invites the reader, who has now almost entirely merged with the narrator, to 'veil your head' to signify their grief. Sure enough, '[i]mmediately you see that the apparition of the Brocken [also] veils his head'. When De Quincey summarily proclaims that this third and final 'trial is decisive', it is deeply puzzling just what has been proven. While the Spectre can now be categorised as an optical illusion, it refuses to fall in with its classification; instead, it veers and vanishes between modern science, ancient superstition and autobiography. The picture is further muddled, moreover, by the emergence of a fourth character. The only amongst the quadrumvirate to receive a proper name, the murderous Mr Symons embarks on 'a hellish career' to exact retribution for the rejection of his advances, egged on by 'a dark figure on his right hand' with distinctly demonic overtones. Four different readings stand side by side, their combination as unlikely as it is suggestive.

The four divergent voices generated by the one apparition are posited in such a way as to establish two centring perspectives. As in his philological system, in which a chiasm of four languages pivots around a dedoubled focal node occupied by Latin and English, De Quincey constructs his ambivalent sense of self into a double focus: as he runs through the personified perspectives he has outlined, he separates the sum of their interactions into two anthropomorphic figures. The first, the Spectre of the Brocken, describes the optic marvel experienced by the empiricist under whom hides an occultist. By contrast, the Dark Interpreter, who evolves out of the Brocken, is the phrase favoured by the bereaved brother and frenzied murderer to capture the dark agencies that propel them into accesses of grief and rage. The transition between these two readings is illocutively performed in the following passage, which calls out the conversion of a natural phenomenon based in objective reality into subjective symbology. If the Spectre names a philosophical paradox, the Interpreter names the application of its impossible structure to writing and thinking:

> in uttering your secret feelings to him, you make this phantom the dark symbolic mirror for reflection to the daylight what else must be hidden for

ever. Such a relation does the Dark Interpreter, whom, immediately the reader will learn to know as an intruder into my dreams, bear to my own mind. He is originally a mere reflex of my inner nature. But as the apparition of the Brocken sometimes is disturbed by storms or by driving showers, so as to dissemble his real origin, in like manner the Interpreter sometimes swerves out of my orbit, and mixes a little with alien natures.[126]

De Quincey's shifts neatly map out a quadrangular structure which on the next level of analysis divides between a Spectre and an Interpreter; between a largely positive image which dramatises an epistemological question, and a predominantly negative figure for a deeply conflicted sense of authorship. This double duality is sutured by a chiastic cross-play of operative categories whose traffic is indicated by references to the phantom's mercurial nature; its tendency to 'mix[] a little with alien natures'. It is this fickleness that unsettles interpretation and continually demands new experiments and readings, whether its instability is ascribed to atmospheric conditions, supernatural causes, the observer's inner turmoil, or a diabolical influence. And it is precisely as such signals are pursued that the ideal object begins to emerge: De Quincey's true figure of idealist composition hides in the articulating hinge between the Spectre and the Interpreter. In the same way, De Quincey's proper voice is not to be found in any one of the perspectives collected in this essay, nor in all of them taken together: it emerges from the negotiation and the unbalancing of all these conflicted identities.

To say that De Quincey names a sign that is forever in internal translation is to say that De Quincey only appears as he translates; as he brokers the push and pull of languages, influences, disciplines and styles. Coleridge, too, recognises that there lies in such negotiation the potential for a reconfiguration of Romantic authorship; an avenue for writers in insecure command of their talents to claim a position at once modest and grandiose. When the latter begins to outline a future life fully devoted to dark interpretation, however, he retreats. In an essay for his journal *The Friend*, which ran from 1809 through 1810, he includes a trilogy of articles on Luther, whom he presents as his literary exemplar. Luther, he reflects, managed to achieve the one thing that he cannot, being too deeply steeped in dejection. Even as Luther was beleaguered by doubts, he 'altered' the world. He employed 'his reason [. . .] in building up anew the edifice of *earthly* society, and his imagination [pledged] itself [to] the possible realisation of the structure'. This ability to trigger a global theological revolution derives from a prescient conception of writership. In Luther, Coleridge recognises the manifestation of a Romantic ideal of performative authorship; of a writer who in his actions embodies his thoughts so much that life and text intermix:

like Hamilton *via* De Quincey, he 'was a Poet indeed [. . .] but his poetic images were so vivid, that they mastered the Poet's own mind! [. . .] LUTHER did not *write*, he *acted* Poems.' This performative authorship must not be understood as a matter of 'genius and *original* power' or 'faith alone', but as a readiness to reduce oneself to the humble posture of the translator, if one who fully appreciates the opportunities inherent in that vocation. Picture a despairing translator in an addled physical state, 'under great irritability of his nervous system' brought on from an excess of sedentary study and a lack of dietary discipline, poring over scattered parchments, each speaking its own language and each replete with suspected errors and baffling hapaxes. This translator, moreover, is feverishly engaged in crafting a median style that might liberate the German-speaking peoples from the burdens of a fossilised Catholicism: he is engaged, then, in grappling with languages as he seeks to distil a medium style that might reconcile their divergent ideas. Here is Luther, visited by a demonic figure as he plunges headlong into the contradictions exposed by comparing different versions of scripture:

> Methinks I see him sitting, the heroic Student, in his Chamber in the Warteburg, with his mid-night Lamp before him [. . .] Below it lies the Hebrew Bible open, on which he gazes, his brow pressing on his palm, brooding over some obscure Text, which he desires to make plain to the simple Boor and the humble Artizan, and to transfer its whole force into their own natural and living Tongue. And he himself does not understand it! Thick darkness lies on the original Text: he counts the letters, he calls up the roots of each separate word, and questions them as the familiar Spirits of an Oracle. In vain! thick darkness continues to cover it! not a ray of meaning dawns through it. [. . .] O honoured Luther! as easily mightest thou convert the whole City of Rome [. . .] as strike a spark of light from the words, and *nothing but words* of the Alexandrine Version. Disappointed, despondent, enraged, ceasing to *think*, yet continuing his brain on the stretch in solicitation of a thought [. . .] he sinks, without perceiving it, into a trance of slumber [. . .] All at once he sees the Arch-fiend coming forth on the wall of the room [. . .] the Ink-stand [. . .] he hurls [. . .] at the intruder.[127]

Like De Quincey, Coleridge turns to 'the fruitful matrix of ghosts' for figures that might explain his poetics. Also like De Quincey, he specifically draws on such spectres to define his writing through translation. In an additional parallel, Coleridge locates his spectre in a hinging moment: in a nearly intractable location between languages, nations, histories, states of consciousness and styles. In a marked contrast to his sometime competitor, however, Coleridge imagines translation as monodirectional: Luther's translation cannot but lead up from matter, from the suffocating throng of 'words and nothing but words' to purely meaningful communication. The apparition that signposts the disintegration of meaning that threatens translation must be abjured posthaste by a wild act of spontaneous writing, an act of faith in the continued powers of pen and ink. As Coleridge sees it, the translator brings man closer to divinity, but his concept of the godhead is entirely spiritual: it is not De Quincey's, who remains committed to an idealist programme of equilibrium.

Having examined De Quincey's highly involved construction of translation through its impact on his authorship, his stylistics and his philosophy, the following pages consider a translation that activates all these angles, examining the practical implementation of a multi-tiered critique of translative reasoning; De Quincey's translation of a novel (not) by Walter Scott, which most realises the dream of a translated text that so disentangles itself from its ancillary position as to achieve a measure of autonomy.

## Notes

1. On De Quincey's editorship of the *Gazette*, see Charles Politt, *De Quincey's Editorship of the Westmorland Gazette, with Selections from his Work on that Journal, from July 1818 to November, 1819* (London: Simpkin, Marshall, Hamilton, Kent & Co., 1890). In 2018, the *Gazette* celebrated its bicentenary, drawing particular attention to its affiliation with Wordsworth and De Quincey. The paper's highest-profile recent article, cited in several international media, is a three-line story reporting an office chair had been set on fire 'on the grassy area, off Maude Street, Kendal'. The conflagration was happily 'extinguished using one hose jet' (*Westmorland Gazette*, 26 January 2007).
2. On the political background of the *Gazette*, see William Anthony Hay, 'Henry Brougham and the 1818 Westmorland Election: A Study in Provincial Opinion and the Opening of Constituency Politics', *Albion* 36, no. 1 (2004): 28–51; and John Edwin Wells, 'Wordsworth and de Quincey in Westmorland Politics, 1818', *PMLA* 55, no. 4 (1940): 1080–128.
3. *Westmorland Gazette*, 1.129; 1.188–9; 1.190; 1.129; 1.190.
4. While De Quincey reads Kant as a closet Tory, he was (and is) widely regarded as 'one of the greatest *liberal* philosophers'. Michael Doyle, *Ways of War and Peace: Realism, Liberalism and Socialism* (New York: W. W. Norton, 1997), 208.
5. *Westmorland Gazette*, 1.285–6.
6. 'Kant on National Character, in Relation to the Sense of the Sublime and Beautiful', *The Collected Writings of Thomas De Quincey*, 14.51, ed. David Masson (London: A. & C. Black, 1897).
7. LYM, 3.97; 3.85.
8. 'Kant on the Age of the Earth', *Collected Writings*, 14.74, ed. David Masson.
9. De Quincey's take on the *Observations* is published under the title 'Kant

on National Character'; *Dreams of a Spirit-Seer* becomes 'Abstract of Swedenborgianism'; and the 'Universal History' is slightly altered to be premised on a 'Cosmo-Political Plan'.
10. Paul Hamilton, *Metaromanticism: Aesthetics, Literature, Theory* (Chicago: Chicago University Press, 2003), 6.
11. For a brief sketch of the immensely fraught discussion on whether Kant registered much of an impact on British Romanticism, see Frederick Beiser, 'Romanticism and Idealism', in *The Relevance of Romanticism: Essays on German Romantic Philosophy*, ed. Dalia Nassar (Oxford: Oxford University Press, 2014), 30–46; Elizabeth Millan-Zaibert, *Friedrich Schlegel and the Emergence of Romantic Philosophy* (Albany: SUNY Press, 2007), 28–52; Manfred Frank, *Auswege aus dem deutschen Idealismus* (Frankfurt am Main: Suhrkamp, 2007), 16–66; and Kathleen M. Wheeler, 'Kant and Romanticism', *Philosophy and Literature* 13, no. 1 (1989): 42–56.
12. Wellek, *Immanuel Kant in England*, which contrasts nicely with F. W. Stokoe, *German Influence in the English Romantic Period, 1788–1818* (Cambridge: Cambridge University Press, 1926), which hardly mentions Kant. Also see Monika Class, *Coleridge and Kantian Ideas in England: Coleridge's Responses to German Philosophy* (London: Continuum, 2012); the essays collected in George McDonald Ross and Tony McWalter (eds), *Kant and His Influence* (London: Continuum, 2005); and Paul Guyer, 'The Scottish Reception of Kant', in *Scottish Philosophy in the Nineteenth and Twentieth Centuries*, ed. Gordon Graham (Oxford: Oxford University Press, 2015), 118–53.
13. J. H. Alexander, 'Learning from Europe: Continental Literature in the *Edinburgh Review* and *Blackwood's Magazine* 1802–1825', *The Wordsworth Circle* 21, no. 3 (1990): 119.
14. Wheeler, 'Kant and Romanticism', 42.
15. Alexander, 'Learning from Europe', 119.
16. For an analysis of Crabb Robinson's work on Kant and others, see James Vigus, Introduction to *Essays on Kant Schelling, and German Aesthetics*, by Henry Crabb Robinson, ed. James Vigus (London: Modern Humanities Research Association, 2010), 1–27.
17. C 1821, 2.52; 2.56; 2.60.
18. Grevel Lindop, *The Opium Eater: A Life of Thomas De Quincey* (London: J. M. Dent, 1981), 229.
19. Roberts, *Revisionary Gleam*, 165.
20. George Gordon Byron, *Don Juan*, ed. A. Cunningham (Philadelphia: Jas. B. Smitth & Co., 1859), [3].
21. KME, 7.49.
22. Review of Edinburgh Review [Part One], 5.285. Emphasis mine.
23. AB, 10.174.
24. BL, 153.
25. LD, 6.74n4.
26. KME, 7.50.
27. LD, 6.74.
28. KME, 7.46-7.
29. LD, 6.74n4.

30. For such a slim volume of work, De Quincey's contributions of the *Post* have attracted considerable scholarly attention. See David Groves, 'Thomas De Quincey and the "Edinburgh Saturday Post" of 1827', *Studies in Bibliography* 55 (2002): 235–63.
31. AB, 10.174.
32. Willich is the author of *Kant's Essays and Treatises on Moral, Political, and Various Philosophical Subjects* (London: William Richardson, 1798–99) and *Elements of the Critical Philosophy: Containing a Concise Account of its Origin and Tendency; a View of All the Works Published by its Founder, Professor Immanuel Kant; and a Glossary for the Explanation of Terms and Phrases* (London: T. N. Longman, 1798). Nitsch wrote *A General and Introductory View of Professor Kant's Principles Concerning man, the World and the Deity, Submitted to the Consideration of the Learned* (London: J. Downes, 1796). Nitsch also published two articles, 'A Sketch of the Philosophy of Dr Kant, Professor of Philosophy at the University of Konigsberg in Russia: By a Disciple of Kant's', *English Review* 27 (1796): 106–11; 354–7; and a letter 'To the Editor of the Monthly Magazine and British Register', *Monthly Magazine* 9 (1796): 702–5.
33. On Nitsch's pivotal (and now almost universally forgotten) role in the British reception of Kant, see Class, *Coleridge and Kantian Ideas in England*, 38–48, 169–90. On Willich, see Wellek, *Immanuel Kant in England*, 11–15. On Wirgman, see Wellek, *Immanuel Kant in England*, 211–42; Stokoe, *German Influence in the English Romantic Period*, 24–6; and Class, *Coleridge and Kantian Ideas in England*, 44–5.
34. Thomas Wirgman, 'Moral Philosophy Reduced to a Complete and Permanent Science, On the Principles of Transcendental Philosophy, As Contained in Kant's "Critic of Practical Reason"', *Encyclopaedia Londinensis* (London: Encyclopaedia Londinensis, 1817), 15.783.
35. This comment is presumably in reference to Willich's inclusion of three philological essays by Adelung in his *Elements of Critical Philosophy*.
36. LYM, 3.87.
37. De Quincey is *au fait* with the various translations that had been produced of (portions of) Kant's work. In his 1836 piece on the 'German Language' for *Tait's*, he notes that 'there is a Latin version of the whole, by Born, and a most admirable digest of the cardinal work (admirable for its fidelity and the skill by which that fidelity is attained), in the same language, by Rhiseldek, a Danish professor' (10.64). The former is Friedrich Gottlob Born, who published *Immanuelis Kantii Opera ad philosophiam criticam Latine vertit Fredericus Gottlob Born* (Leipzig: E. B. Schwickert, 1796–8). Though he is also mentioned by William Thomson (*Outline of the Laws of Thought* (London: William Pickering, 1842), xi), I have not been able to identify who 'Rhiseldek' might be. There were several more occasional essays and translations in English than De Quincey lists in the 'English Notices of Kant' section of the 'Letters': for a fuller impression, see Class, *Coleridge and Kantian Ideas in England*, 17–48; 216–17. Interestingly, De Quincey does not mention the translations by John Richardson, confirming Class's observation that the latter's work did not 'receive particular notice in Coleridge's intellectual circles', and 'met with utter silence from the press'. (13)

38. KME, 7.87.
39. The original *London* article (and perhaps De Quincey in the original he sent to the printers) spells his name Villars.
40. This, again, is a misspelling in the *London*, which prints Dégérando.
41. De Quincey was not aware that de Staël had received her Kant through Crabb Robinson.
42. *The Edinburgh Review* 47 (1828): 134.
43. Review of Edinburgh Review [Part Two], 5.296. De Quincey launches another attack in KME, 7.48–9.
44. Wellek, *Immanuel Kant in England*, 173.
45. LD, 6.74n4.
46. KME, 7.48.
47. KME, 7.50.
48. Kant's Abstract of Swedenborgianism, *The Collected Writings of Thomas De Quincey*, ed. David Masson, 14.61.
49. KME, 7.52; 7.65.
50. Kant on National Character, 47.
51. Kant on National Character, 56.
52. KME, 7.54; 7.65–8.
53. BL, 153–4.
54. Quoted by James Anthony Froude, *Thomas Carlyle: A History of the First Forty Years of His Life, 1795–1835* (London: Longmans, Green, and Co., 1891), 196–7.
55. KME, 7.70.
56. KME, 7.51–3.
57. He may have taken this from Herder, who also focuses a philosophical critique of the Kantian method through its stylistics. See De Quincey's essay on Herder, 'Death of a German Great Man', 114–24.
58. The critical literature on this distinction is extensive. Notable contributions include Tim Fulford, 'De Quincey's Literature of Power', *The Wordsworth Circle* 31, no. 3 (2000): 158–64; Frederick Burwick, *Knowledge and Power*, esp. 1–23; and Brian McGrath, 'Thomas De Quincey and the Language of Literature: Or, on the Necessity of Ignorance', *Studies in English Literature, 1500–1900* 47, no. 4 (2007): 847–62.
59. LYM, 69–70.
60. Immanuel Kant, *Critique of Judgment*, trans. J. H. Bernard (New York: Macmillan, 1951), 172.
61. KME, 7.51.
62. ER, 6.182.
63. SEL, 17.65.
64. S, 12.22.
65. KME, 7.51–2.
66. AB, 10.161.
67. S, 12.22.
68. SEL, 17.67.
69. Thomas Carlyle, *Lectures on the History of Literature: Delivered by Thomas Carlyle April to July 1838*, ed. J. Reay Greene (London: Ellis and Elvey, 1892), 205.
70. SEL, 17.68.

71. AB, 10.162.
72. Coleridge, 10.80.
73. BL, 155.
74. Grevel Lindop, *The Opium Eater: A Life of Thomas De Quincey* (Oxford: Oxford University Press, 1985), 132.
75. David L. Clark, 'We "Other Prussians": Bodies and Pleasures in de Quincey and Late Kant', *European Romantic Review* 14 (2003): 261–87; Paul Youngquist, "De Quincey's Crazy Body," *PMLA* 114, no. 3 (1999): 346–58.
76. AB, 10.163.
77. Wellek, *Immanuel Kant in England*, 176.
78. AB, 10.164–5.
79. C 1821, 2.63.
80. AB, 10.165; 10.164.
81. See Youngquist, 'De Quincey's Crazy Body'; and Bruno Clément, 'Kant est-il mort comme il a vécu? A-t-il vécu comme il a écrit?', in *Vie philosophique et vies de philosophes*, ed. Bruno Clément and Christian Trottmann (Paris: Sens & Tonka, 2010), 79–94.
82. *Les derniers jours d'Emmanuel Kant*, trans. Marcel Schwob (Paris: L'Herne, 2013); *Die letzten Tage des Immanuel Kant*, trans. Cornelia Langendorf (Berlin: Matthes & Seitz, 1991).
83. LD, 6.75. Ehregott Andreas Christoph Wasianski, *Immanuel Kant in seinen letzten Lebensjahren: Ein Beytrag zur Kenntniß seines Charakters und häuslichen Lebens aus dem täglichen Umgange mit ihm*, vol. 3 of *Über Immanuel Kant* (Königsberg: Friedrich Nicolovius, 1804). Ludwig Ernst von Borowski and Reinhold Bernhard Jachmann respectively wrote the first and the second volumes for the three-volume series in which Wasianski published his account, titled *Darstellung des Lebens und Charakters Kants* and *Immanuel Kant geschildert in Briefen an einen Freund*. Friedrich Theodor Rink is the author of *Ansichten aus Kants Leben* (Königsberg: Göbbels & Unzer, 1805).
84. LD, 6.76. The latter series of authors, each of whom contributes entries to the memorial literature sparked by Kant's death, barely feature at all in De Quincey's text: their invocation mostly serves to exaggerate the translator's intellectual labour. Only Jachmann is referenced in 'The Last Days', twice, to refute an assertion made by Wasianski.
85. See Chapter 2.
86. LD, 6.93; 6.73; 6.75.
87. Quoted in Manfred Kuehn, *Kant: A Biography* (Cambridge: Cambridge University Press, 2002), 14.
88. Immanuel Kant, 'The Conflict of the Faculties', in *Religion and Rational Theology*, trans. and ed. Allen W. Wood and George di Giovanni (Cambridge: Cambridge University Press, 1996), 233.
89. Immanuel Kant, *The Metaphysics of Morals*, in *Practical Philosophy*, trans. Mary J. Gregor (Cambridge: Cambridge University Press, 1996), 422–37.
90. LD, 6.82.
91. LJ, 140–1.
92. LJ, 38; 172–7.

93. Manfred Kuehn, *Kant*, 416.
94. Clark, 'Prussians', 265.
95. Immanuel Kant, 'Conflict', 324; 317; 325.
96. LJ, 215; 38.
97. LD, 6.82; 6.100.
98. LJ, 32.
99. LD, 6.81; 6.86; 6.96; 6.100.
100. LJ, 137.
101. LD, 6.95.
102. Kant, *Metaphysics*, 551.
103. On pseudo-translation, see Chapter 5 in this book.
104. Charles Rzepka and Paul Youngquist, 'De Quincey and Kant', *PMLA* 115, no. 1 (2000): 93–4.
105. Youngquist, 'Crazy Body': 350.
106. WH, 17.155; 17.173; 17.145; 17.173; 17.156; 17.175; 17.162; 17.159; 17.153.
107. C 1822, 2.81.
108. WH, 17.160; 17.152–53; 17.148; 17.159; 17.149; 17.170; 17.167–8.
109. Brevia, 229. First two emphases mine.
110. Baudelaire, *Les Paradis Artificiels*, 52.
111. SdP, 15.182.
112. For context, see Eleoma Bodammer, 'Writing on the Brocken, in the Brocken: The Poetry of the Inn's Albums', *Publications of the English Goethe Society* 82, no. 1 (2013): 42–64.
113. David Brewster, *Letters on Natural Magic: Addressed to Sir Walter Scott, Bart* (London: John Murray, 1832), 129; 127–33.
114. SdP, 15.182.
115. Brewster, *Letters*, 153–4.
116. David Hume, *An Enquiry Concerning Human Understanding: And Other Writings*, ed. Stephen Buckle (Cambridge: Cambridge University Press, 2007), 114; 99. As will become apparent, De Quincey disagreed with Hume on the reading of miracles, publishing a detailed rebuttal in 1839. See Frederick Burwick, 'Coleridge and De Quincey on Miracles', *Christianity and Literature* 34, no. 4 (1990): 387–412.
117. 'Letters from Germany', *The New Monthly Magazine* 3 (1835): 3.216.
118. SdP, 15.183.
119. Coleridge, *Aids to Reflection*, *The Collected Works of Samuel Taylor Coleridge*, ed. John Beer (Princeton: Princeton University Press, 1993), 9.227.
120. Coleridge, 'Constancy to an Ideal Object', *The Poems of Samuel Taylor Coleridge*, ed. Derwent Coleridge and Sara Coleridge (Leipzig: Bernhard Tauchnitz, 1860), 297–80.
121. Coleridge, *Aids to Reflection*, 9.227.
122. Coleridge, *Lectures on Shakespeare (1811–1819)*, ed. Adam Roberts (Edinburgh: Edinburgh University Press), 102.
123. Coleridge, *Lectures on Shakespeare*, 102.
124. BL, 6.
125. The precise standing of these final few paragraphs is a matter of dispute. Japp hypothesises them to be a suppressed section of the 'Suspiria' which

ought to have been included before its section on the 'Apparition'; in the recent Lindop edition, however, they are printed behind the latter as a more organic endpoint. The uncertain status of the passage imparts interpretative flexibility to De Quincey's fourfold constellation of discourses, further enhancing the disorienting effect generated by the hypermobile construction. See Alexander H. Japp, 'Introduction, with Complete List of the "Suspiria"', *De Quincey's Posthumous Works*, 1.
126. SdP, 15.184; 15.183; 15.184; 15.569; 15.185.
127. Coleridge, *The Friend: A Series of Essays* (London: Gale and Curtis, 1812), 143; 140; 140–2.

# Chapter 4

# The Ghost of Cutler's Stockings: The Idea of Translation

## Freely Translated from the English

Towards the end of 1823, the first volume of a new historical novel by Walter Scott is published. This event did not initially strike anyone as hugely significant: Scott was a prolific author, easily managing a yearly triple-decker. This one novel is different, however; so much so that it ignites a critical furore in the immediate aftermath of its publication. What is at stake in this debate is not the book's quality, but its mysterious provenance. For reasons left suspiciously unaddressed by the novel's paratextual matter, it is printed not in Edinburgh or London but in Berlin – even more startlingly, the work is published not in English but in German. If the offending publication is to be taken at its word – a dangerous proposition in dealing with the Great Unknown – this book is a translation from an original as yet oddly absent from the British catalogues. It was not unheard of for translations to beat their originals to the market, but the fashion in which the text advertises its translated status must give pause: it is uncommon for Romantic translations to direct their readers' attention to their derived condition, and it is even more jarring for putative translators to announce themselves by name, especially through the conceit of partial suppression normally employed when real-life persons enter fictional plots.[1] Yet here it is: *Walladmor: Frei nach dem Englischen des Walter Scott von W... s.* That is, *Walladmor: Freely [translated] from the English of Walter Scott*, by W... s. When the first volume is joined by the obligatory complement of a further two parts in early 1824, the latter of which further foments confusion by carrying questions of authorship into its narrative, the critical debate grows even more urgent.[2] Sensing the appositeness to his own work of this collective puzzlement over the exact status of a translation, pretended or otherwise, De Quincey adds to the growing body of commentary three interventions of his own: a review article, a retrospective account and an English translation of the German-Scotch novel. It is in the course of his engagement with *Walladmor* that he achieves his richest exploration of the stylistic and philosophical potential of translatorial writing.

If *Walladmor* does eventually turn out a 'Scotch novel[] made in Germany', it would be 'by no means the only example'.³ The contemporary craze for all things Scott spawned a legion of imitators dashing off novels in the *Waverley* mould, many of them strategically vague on questions of provenance – so many, in fact, that readers soon grew wary of counterfeit merchandise. 'While the fraudulent imitation of celebrated authors is rampant in the Romantic period', Esterhammer observes, 'Scott forgeries were [. . .] produced with particular enthusiasm in various languages until the mid-nineteenth century.'⁴ Aided by Scott's refusal to attach his name to his novels, just about every nation began churning out publications modelled on the vogue's namesake deity. Indeed, 'I should not be surprised to hear that some man had undertaken to demonstrate the *non*-existence of Sir Walter Scott', De Quincey records, alleging that 'the mysterious author of Waverley has in our own days been detected in persons of so many poets and historians the most opposite to each other, that by this time his personality must have evaporated into a whole synod of men'.⁵ The proliferation of Scott-like and Scott-lite creatures, the *Allgemeine Literatur-Zeitung* remarks in 1826, in a retrospective piece on the *Walladmor* polemic, is a function of the 'Scottomania' that has gripped the West. This explosive obsession

> runs rampant not only in Scotland and England [. . .] but also in Germany and France, and even in the New World, accompanied by a variety of more and less alarming symptoms and crises. In Germany it is presently raging amongst the translators as an inflammatory disease of the nerves [*hitzige Hetzkrankheit*]; among the ludicrously cheap publishers as a constant pursuit of speculation; and as a rampaging devourer of paper; not to mention the evils it exacts on our writing men and women through the blandishments of imitation. After all, those today with the capacity and the willingness to read novels [. . .], what else would they desire than something by Scott, or after Scott, or like Scott? [. . .] In this way many speculative translators and publishers have smuggled into Germany goods that have as little of the Scott and the Scot in them as an adventure under the Berlin linden trees.⁶

Inspecting the prepositions available to contemporary criticism to qualify the precise connection of *Walladmor* to Sir Walter – is it to be considered 'something *by* Scott, or *after* Scott, or *like* Scott'? – many assert the work must be a forgery, perhaps produced by Washington Irving, or Coleridge or some such hackish animal. The resulting confection must subsequently have been translated into German to exploit a market eager for Scottish fare but deprived of information from British literary circles.[7] This conspiratorial hypothesis is particularly prevalent in the German reviews, in which writers, grievously aware of a national disadvantage in historical writing, were quick to suspect a hoax. '[W]hen at that time the first volumes of Walladmor appeared', the *Zeitung* reminisces,

> most connoisseurs of Scott believed it simply had to be yet another trick being played on the German public. Those men of letters who knew the English book market affirmed that there was in England not a single Scott novel, or a novel of any other type, called *Walladmor*.[8]

Several British periodicals also subscribe to this theory, with the *Westminster Review* offering a particularly vivid narrative. Noting that Scott had been dithering over *St Ronan's Well*, finally published on 27 December 1823, and that this implied a German translation would incur a delay deleterious to the profits of European publishing houses whose accounting revolved around the biannual Leipzig fare, the *Westminster* imagines the following scene:

> [i]t appears that the great half-yearly book-fair at Leipsic cannot go on to the satisfaction of the parties concerned, without a new novel professing to be translated from the pen of our British Unknown; and that, at the last Easter congress of continental booksellers, their high ally in Edinburgh [Archibald Constable] had [...] not supplied them with the legitimate means of gratifying this appetite. It is to be hoped that there are more 'great unknowns' in the world than one; and it would be strange indeed if Germany had not her share of them [...] to one of these the Berlin publishers applied, to furnish their stalls with a stipulated quantity of historical romance, fabricated after the true Scottish fashion [...] the above bargain was made, the commodity manufactured and called *Walladmor*.[9]

Others insist the work to be the real McCoy, conjecturing that Scott's original has been nabbed by a Continental competitor, whisked off to Germany, and hurriedly translated. '[T]he German newspapers announced "a new romance by the author of Waverley", as about to issue from the press of Leipsig. There was some ground for suspecting that a set of suspended sheets might have been purloined and sold to a pirate', John Gibson Lockhart recalls.[10] Those amongst the German literati less predisposed to paranoia argue that 'English publishers often share the proofs of new works by Scott with friendly traders in Germany, and a similar explanation no doubt applies to this novel.'[11] The scenario proves plausible enough to persuade even British reviewers with readier access to authoritative sources. One reviewer is so convinced that *Walladmor* must be genuine that he challenges any who would question the novel's origination:

> [w]e challenge the publishers to state such minute circumstances as will convince us of its German origin. We call upon them to publish the German author's name. We do not believe they can do so; or if they do produce a name, will they prove to us that the book was not originally written in English, and sent over to Germany to assist in supplying the cormorant stomachs of German novel readers? [. . .] It has been asserted in the public prints, and never contradicted, that real Scotch novels appeared in Germany before they showed themselves in the British metropolis, and why may not Walladmor be one of those?[12]

Finally, others still, arguing that Scott's novels abound in games of identity, reckon that the originator of the publication must be none other than Scott himself. Such readings draw on obvious echoes between *Walladmor* and the early days of *Waverley*, which had also propelled readers into perplexities when they sought to determine the books' creator. While in 1824 Scott's role had been securely established, he continued to dissemble his paternity until 1827, joyously obfuscating the question by penning prefaces designed to disperse his books' authorship over a cast of characters. Reviewers and fellow writers proved remarkably patient with such posturing, perpetuating Scott's paratextual fictions by referring to him as 'the Great Unknown' or some other ritual circumlocution, often exploiting the close similarity between Scottish and Scott-ish (*scottisch* and *schottisch*) to hint at ways in which the former shades into the latter. Scott's identity was structured as a public secret, in which all readers were made complicit. As De Quincey summarises its paradoxes,

> [w]hatever disguise an author chooses to assume, it is a point of good breeding to respect it [. . .] Sir Walter is not under any necessity of avowing himself the author, but no man who does not mean to insult [Scott] is now at liberty to doubt whether he is.[13]

It is not far-fetched to read *Walladmor* as the latest chapter in Scott's deceptions. What is more, Scott is disinclined to confirm or deny the attribution. In a letter dated 4 March 1824, he disowns any link to *Walladmor*, instead conjecturing that the anonymous author of *Waverley*, with whom he had been spuriously equated, must now have been joined by yet another such parasitical entity, albeit once removed. Indicating his awareness 'of a German novel professing to be translated from the English and bearing my name at full length on the title-page', he laments 'that I must not only bear my own faults, and, in the opinion of many, those of that unknown gentleman, but also all the devices with which the invention of others continue to load either him or myself'.[14] This sort of double-dealing, exceeding Scott's usual delight in sparking public confusion, proves too rich for some readers, who surmise that Scott, finding that his 'wayward coquetry to make [his novels] deeds without a name' in order to 'render[] his identity the more notorious', had lost some of its pull, decided to one-up himself. Previous Scott novels were sometimes accused of mystifying their authorship to enhance their saleability: as one 1820 editorial notes, Scott was contriving to 'rais[e] popular attention at a cheaper rate than by cleverness alone', in that *Waverley* 'itself scarcely excites so much curiosity as the question who is the author'.[15] *Walladmor* attracts even greater suspicion. One irate critic alleges that Scott crafted 'this wretched piece of puffery', this 'impudent imposture upon the literary world', in order to '*puff* the fast-fading embers of his popularity, which of late has glimmered dimly in comparison with its former blaze'.[16] '[T]he articles', as the *Zeitung* laconically summarises the affair, 'became ever more confused and ever more bizarre.'[17]

If *Walladmor* provokes such fervid disputation, it is because not one of the most evident hypotheses really covers the particulars of the case. The travails of one German critic, so stumped that he thrice reconsiders his assessment, are instructive. Upon receiving the first volume, he condemns the work as a swindle. When he reads the second part, he issues a public apology for his earlier outrage and accepts the novel as Scott's legitimate offspring. Finally, upon receiving the third instalment, he recants both his condemnation and his endorsement, deciding that the book so cleverly hoaxes its reader it ought to classed under a separate rubric.[18] A number of British periodicals agree with this assessment. None shows greater acuity than the *Literary Gazette*, whose issue for 27 December 1823 is the first to alert Britain to whispers of a German Scott, albeit under the mistaken impression that the text must be a preemptive *soi-disant* translation of *St Ronan's Well*; a story masquerading as a forthcoming novel that reproduces only such plot points as had already been rumoured, granted a new title so as to confound bothersome questions. In an appended note to its review of Scott's *St Ronan*, the *Gazette* offers a few details of the interloper's plot, suggesting that the German writer must have learnt that Scott's next novel was to risk a new approach in setting itself in the nineteenth century, a period he had not risked before.[19] This, as the *Gazette* indicates, is as far as the similarities go:

> it is a curiosity of literature that a pseudo-translation of this novel reached London before the original. It is entitled *Walladmor* and published by Herbig,

Berlin. The first chapter is an account of the explosion and wreck of the Steam-packet Halcyon, off Bristol; and details with some attempt at effect, the struggles of two of the passengers in endeavouring to save their lives on the same cask! The whole is indeed a Tale of a Tub.[20]

While its accusations are misdirected, in naming *Walladmor* a pseudo-translation, the *Gazette* has hit on *le mot juste*.[21] The German oddity, it soon becomes apparent, is an original creation that frames itself as a derivation. What appeared a free translation has turned out to be entirely free; a self-conscious masque, performed by an author whose real name is determined, after further sleuthing, to hide under a double pseudonym: W... s is Willibald Alexis is Georg Wilhelm Heinrich Häring.[22] This qualification does much to clear up the practical matters of classification and attribution, but *Walladmor* is far from exhausted. Periodicals continue to contemplate this strange novel; only now they struggle to explain not the *mode* of its existence, but the *motives* for its decision to disguise itself. In addition to the economic motives to which most critics default, another line of interpretation lies open to those better acquainted with the conceit. The classical theory of the mode, based on its popularity amongst eighteenth-century *philosophes*,[23] holds that pseudo-translation is a framing device used to disclaim culpability for contents and forms that might otherwise meet with a hostile reception. The 'fictitious translation', Gideon Toury therefore argues, attempts to

> put the cultural gatekeepers to sleep by presenting a text as if it were translated, thus lowering the threshold of resistance to the novelties it may hold in store and enhancing their acceptability, along with that of the text incorporating them as a whole.[24]

Alexis's exercises in mimicry might thus be explained away through the same mechanisms that account for the profusion of pseudo-English Gothic romances in nineteenth-nineteenth Russia; that is,

> in order not to be rejected [...], the texts [...] had to draw their authority from an external tradition, and a very particular one at that [...] Many of those were 'novels by Ann Radcliffe', who was at that time regarded in Russia as the epitome of the genre.[25]

It is clear that *Walladmor* is designed for commercial success, if only because it has a second print run as early as 1825 and sparks translations into Dutch, Swedish, Polish, English and French. And it is also apparent that Alexis desires to found a homegrown tradition of historical writing: even now, he continues to be regarded as 'a pioneer in the composition of the real historical novel in Germany'.[26] Yet neither of these perspectives can explain why the novel so energetically exploits the mode of pseudo-translation. While this text appears to have been created in imitation of Scott, either to reap the monetary or the literary dividends from this association, it also appears intent on achieving far more. *Walladmor* may have 'Scott down to a T – his plotting, his characters, his excursuses, even his mottos',[27] so much so that 'critics have seen it abound in *Waverley* topoi',[28] but it exhibits much greater ambitions. Recognising the novel's breadth of vision, the *Eclectic Review* opens its assessment by lamenting the predictability of novels in the Scotch mould, reflecting this one specimen may well outdo them all:

> The astonishing popularity and well-earned success of the class of fictions called [. . .] 'the Scottish novels' [. . .] are rare singularities in the history of our light literature. [. . .] The school is completely fixed, the taste universally diffused. [. . .] during the intervals of the parturient throes of the great Northern romance-writer, we must put up with the feebler products of the imitators who, with more or less grace, wear his livery, and study, as in a sort of literary high life below stairs, the air, the attitudes, and the manners of their master. [. . .] We spoke slightingly of the imitators of the Waverley novels; but, in this tribe, we will not class several specimens of the school which have recently attained the highest ranks of that secondary merit. [. . .] We scarcely know whether the Writer of Walladmor can be legitimately ranked amongst the imitators of the Waverley school. The plan and sketch bear evident traces of resemblance, but, in the filling up of his outline, he is original and inventive, far beyond the aspirings of an intentional copyist. [. . .] Walladmor appears to have been, at first, devised as a playful piece of waggery upon the Scottish novels.[29]

The *Eclectic*'s anonymous critic delivers a verdict often applied to texts that resist categorisation: he classes *Walladmor* as a parody; a humorous text dependent upon a set of accepted genre conventions. There is certainly much entertainment to be found in the critical befuddlement sparked by Alexis's brazen exploitation of Scott's pseudonymity. But *Walladmor* also does more: this is a text that incessantly thematises its status as a pseudo-translated novel. It is for this reason that this text, almost alone amongst the torrent of masked novels that appear from the eighteenth century forward, whips up such critical attention even to the present day.[30] Alexis has created a text whose analysis is pursued as a proxy for the legal, literary and philosophical questions sparked by that broad group of texts which live in a state of anonymity, derivativeness and translation: *Walladmor*, in short, operates as a proxy for what Russett has demonstrated amounts to a broad tradition of texts whose mode integrally involves the complication and obfuscation of notions of identity and authenticity.[31]

Much as Scott does for his own novels, Alexis lays the foundations for his book's reputation as 'the most daring, and in literary terms, the most interesting'[32] of the ersatz-Radcliffes and quasi-Scotts by designing an involved apparatus of paratexts. The first volume hints at the games to come: the novel opens on a prolonged dedication 'by one of his quietest worshipers' to an entirely fictitious Sir James Barnesley of Ellesmere, whom pseudo-Scott thanks for hosting him during a tour of Wales in which he collected the 'images and thoughts' that inspired the present novel. This inscription is followed by a foreword which tantalisingly defers any declaration of the novel's authorship to its last paragraph, in which the pretended translator briefly steps forward, and the text finally categorises itself a translation. In addition to pseudo-clarifying the text's attribution, the preface serves to situate the epithet *free* under which it has chosen to travel by defending it as a show of humility; a self-conscious signal that the translation may regrettably not be fully accurate. This remark naturally leads into a brief meditation on the mystery of the novel's origination, which is flagged only to be dismissed until the *Walladmor* edifice has been completed:

> The public will be informed only when the work has been completed of the reasons why we are able to have the novel *Walladmor* appear in German garments before it has presumably left the Edinburgh presses, perhaps even before it has appeared in Paris. I call this translation *free* in order to escape the requirements of the strict school of translation, and I pray you will excuse the printing errors that have resulted from the distance from the original place of publication.[33]

When Alexis learns of the critical ferment that his first volume is starting to attract, he jumps at every opportunity to confound the public further. The third instalment of *Walladmor* opens with another aberrant dedication, which names a third player in the novel's genesis. The first volume's dedication 'to James Barnesley, Baronet, by one his quietest worshipers, the author' transforms into a translator's recommendation of his latest work to 'Walter Scott, Baronet'. In the new foreword that follows this highly unconventional gesture, the pseudo-translator assumes the speaking part previously granted to the pseudo-author. His name still half-suppressed, W... s argues that the novel's unusual opening is another sign of its freedom. The latter term, still nominally attached as a modifier to *translation*, increasingly appears to designate a process of concealed takeover:

> it may be unusual, but not entirely unheard of, that a translator would dedicate his translation to the author of the original, and since he flatters himself that the present translation is not an ordinary one, the translator of Walladmor has taken this unusual freedom.[34]

Alexis extends his manoeuvring beyond the confines of his creation. He anonymously publishes his very own review of *Walladmor*, which he combines with a mock-assessment of the genuine *St Ronan's Well*, quoting passages from his own work in illustration of Scott's poetics.[35] He also issues an open letter in defence of his book's authenticity, headed 'To Some Weak Souls: A Letter by the Translator of Walladmor'[36] and, in the chapter of his memoirs that details his Scottish exploits, recalls sending a note to one critic who had proclaimed *Walladmor* an imposture, warning him that 'the thing could take a turn he could not yet foresee, which would have his shots rebound on himself'. The critic in question promptly retracts his previous judgement. 'Does it occur often that a reviewer of his own free will has it printed that "I made a mistake"', Alexis asks with relish, since

> [t]his one did just that: with noble candour he reversed his whole review, and [. . .] heaped on what he had previously denounced as a talented deception an amount of praise that exceeded my own estimations.[37]

Feeling his pseudo-ploy still has not exhausted its staying power, Alexis risks a second set of Scotch novels in 1827, *Schloß Avalon: Frei nach dem Englischen des Walter Scott vom Übersetzer des Walladmor*,[38] and plans another publication that prolongs his investigations of the trope of translation, published in outline as *The Strange Adventure of a German Traveller in England: A Critical Novella by the Translator of Walladmor*.[39] In short, Alexis extends and expands the games of identity and authorship previously pursued by the Great Unknown by transposing them into the mode of translation.

Not only does W... s, or Alexis or Häring, position his creation through elaborate paratextual gestures; he actively carries his peripheral mischief into his narrative: subtly at first; overtly before long. In its first instalment, the novel still seems conventional enough; a serviceable but unexceptional entry into the genre of historical fiction which tells the tale of the eponymous house of Walladmor. A noble dynasty is threatened with extinction when its last scion, one Sir Morgan, has his heirs misplaced; after sundry adventures, the Walladmors are restored to glory when Morgan's twin sons prodigally return in adulthood. The action takes place in Wales in the early 1820s, albeit a version of Wales, as the book's British readers are quick to note, beset with an array of 'vagaries'.[40] Walladmorian Wales is characterised by inaccurate geography, bewildering local customs and unorthodox spellings. While reviewers take some exception to such infelicities, they are generally happy to overlook them. '[T]he case of a man's swimming on his back from Bristol to the Isle of Anglesea' may be 'more than the most indulgent public could bear'; all in all, however, such 'topographical sins dwindle into peccadilloes in a romance'.[41] These errant signals gather into a more urgent case for critical reconsideration when *Walladmor* advances into its second and third volumes: both these instalments exploit the potential for metafiction by developing its cast of characters into personifications of the structures of duplication and substitution that subtend Alexis's pseudo-translational methods. One of Sir Morgan's heirs, rechristened Bertram by his adoptive nation, ends up a citizen of Germany; the other son remains in Wales, where he has been renamed James Niklas or Nichols, the orthography of his surname changing according to no apparent principle. Bertram is an aspiring author, come to Wales to gather cultural and historical material for a historical novel. James, by contrast, has been adopted by a local band of pirates, and is now the leader of the book's playbill of smugglers, beachcombers and thieves. While these two vocations may appear as unrelated as the nations of Germany and Britain (or Wales), *Walladmor* implies that they are different expressions of the same underlying structures. Bertram and James are twins, identical ones at that, and both have been banished to the periphery, to a place outwith the borders which established English society has drawn for itself. The two characters' kinship grows even more suggestive when their estranged father enters the plot. Sir Morgan has chosen for his own career the magistracy; a line of work whose essence it is to oppose James's nefarious plans. Given the siblings' physical similarity, moreover, Bertram finds himself the target of his father's policing of the borders between the real and the fake. Sir Morgan is not aware that he is pursuing his own offspring, and he is even less cognisant of his confusion of Bertram for James. This ignorance is mirrored by his sons, who inexplicably fail to deduce their shared parentage from the striking resemblance between themselves or their father. The Walladmor genealogy is obscure to those involved in the fiction, then, but its implications are plain enough: novelists, pirates and officials perform their duties in very different spheres, but are all engaged in organising forms of circulation between and within communities which interface and collide with one another. Sir Morgan may have the facts wrong when he hauls Bertram into court, but his legal intuitions are sound: his German-British son is engaged in plans that approach very nearly to his Welsh son's illicit dealings. The former, after all, has his sights on a novel in the vein of *Waverley*, and his journey to Wales has been undertaken to export marketable figures and adventures before the Great Unknown gets to them. James and Bertram make for a double figuration of non-traditional, peripheral forms of circulation, allegorising how these parasitise upon traditional channels, embodied in their turn by an envious progenitor.

Eager to up its suggestiveness even further, the novel's third instalment invests a previously marginal character with extraordinary metafictional resonance. Enter Thomas Malburne, a mysterious personage whose wiles so baffle the novel's other characters that they devise a range of extraordinary hypotheses regarding his identity. He dogs Bertram for reasons that initially remain unclear, repeatedly intruding into his life with jarring suddenness. As the novel hurtles to its conclusion, he grows ever more invasive, at one point even transgressing into Bertram's dreams:

> Last night I dreamt that I was walking by the lake. He suddenly stood behind me and pushed me, saying these words: Here I must walk, as I am a rightful descendant [*Hier muß ich spazieren, denn ich ben vollbürtig*]! I fell off the cliff, and I awoke. [...] It seems to me that he is an evil demon, patiently watching each of my deeds in order to serve as my prosecutor to some secret tribunal. But at other times I am tormented by a fear that he is no grim demon, but a spirit of truth, come to teach me about the nature of lies and deception.

In this proleptic passage, Malburne trespasses into an intercalated story, a lower-level fiction embedded within the larger narrative. Having arrived there, he promptly rewrites a picturesque dreamscape into a vignette that allegorises the moral and legal stakes of authenticity. Malburne sits in judgement of Bertram's pretensions to the authorship of his own dream; finding the latter wanting, the former summarily ejects the latter from the fiction he had been constructing, brusquely appropriating the dreamlike tale. Before long, the novel's overarching narrative concludes in similar fashion: Malburne reveals to Bertram the truth of his parentage in exchange for the latter's promise that he will cede the copyright to the historical novel he was planning to compose. This transfer wraps up both the plot of *Walladmor* and the questions that surround its origins. In the dream episode, the only motivation that Malburne volunteers for his assumption of authority is his *Vollbürtigkeit* – the fact, that is, he is a full relative of Bertram's. While intractable to the nonplussed Bertram, to readers awake to the controversies swirling around the book he is presently perusing, Malburne's coded language renders him a privileged character, possessed of a consciousness that propels him beyond the confines of the plot. While he announces this status in the language of familial connection used throughout the novel to allegorise the interactions of various spheres of the literary system, he operates to a filiation that relates to the genesis not of the fictive house of Walladmor, but of the fiction of *Walladmor* as such. It is not the surface story of the fall and rise of a Welsh family that properly constitutes the drama of this novel, then: the crux of its plot is located outside its fictional world, in its readers' grasping attempts at defining this strange artefact and the poetics of translative writing that it represents.

The final moments of *Walladmor* fully push forward its metafictional design. Having suffered one bewilderment too many at the hands of Malburne, and inspired by a brief meditation on the importance of literary authenticity, the aspiring historical novelist orders his pursuer to disclose his identity, demanding, as he puts it, to hear 'the voice of truth'. Undeterred by Malburne's protest that fame rather than truth ought to be the purpose of literary endeavours, Bertram keeps pressing. His interlocutor finally confesses his constant intrusions proceed from a desire to head off Bertram's exportation of romantic materials to Germany. Malburne confesses that has learnt of the latter's plan 'to collect materials for a novel in the style of those [books] published in Edinburgh, which people generally, if completely falsely, attribute to Walter Scott'. He is even aware that Bertram has covertly been composing poems and short dialogues during his sojourn in Wales in preparation for this massive transfer. On the edge of a discovery so momentous that he finds himself dumbstruck, Bertram again asks Malburne to disclose his true identity:

> Sir! who are you? [...]
> I am the author of Waverley.
> Bertram jumped back, as though he had been struck by the most terrible electrical shock, and, finding his courage himself only after several minutes had passed, again approached the other man, and, as if carefully testing whether he could be trusted, he stammered in tones bespeaking great doubt – of Guy Mannering, The Antiquary, Rob Roy, The Tales of My Landlord? –
> Showing no signs of perturbation, the stranger continued when Bertram faltered:
> And also of Ivanhoe, The Monastery, The Abbot, The Pirate, The Fortunes of Nigel, Peveril of the Peak, Quentin Durward, and so on.
> So you are not a mystical person after all.
> I eat roast beef and drink port.*
> Whatever the case may be, my good sir, who I am unable to name, but to whose famous name I owe respect, I do hope that by 'and so on' you do mean yet another novel, which I have already fragmentarily written down, as these documents will prove.
> * Kindest reviewer! Surely you will not spoil this remarkable discovery to the reader in your review. – *Translator's note.*[42]

Thomas Malburne is revealed to be Walter Scott. Or rather, he is revealed to be the Great Unknown, the persona that Scott assumes when he writes himself into his fictions, or when others refer to him in this official capacity. A duel for authorial precedence ensues in the wake of this auto-decryption, in which Bertram and Malburne quote to one another passages from the preceding narrative of *Walladmor* in order to prove their authorial primacy. In his *Memoirs*, Alexis claims that his *Walladmor* was always intended to crescendo in this scene: when he summarises the story, he ignores the prodigal plot, highlighting the fraught interaction of Bertram and Malburne and its climax in close combat. 'Two people were to be involved in all sorts of complicated, highly Romantic events, a young German and a mystical Briton', he writes:

> Both appear as collectors. The former sets out to collect material for an English novel in the manner of Scott, and keeps on stumbling into a stranger, who gets in his way because he wants the same thing, until at the end it turns out that it is the Great Unknown [*der große Unbekannte*] himself. Now it was all about the question whether the little unknown has the same rights to work [this material] as the Great Unknown.[43]

Just as Malburne substitutes for the Great Unknown (that is, for the cover under which Scott travels when he enters into literature), Bertram may be read as a replacement for Alexis (that is, for the nom de plume adopted by Häring). These thrice two characters meet in a highly meta-fictionalised version of Wales, reimagined as the geographical correlate of a text bedevilled by questions of mediation and authority. Just as the battle for ownership is ultimately decided in Malburne's favour, so must Alexis *qua* pseudo-translator cede priority to Scott when his novel's plot is unravelled. And just as Malburne *annex* Scott cannot be pinned down by the narrative, so, too, does Alexis *casu quo* Bertram refuse textual circumscription, appending to the scene of battle a footnote in which he recovers from an ostensible defeat by addressing potential reviewers.

Bertram's multi-personal encounter with Malburne caps off the many-layered experiment that is *Walladmor*. More importantly, the scene also showcases the tools Alexis employs to construct translation into a literary mode. This effort hinges on the creation of a textual space in which oppositional pairs – Scotland and Germany, original and copy, and so on – are played off against each other, with translation emerging as the logic that connects two apparently incommensurate items into a productive dialogue. Moreover, Alexis cultivates translation not as an auxiliary, but as end in itself, instinct with its own tropological and aesthetic potential. In featuring as the plot's deciding event Malburne's assertion of authorial priority, the novel makes visible the double bind of its programme for a poetics of translation: translation yearns to shed its secondariness, but always finds itself forcibly reinscribed into that position.

In designing his book to be visibly and irreducibly in translation, Alexis is out to improve on his inspiration: in cultivating translation, he contributes considerably to the Romantic model of fiction as it was developed by Scott. While there are precedents in Scott for transgressive characters, obtrusive narrators and obfuscated authors, they typically remain restricted to the paratextual level; to prefatory matter and curated public interventions. It is, as Burwick argues, 'quite another' matter for the Great Unknown 'suddenly to intrude upon the narrative and confront the hero in the midst of action'. One way to frame this fresh spin on a familiar method is to argue that Alexis, notwithstanding the Scott-like overlay in which he veils his experiments, is here acting on a peculiarly German interest in 'the processes of engendering and disrupting illusion', as opposed to a British preoccupation with 'the limits and deceptions of language'.[44] This renationalising reading collides with key aspects of Scott's conception of historical writing, however. As Ann Rigney observes, Scott is highly attentive to questions of 'hybridity', and while he specifies that hybridity primarily as a play between 'fact and invention',[45] it also propels his writing towards a 'novelistic practice [. . .] that constantly produces its own theoretical reflection' on such issues as writing, authorship and narrativity.[46] This suggests that Alexis's difference from Scott is one of degree: in being mediated through a German filter, Scott's ironies grow into more radical shapes; into an out-Scotting of Scott: *Walladmor* ambitions to effect the consummation of what is only half-gleaned in, for instance, the 'Prefatory Letter' that opens *Peveril of the Peak* or the 'Introduction' that sets the stage for *The Bride of Lammermoor*. As Alexis sees it, Scott could never have achieved this culmination on his own, since the extension of his ironic method into the texture of the novel is premised on an act of translation. In the model of creative translation that Alexis here proposes, then, the Scotch novel must be made German before it can be fully Scottish, just as Scott must be remade into Alexis before he can truly tap into his own potential. As De Quincey appropriates this logic, he will extend this argument, noting that Alexis, too, requires repatriation in order to grow into himself.

## And Now Freely Translated from the German

Having caught wind of the prodigiously suggestive *Walladmor*, De Quincey eagerly seeks access to the novel. When in September 1824 he learns that Scott has ordered a copy from Berlin, he writes to James Augustus Hessey, one half of the Taylor and Hessey duo who manage the *London Magazine*, to request his support in soliciting the book from its British importer. 'We *must* have "Walladmor" (that is yᵉ name in the Leipzig Catal.) if Heaven or Earth can get it', he impresses on Hessey, promising to furnish '[a]n abstract of the novel', which ought to be 'of universal interest from the circumstances' of the curious case. The bookseller obliges, but allows De Quincey no more than '24 hours [. . .] within 36 hours of receiving it at most'.⁴⁷ Enthused by the potential of *Walladmor*, the latter manages to resist the temptations of procrastination that so often thwart his projects: the *London* for the following month duly features a full review of *Walladmor*. The article is in the standard style of the time: it is an assemblage of quotes loosely jointed by commentary, the former 'translate[d] not merely *from* the German – but also *into* English, a part of their task which translators are apt to forget'.

De Quincey's review wastes no time in pronouncing on the nature of the text under investigation. '"*Freely* translated!"', he exclaims by way of opening; '[y]es, no want of freedom! All free and easy!' While he proceeds to provide a detailed précis of the narrative, 'mounted [. . .] *en croupe* behind the novelist in character of translator', he refuses to judge the novel on the merits of its surface narrative, instead focusing on its deeper drama. Admittedly, there is 'great life and stir in the movement of the story', and there is also 'much dramatic skill in devising situations; and an interest given to some of the characters'. In this one historical novel, however, such accomplishments count for little. The true centre of gravity, De Quincey intimates, is to be found in the polemic excited by the book's paratextual apparatus. In order to explain the genesis of *Walladmor*, the review initially appears to subscribe to the commercial conspiracies conjectured by most other critics. An unnamed cabal of German booksellers, united by a common desire for stable bottom lines, 'had come to an agreement, one and all, that Sir Walter Scott was rather tardy in his movements'. Since 'at all events there must be a Scotch novel against the Leipsic fair', they resolved to fabricate one. While the preferred product is 'the genuine foreign article', an alternative might be found in 'a *home* manufacture brought as near in strength and colour as "circumstances" would permit. A true Scotch novel, if possible: if not, a capital hoax!' Another popular scenario to explain the book's publication is also touched upon, padded with further imagined details to enhance its implications. Obliquely referencing the story of piracy signalled by Lockhart and courted by Alexis's ambiguous introduction to the first volume, De Quincey remarks that if Scott really had written *Walladmor* only to have its proofs stolen, this would have entailed the publication of a copy before its original. Translating the stand-off of Bertram and Malburne into print-cultural terms, he vividly imagines a sequence of increasingly elaborate manoeuvres as original and translation face off in the international book market, finally amounting to the construction of a chiastic architecture in which languages and versions incessantly swap places:

> Through some quarter or other it was said that a duplicate of every proof sheet, as it issued from the Edinburgh press, was forwarded to a sea-port town on the continent, and there translated into German. Now it was the design of the pirates to put this German translation into another conspirator's hands who was to translate it into good English: he was ready to swear (and truly) that he had nothing to do with piratical practices upon English books; for that he had translated from a known and producible German book. The German book was in regard to him the authentic archetype. [. . .] To keep up the ball, an opposition party in London designed to carry on the series of reverberations by translating the pirated English translation back again into excellent German, and launching this decomplex pirate in the German market against her own grandmother the old original pirate. Accidents favouring, and supposing the wind to be against Mr. Constable (who of course sends the copies for London by sea), – it was conceived possible that a German daughter, an English grand-daughter, and a German great-grand-daughter might all be abroad in London before the Edinburgh mother arrived; who would thus have found herself an old woman on reaching Mrs Hursts' and Co., and blessed with several generations of flourishing posterity before she was fully aware of her own existence.[48]

Given De Quincey's evident appreciation for Alexis's daring experiment, it is remarkable that he offers such a reactionary reading of the novel's narrative, expressing particular disagreement with the character upon whom turn the book's metafictional gestures. 'We are extravagantly fond of sport', he writes in the tones of a thoroughly humourless person: 'many a time have we risked our character as philosophers by the exorbitance of our thirst after "fun."' But Malburne is a different matter. Citing at some length the revelatory conversation between Bertram and Malburne at the end of the book, he sternly observes that such scenes may be 'part of the general hoax', but verge on slander insofar as they indirectly accuse Scott of the literary crimes that De Quincey would go on to accuse Coleridge of. When Malburne is seen to intrude on private affairs and scuttles off with Bertram's proto-plot, this is carrying the joke too far. Alexis 'ought to apologise to Sir Walter Scott by expelling the part [of Malburne] from his next edition',[49] lest a well-meaning British reader take it upon himself to defend Scott's honour. 'I don't know but some of us will be making reprisals', he adds.[50]

De Quincey soon takes charge of the British counter-offensive against Alexis's skullduggery. Noting the interest in *Walladmor*, Taylor and Hessey commission its reviewer to translate the novel into English: the resulting book is anonymously published in 1825, under the parodic title *Walladmor: Freely Translated from the German into English and Now Freely Translated from the German into English*. This curious book, too, triggers some perplexity among its reviewers. At this point, the infamy of *Walladmor* is such, however, that this bafflement appears at least partly performative. In many accounts, De Quincey comes to inhabit a function akin to Alexis's: shielded by anonymity, he is presumed to be a character in the masque designed by the Great Unknown. Some readers genuinely appear at a loss, with some presuming the prodigal emergence of a British *Walladmor* must attest to the novel's coveted parentage: De Quincey's *Walladmor*, that is, is taken to be Scott's original prior to its abduction. Others allege that even if the work does not originate from Abbotsford, at least it must boast some as yet mysterious British derivation. The *Newcastle Magazine* hedges its bets by arguing that a work of this quality could not but have been originally composed by a native artist. *Walladmor* is clearly the rightful progeny of Scott, or at most of a creator once removed:

> There is nothing in the style to prevent it – the scenery is in some parts as well described as the Great Unknown could have described it – there are a few inconsistencies from carelessness, too, which do not diminish the probability of the case. There is only one thing a little against this supposition. The characters are not so elaborately wrought up as in the authenticated works. But this may be thus accounted for. The original Walladmor may have been transmitted to Germany, translated in all its pristine ponderosity, and afterwards reduced to its present miniature proportions, in order to add a little in England to the heap of its German accumulation. At all events, Walladmor bears internal evidence of an English, or at least a British origin.[51]

Similarly balancing between hypotheses, the French version of De Quincey's translation, a triplicating modulation to De Quincey fantastic scenario of redoubled circulation, opts for an artfully ambiguous title: *Walladmor, Roman attribué en Allemagne à Walter Scott: traduit de l'anglais par M. A. J. B. Defauconpret, traducteur de la collection complète des romans historiques de Sir Walter Scott.*[52] The continuing confusion legible in these responses is all the more remarkable in that De Quincey exaggerates Alexis's stratagems, rendering the true objectives of the novel even more transparent. Not only does the English addition to the novel's subtitle mirror its German inspiration, thereby broadcasting the work's status as a parodic translation; there is also, true to the model set out by Alexis, a long prefatory advertisement, included ahead of each of the novel's volumes, in which the British translator is pained to dispel any remaining mysteries. The current work, De Quincey writes in a dry style that foregoes the imaginative enthusiasm he displays in his review, was originally produced in the German language, as a *soi disant* translation from Sir Walter Scott, to meet the demands of the last Easter fair at Leipsic. [. . .] If it happens [. . .] that an author fails to meet [the] obligations of the Leipsic fair, – obliging persons are often at hand who step forward as his proxy by forging something in his name.

Initially denouncing the German *Walladmor* as larcenous, the introduction hastens to offer an apology for organising its importation. The standard excuse of moral education by example is conspicuously absent; instead, the anonymous translator openly admits to commercial motives, in that '[a] work, produced to the German public and circulating with success under such assumptions, must naturally excite some curiosity in this country; to gratify which it has been judged proper to translate it'. A second preface, modelled on Alexis's dedication to Scott but addressed to 'W***s, the German "Translator" of Walladmor' and clearly intended for his readers' perusal rather than Alexis's, offers a second explanation. De Quincey mainly uses this second dedicatory epistle to proclaim his independence from the source text, unabashedly emphasising the egregious liberties he has taken in translating Alexis's original. 'You will be surprised', he informs pseudo-Alexis, 'that your *three* corpulent German volumes have collapsed into *two* English ones of rather consumptive appearance.' These numbers are significant: a two-volume novel is an unconventional format throughout the nineteenth century, especially for novels aspiring to the Scott imprimatur. Defauconpret, for one, is so dismayed by the diminution that he redistributes the chapters into three volumes. Demonstratively sensitive to the 'affront' Alexis or his publisher might take, the translator claims that he has reduced only to improve. 'The English climate, you see, does not agree with' many of Alexis's questionable decisions, forcing the jettisoning of so many of them that the novel has effectively been remade into something only tangentially connected to the original:

> The truth is this: on examining your ship, I found that the dry rot had got into her: she might answer the helm pretty well in your milder waters; but I was convinced that upon our stormy English seas she would founder, unless I flung overboard part of her heavy ballast, and cut away some of her middle timbers, which (I assure you) were mere touchwood. I did so; and she righted in a moment: and now, that I have driven a few new bolts into her – 'calked' here – and 'payed' her, I am in hopes she will prove sea-worthy for a voyage or so.

The preface lists several 'changes which I have been obliged to make in deference to the taste of this country'. Unproductive asides, loose threads, awkward characters, unstable diction, unmodish epigraphs – all must go. Some of these alterations proceed from a better appreciation of what is required for a good novel, like a heavily reworked chronology or a more carefully delineated plot structure; others derive from the translator's personal preferences. De Quincey takes care to signal the latter at some length, noting, amongst other defects, the overwrought sentiment which also offended him in Goethe, which prompted him to take 'the liberty, in the seventh chapter, of curing Miss Walladmor of an hysterical affection'. He also relocates many scenes, often choosing areas with which he is familiar. 'Upon Penmorfa sands I once had an interesting adventure, and I have accordingly accommodated Penmorfa'; in another case, '[t]o the little town of Machynleth [sic] I am indebted for various hospitalities: and I think they will acknowledge that they are indebted to me exclusively for [granting them in this book] a mayor and corporation'. Most of all, De Quincey's modifications target those aspects of the plot that are metafictional in effect: when he reframes *Walladmor* for British readers, Malburne is unceremoniously expunged, as is his pivotal encounter with Bertram, who now finds himself shorn of novelistic ambitions. De Quincey, in short, as he gleefully signs off his dedicatory overture is an 'obedient (but not quite faithful) TRANSLATOR': he cuts an autonomous figure, almost always favouring his own biases over those of his 'principal'.[53]

As the wayward interpreter correctly surmises, Alexis is undecided between displeasure and astonishment when he finds his work traduced. In his *Erinnerungen*, he speaks of his delight to learn he has been reviewed in Britain in an article which he even takes to be by Scott (but is really by De Quincey). And he is gratified beyond measure to find himself translated into English, the language that ranks as the most prestigious for his preferred genre, by a person whom he wrongly hypothesises to be a close friend of Scott's. However, he is deeply disappointed to be criticised for his take on Scott's involutions, and to read a text entirely denuded of key passages:

> I do not recognise my novel in the English Walladmor, because it excises what is properly mine [*mein Eigenthum darin*], the 'earnest parody', as the Swedish translator puts it. The Great Unknown does not appear, nor is Bertram a young German author who travels the world to write a novel in the style of Scott.[54]

By Alexis's standards, the current British *Walladmor* is a failure. Alexis therefore professes a continued hope for an English translation that might adequately convey both his mastery of the historical mode as well as his successes in using his mentor's principles to break new ground. It is easy to sympathise with this disappointment; to argue that De Quincey's '*very* free translation' bespeaks an inability to recognise 'those very qualities in the novel which make it readable'; those touches, that is, that deviate from the established mould of the Scott novel by overcharging its metafictional elements.⁵⁵ Thus to read the English *Walladmor* as a bowdlerisation is perhaps to take seriously De Quincey's morally and artistically conservative tone. This is further borne out by a postscript affixed to the novel's second volume, which offers the reader another 'word of explanation' in order to contextualise the decimation of the original. '[T]he reader', the translator reflects, 'will else find it difficult to understand upon what principle of translation *three* "thick set" German volumes can have shrunk into *two* English ones of somewhat meagre proportions.' As in his dedicatory preface, De Quincey posits that

> [i]n general I have proceeded as one would in transplanting a foreign opera to our stage: where the author tells the story ill – take it out of his hands, and tell it better: retouch his recitative; bring out and develop his situations.

A judicious interfusion has previously been shown to be central to De Quincey's methodology; in this one case, however, the author's errors are allegedly so many that a merciless rewriting is in order, lest the British body literary be subjected to a deleterious influence. Revisiting the image of inoculation, but restricting its meaning to the medical register, he writes of Alexis's mistakes as a stultifying force: 'translated into English, bottled, and corked up, they would furnish *virus* enough, if distributed by inoculation amongst the next three thousand novels of the English press, to ruin the constitution of them all'.

The question is whether De Quincey is entirely sincere in presenting his take on Alexis's daring inventions as reactionarily anglocentric. His translation preserves many provocative innovations, even compounding them with some paratextual trickery of the interpreter's own devising: De Quincey's postface and introductory address to Alexis mark complications not yet entertained by the German writer. The English version also compensates for its heavy-handed obliteration of metafictional decorations by introducing some new material, adding to Alexis's parodic hits some gags of its own. In the English *Walladmor*, Bertram happens to read a copy of the very book in which he features as a character; 'the *first* volume of Walladmor, a novel, 2 vols. post 8vo.; the second not being then finished'. Bertram even professes admiration for the very novel in which he is a character, naming the latter as his preferred work of fiction through an internal citation: 'his favourite volume, we understand. was in "post 8vo"'.⁵⁶ However vehemently De Quincey may object to personal satire, he is positively disposed to those aspects of his fiction in which he spies a practical method for asserting a translatorial identity and a translational poetics. Even if he notes in his concluding comments that he 'began to fear that if, in addition to a new end, I were to put a new beginning and a new middled, – I should be accused of building a second English hoax upon the primitive German hoax', this stacked architecture is precisely what he hopes to achieve, most notably in his titular and paratextual advertisements of the degrees of separation between his translation and Alexis's original.

In the final comments which De Quincey volunteers on the events surrounding *Walladmor*, contained in a subsection to his 'Autobiography of an English Opium-Eater' published in *Tait's* between 1834 and 1838, his English translation is declared 'no more a translation from the German than the German from the English'.[57] This is less an admission than it is a boast: faced with a German copy that lacks an English original, De Quincey aspires to produce an English copy that lacks a German original. A long process is required to wrest such independence from the source material. In his dedicatory letter, the infidel translator notes many further acts of translation will be required, projecting an endless series of reciprocating acts of transfer, in which two interpreters rewrite each other's texts in infinite relay. '"[M]ine dear Sare", De Quincey writes, imitating a German accent,

> could you not translate me back again into German [. . .] and then I give you my word of honour that I will again translate you into English. [. . .] Jusqu'au revoir! my dear principal: hoping that you will soon invest me with that character in relation yourself.[58]

If Alexis proclaims his freedom from Scott, De Quincey does him one better: far from rejecting Alexis's expansion of Scott's ironies, he positions the English *Walladmor* as an elaboration of the German elaboration of Scott. If Scott requires percolating through a German filter in order to bring out the extent to which his poetics secretly revolve around the problem of translation, so, too, does Alexis's intensification of Scott require a transplantation to British soil in order to come into its own. This imagination of translation is properly chiastic in that it combines horizontality with verticality; the palimpsestic with the palimpsestuous: different versions of *Walladmor* stand side by side, each competing for attention and priority, even as they constantly move to obsolete one another. De Quincey intends for this *fort* and *da* between Britain and Germany to be an endlessly reiterative figure-of-eight whose gyrations generate a reinvigorating electrification of the languages, literatures and nations caught up in its exchanges. As *Walladmor* is translated, retranslated and re-retranslated, the book continually achieves a better expression of the nature of translation, even as each new version fails to actualise its complete potentiality. Lest it be presumed that this layout hypostatises some final text that might synthesise Britishness and Teutonicity, which would entirely abrogate the dichotomy of original and copy, De Quincey impresses on his reader the fatal consequences of any such climactic fusion: 'Shocking! I abominate the omen [. . .] What, my two volumes, post 8vo. "vanish into nought?" [. . .] No, no: [. . .] The two Florimels will never meet; and the fatal result of "melting", and "vanishing into nought", will thus be obviated.'[59] The idea of translation that is revealed in the maddening circulation of *Walladmor* is not to be understood to equate to a specifiable text or principle – it is in the very motions of communication and misunderstanding, in the active performance of its actions, that it properly resides.

### Fugue: Founded on the Preceding Theme

In *Walladmor*, De Quincey detects a potent illustration of the poetics of translation he envisages; most of all, he recognises the beginnings of a counter-Kantian, thoroughly idealist project. Furthering this analogy, he uses his introductory letter to Alexis to highlight the equivalence between pseudo-Scott and an as yet hypothetical pseudo-Kant, noting both are their respective nations' most desirable pseudo-exports. 'What should you say to it in Germany', he asks of Alexis,

> if one of these days for example you were to receive a large parcel by the 'post-wagen' [mail coach] containing Posthumous Works of Mr Kant. I won't swear I shall make up such a parcel myself: and, if I should, I bet you anything you choose that I hoax the great Bavarian professor [Schelling] with a treatise on the 'Categorical Imperative' and 'The last words of Mr Kant on Transcendental Apperception.' – Look about you, therefore, my gay fellows in Germany; for, if I live you shall not have all the hoaxing to yourselves.

This may be read as an announcement of De Quincey's 'The Last Days', which is to appear two years after *Walladmor*. A more intriguing option, however, is to parse these lines as announcing a programme of German/British translation and retranslation which is to inoculate both literatures with translative models of textuality and writing. Moreover, De Quincey's philosophical profile suggests his invocation of a specifically Kantian pseudo-translation holds additional implications. Just as the German *Walladmor* pseudo-translates Scott, at once honouring his innovations and extending them, so does De Quincey use his *Walladmor* to evolve Kant. The concrete philosophical stakes of translation as they manifest in the novel's projected circulation and transformation are allegorised by the philosophical chestnut of Sir John Cutler's stockings; a homespun variation on the thought experiment of Theseus' ship which maintains its basic identity even as it is constantly repaired. Just as Sir John's footwear is continually darned and redarned by his maid, so much so that it is now materially entirely different from its first iteration, it is inherent in translation that it completely refashions the original. Even though its labour is menial and ancillary, the latter even literally so, translation baffles categorisation:

> We have a story in England, rather trite here, and a sort of philosophic common-place [...] but possibly unknown in Germany: and, as it is pertinent to the case between ourselves, I will tell it: the more so, as it involves a metaphysical question [...] Sir John Cutler had a pair of silk stockings: which stockings his housekeeper Dolly continually darned for the term of three years with worsted: at the end of which term the last faint gleam of silk had finally vanished, and Sir John's silk stockings were found in their old age absolutely to have degenerated into worsted stockings. Now upon this a question arose among the metaphysicians – whether Sir John's stockings retained (or, if not, at what precise period they lost) their 'personal identity.' [...] – Some such question, I conceive, will arise upon your account [...] Meantime, [...] could you not [...] darn me as I have darned you? [...] Darn me into two portly volumes: and then I give you my word of honour that I will again translate you into English, and darn you in such grand style that, if Dolly and Professor Kant were both to rise from the dead, Dolly should grow jealous of me – and Kant confess himself more puzzled on the matter of personal identity by the final Walladmor than ever he had been by the Cutlerian stockings.[60]

De Quincey here claims that he has achieved something extraordinary in translating Alexis; a text, that is, which is the outward manifestation of the metaphysical idea of translation. As a logical consequence of his destruction of any thoroughfare between thought and matter, Kant judged it impossible to create a hypotypotic text in which the two might come together;[61] and while Coleridge and Carlyle had conjectured translation might offer an escape, they had been unable to hit on any examples. If *Walladmor* is considered in aggregate, as a composite performance of recursive retranslations that stretches into infinity, it emerges as a text that both maintains and sublimely suspends Kant's strict dichotomisation. In complicating the boundaries between primary and derived creation, meaning and matter, and object and subject – each of which has preoccupied one of this book's three previous chapters – the translated text orchestrates a momentary melding of the categories so strictly policed by Kant, situating a lucid interval of undivided thought in the infinitesimal pause that marks the fugal transition of one extreme into another. De Quincey's inoculative concept of translation is soundly English, as soundly English as Sir John's namesake stockings, but it lacks motive power without reference to, implementation in, and re-importation from a German context: translation must itself rely on translation in order to fully understand itself. This addition of a foreign factor also changes the purport of allegory of the stockings: Dolly darns alone; De Quincey and Alexis darn in relay, each pursuing their own audience and their own objectives as they translate one another.

Conscious of the text's possibilities, De Quincey frames *Walladmor* as a demonstration of translation's potential to become a philosophical and literary mode in its own right, if one that can never hope to grow into a fully separable genre. This is most evident from his efforts to liberate translation from the reading that perhaps most clings to it – the presumption, that is, that translations originate not in visionary creation but in much lowlier motives of commercial gain, and should therefore not be taken seriously or read critically. Translation, in this perspective, is an occupation to be pursued as a career only by those authors who lack the wherewithal to produce the truly worthwhile stuff. De Quincey initially appears to present himself precisely in this character; as a luckless poet forced by unpropitious circumstances to read, review and, most ignominiously of all, translate. He pauses at length on the economic logic underlying his travails with *Walladmor*, presenting a sample of his murderous schedule. In his review, he notes that he was tasked with reading 'three volumes containing 883 pages [. . .] in 32 hours'.[62] In the retrospective account included in his 'Autobiography', he recollects that he was contractually obliged 'to keep up with the printer', even as he attempted to turn a particularly badly written original into something that might sell to the discerning British public:

> three sheets, or forty-eight pages I made sure of producing daily; at which rate, a volume would be finished in week, and three weeks might see the whole work ready for the public. Never was there such a disappointment, or such a perplexity. Not until the printing had actually commenced, with arrangements for keeping several compositors at work, did I come to understand the hopeless task I had undertaken. Such rubbish [. . .] no eye has ever beheld as 950, to say the very least, of these thousand pages. [. . .] I thought it better to pursue the task; mending and retouching wherever that was possible; but far more frequently forging new materials [. . .] There were absurdities in the very conduct of the story and the developement of the plot, which could not always be removed without more time than the press allowed me; for I kept the press moving, though slowly – namely, at the rate of half-a-sheet (eight pages) a day. In some instances, I let the incidents stand, and contented myself with rewriting every word of the ridiculous narration, and the still more ridiculous dialogues.[63]

Having advertised his interventions, De Quincey moves to quash any misconstrual of such interventions as proof of creative liberty. Instead, he stresses his subservience to the pace of the press and the whims of editors, both of which enforce a strict regimen of timely contributions.

It is doubtful that he kept to this scheme as conscientiously as he suggests, but such realities matter little: this is an author out to reduce himself to a clerk. De Quincey's preface to *Walladmor* does much the same for Alexis, behind whom his translator conjectures a sweatshop of writers engaged in manufacturing deceptive produce in a division of labour in which each author is assigned his own set of duties. This set-up would explain the patchwork style of the novel, in which long expostulations on genealogy and astronomy alternate with swashbuckling action. Failing sufficient 'time for the quickest hoaxers to compose three volumes before the Leipsic Fair', a studio of hacks provided a solution:

> two men must do what one could not. [. . .] This I conceive to have been the pleasant arrangement upon which 'Walladmor' was worked so as to fetch up the ground before the fair began; and thus ingeniously were two men's labours dovetailed into one novel: 'aliter non fit, Avite, liber'.[64]

Scott activates much the same industrial hypothesis in his second recorded reaction to his German double. In his 1825 novel *The Betrothed*, he includes by way of prologue the fictitious minutes of 'a general meeting of the shareholders designing to form a joint-stock company, united for the purpose of writing and publishing the class of works called the Waverley novels'.[65] The entrepreneurs resolve to orchestrate the total commodification of historical romance by investing in 'a little mechanism' designed according to the insights of 'the immortal Adam Smith, concerning the division of labour'. A loom is commissioned, adapted to the weaving of historical fiction from the conventions that Scott's imitators rely upon to compose plausible surrogates. Much as an engine can be built 'where they put in raw hemp at one end, and take out ruffled shirts at the the other', a jenny might be conceived that will save 'some part of the labour of composing these novels [. . .] by the use of steam' and from a stock of raw clichés:

> It is to be premised that this mechanical operation can apply only to those parts of the narrative which are at present composed out of commonplaces, such as the love-speeches of the hero, the description of the heroine's person, the moral observations of all sorts, and the distraction of happiness at the conclusion of the piece. [. . .] by placing the words and phrases technically employed on these subjects in a sort of framework [. . .] and changing them by such a mechanical process as that by which weavers of damask alter their patterns, many new and happy combinations cannot fail to occur, while the author, tired of pumping his own brains, may have an agreeable relaxation in the use of his fingers.

A test case for the mechanisation of literature is already abroad. Consider as an example, one capitalist urges, a recent pseudo-Scott published in

Germany, titled *Walladmor*. It is evident, the financier argues, that this book has been fabricated in obeisance to the forces of the market; a 'Romance, by the Author of Waverley, having been at that time expected [. . .] but finding that none such appeared.' It is also clear that the book's compositors must have used a 'steam engine' or some such contrivance: the assembly agree that the German confection is of subpar quality, and are joined in this harsh valuation by the quasi-anonymous author who voices similar judgement in a footnote ('there are good things in Walladmor, I assure you, had the writer known any thing about the country in which he laid the scene'). Dispiritingly for authors bent on painstakingly crafting a superior book, however, the investors note that the work's embarrassing errors have in no way reduced its marketability, least of all amongst its intended non-British readership, 'where folks are no better judges of Welsh manners than of Welsh crw'. The implication is evident: the Great Unknown, a true Scotsman who enjoys the added benefit of non-mechanisation, is certain to create a far superior text, if one that is slower in its production. And yet Scott is also happy to diminish his authorship by equating his work with its manufactured counterparts, noting that even *The Betrothed* 'will scarce meet the approbation of the Cymmerodion' due to its culpable lack of historical research and uncertain grasp of local colour.[66] Scott, then, uses *Walladmor* in the same manner as Alexis or De Quincey, albeit to different ends: if Alexis designs the text as an intensified take on Scott, and De Quincey draws on it to explode problems inherent in Kantian philosophy, Scott primarily reads *Walladmor* as a dramatisation of a conflict between aesthetic and commercial discourses that increasingly troubles Romantic writing – *Walladmor* is as a composite text, inviting a range of performative interpretations.

Far from defending his work against accusations of commercialism and anti-aestheticism, Alexis encourages them, openly doubting the aesthetic merit of his exertions. The prefatory dedication to Scott with which Alexis opens his third volume, translated in full by De Quincey, presents the novel as a product of the harsh regime of mechanical reproduction under which translators must now toil. Alexis portrays himself as a labourer, obligated to produce material at breakneck speed for fear of being replaced. The operative terms in translation are not quality, fidelity or creativity, but 'haste' and competition: enslaved by the developing industrial apparatus, the fate of the modern translator is a 'melancholy affair'.[67] Alexis, quoted here in De Quincey's translation, laments at length his duty to sate a manic market, which necessitates the production of subpar material:

Ah Sir Walter! – did you but know to what straits the poor German translator of Walter-Scottish novels is reduced, you would pardon greater liberties than this. *Ecoutez*. First of all, comes the bookseller and cheapens a translator, in the very cheapest market of translation-jobbers that can be supposed likely to do any justice to the work. [. . .] You see, Sir Walter, into what 'sloughs of despond' we German translators fall with the sad necessity of dragging your honour after us. Yet this is but a part of the general woe. When you hear in every bookseller's shop throughout Germany one unanimous complaint [. . .] [on] diminished sale on the one hand; and on the other hand the forestalling spirit of competition among the translation-jobbers, bidding over each other's heads as at an auction, where the translation is knocked down to him that will contract for bringing his wares soonest to market; – hearing all this, Sir Walter, you will perceive that our old German proverb '*Eile mit Weile*' (i.e. Festina lente, or *the more haste, the less speed*) must in this case, where haste happens to be the one great qualification and *sine-quâ-non* of a translator, be thrown altogether into the shade by that other proverb – 'Wer zuerst kommt mahlt zuerst' (*First come first served*). I for my part, that I might not lie so wholly at the mercy of this tyrant Haste, struck out a fresh path – in which you, Sir, were so obliging as to assist me.[68]

As he seeks to pseudo-exculpate his work for its pseudo-errors of translation by pointing to the extortionate conditions under which they both pseudo-labour, Alexis and De Quincey offer an important gloss on their titular invocations of freedom. If the novel's translators are to be believed, *Walladmor* announces itself as *frei* and as twice *free* not because it proudly seeks to claim independence or originality, but because it seeks to flag its guilty awareness that it has been unable to fulfil the brief of fidelity from which translations derive what little respectability they have.

The predicament faced by Alexis, De Quincey and Scott revolves around the apparent conflict between, on the one hand, the wide circulation required of a text if it is truly to reinvigorate the nation and, on the other, the fatal influence of the commercial processes required for such a wide circulation. The solution as Alexis and Scott half-glean it, and De Quincey expands it, is to submit oneself to the very logic one seeks to resist. In order to push back against the pressures of industry and thereby assert the literary, stylistic and philosophical potential of translation, the preconceptions that operate against it are to be challenged from the inside by creating a text that appears tailored to the demands of the market even as it defies those demands, piggybacking on commercial processes to broadcast a novel poetics to as wide a readership as possible. The advantage of translation, Alexis muses, is that it bears material traces of its being caught in the processes of mechanistic commercialisation: it abounds in errors; those same lapses and mistakes that ostensibly lead to the *frei* epithet. '[T]he sheets, dripping wet as they arrive by every post from the Edinburgh press', Alexis writes *via* De Quincey,

> must be translated just as they stand with or without sense or connexion. Nay it happens not unfrequently that, if a sheet should chance to end with one or two syllables of an unfinished word, we are obliged to translate this first instalment of a future meaning; and, by the time the next sheet arrives with the syllables in arrear, we first learn into what confounded scrapes we have fallen by guessing and translating at hap-hazard.

Much may grow from errors of translation. The word *Smith-*, for instance, might reasonably be expected by a translator to refer to a blacksmith, a *Schmiedemeister*. This *Smith-* may also morph into *Smithfield matches*, however; that is, marriages of convenience. Too pressed for time to ponder the subtleties of English capitals and hyphens, Alexis translates into being a blacksmith wholly absent from the original, who promptly grants the protagonist a rustic backstory of which readers of the original will remain wholly unaware. The blacksmith is an evident error, but he is not any kind of error: the *Schmiedemeister* could *only* show up in translation, where he figures as an emergent event; as an accidental half-presence, generated when the commercialised, unbalanced, non-aesthetic circulation of literature is left to pursue its totalising imperatives. The smith is a creature indicative of the pressures of industry, but he is also a creature disruptive of those pressures: he disturbs the assumed continuity between original and copy on which imitations and translations rely for their marketability – in effect, the smith is a creature of pure translation. As more such contingent smiths come to occupy the text and distort it into a very different document, the translation achieves a measure of creative separation from the demands of the market. In his translation of *Walladmor*, De Quincey consequently devotes considerable attention to this anecdote: it is the single instance he chooses to expand rather than compress, adding for dramatic effect that 'the translated sheet had been already printed off, with the blacksmith in it (lord confound him!); and the blacksmith is there to this day, and cannot be ejected'.[69] Drawing on the etymologisation of text as textile, he adds in postscript that '[i]t is a most delicate operation to take work out of another man's loom, and put work in: joinings and sutures will sometimes appear; colours will not always match'. It is this felicitous defect, this arresting gap between original and copy, that translation enshrines, and that Romantic translations like *Walladmor* exploit to define their project for a reinvigorated and reinvigorating text. The *Walladmor* affair has only begun to assert this ghost in the machine, but with every translation, it asserts its presence, and with every retranslation, it grows in force. Even a commodity like *Walladmor* can conjure up a dark interpreter with transformative potential, much as an author as proverbially little as De Quincey can write a body of work that breathes new life into thought.

It is precisely as De Quincey gleans the pure language of translation given spectral shape in the adventitious blacksmith that he can, and must, extricate himself from his most daring experiment in translation. 'The truth is', he volunteers as a parting gift,

> [t]he truth is – I have altered; and altered until I had not the face to alter any more. The ghost of Sir John Cutler's stockings began to appear to me, and elder ghosts than that – the ghost of Sir Francis Drake's ship, the ghost of Jason's ship, and other celebrated cases of the same perplexing question: metaphysical doubts fell upon me.[70]

As translation explores those things that may be said to be unique to its modality, none of them ordinarily regarded as a solid foundation for Romantic authorship – its keen sense of the commodification of modern writing, its creation of troublesome errors, its appreciation of the stylistic and linguistic divergence within and between languages, its attempts at balancing creativity against imitation, and so on – it properly grows into its own. And as the Romantic translator redoubles his efforts, if only by conjecturing entirely theoretical options, he approaches ever more nearly to understanding and actualising a mode of existence founded on the idea of translation. This idea, as De Quincey here records, is ultimately impracticable, paralysing those few practitioners intrepid enough to spin off translation from the pragmatic structures of exchange it normally orchestrates by threatening a disintegration, or overintegration, of language. The idea of translation achieved in *Walladmor* ultimately defeats it: in the final analysis, what is at stake in De Quincey's career-long practical and theoretical explorations of translation, is a mode of metaphysics, of style, of authorship, that cannot sustain itself beyond brief gestures from which spectral intimations of undivided thought may be gleaned: the yearning for those gestures, however, is enough to animate an entire career in writing.

### Notes

1. See Norbert Bachleitner, 'A Proposal to Include Book History in Translation Studies: Illustrated with German Translations of Scott and Flaubert', *Arcadia: International Journal for Literary Studies* 44, no. 2: 420–40.
2. For a brief overview of the different translations, see Lionel H. C. Thomas, '"Walladmor": A Pseudo-Translation of Sir Walter Scott', *The Modern Language Review*, 46.2 (1951): 218–31, esp. 231, n2–4.

3. George Saintsbury, 'The Historical Novel', *Macmillan's Magazine* 70, no. 10 (1984): 19.
4. Angela Esterhammer, 'Identity Crises: Celebrity, Anonymity, Doubles, and Frauds in European Romanticism', in *The Oxford Handbook of European Romanticism*, ed. Paul Hamilton (Oxford: Oxford University Press, 2016), 782.
5. W, 4.272.
6. *Allgemeine Literatur-Zeitung* 113 (1826): 66.
7. See, respectively, *Abendzeitung Wegweiser* no. 11 (1824); and *Zeitung fur die elegante Welt* (1824), no. 176. For further details regarding the critical reaction to the novel, see Thomas, 'Walladmor', 218–31.
8. *Allgemeine Literatur-Zeitung*, 66.
9. *Westminster Review*, 3–4 (1824): 273.
10. John Gibson Lockhart, *Memoirs of the Life of Sir Walter Scott* (Edinburgh: A. & C. Black, 1851), 550. Lockhart assumes that the sheets smuggled to Germany must have been the proofs of *The Betrothed*. This is impossible: work on *The Betrothed* did not begin until June 1824, and the manuscript did not arrive at the printers until spring 1825.
11. *Allgemeine Literatur-Zeitung* (1826), no. 113: 66.
12. *The Newcastle Magazine* 4, no. 4 (1825): 169.
13. W, 4.259.
14. Walter Scott, *Familiar Letters of Sir Walter Scott* (Boston: Houghton Mifflin, 1894), 191–2.
15. *London Magazine* (1820), 2: 11, 517.
16. *The Monthly Critical Gazette from 1825* (London: Knight and Lacey, n.d.), 2.455–6.
17. *Allgemeine Literatur-Zeitung* (1826), no. 113: 66.
18. Thomas, 'Walladmor', 218.
19. While the *Gazette* is not yet aware, the decision to situate the narrative of *Walladmor* in Wales, another setting Scott had not yet attempted, may have been prompted by rumours Scott's next novel after *St Ronan* would explore that locale. *The Betrothed*, published in 1825, had been completed in manuscript by December 1824.
20. *The Literary Gazette: A Weekly Journal of Literature, Science, and the Fine Arts* (1823), no. 362: 818.
21. For definitions of pseudo-translation, see David Martens and Beatrijs Vanacker, 'Scenographies of the Pseudo-Translation I: Literary Issues of a Marginal Device', *Lettres Romanes* 67, nos. 3–4 (2013), 347–58; and Tom Toremans and Beatrijs Vanacker, 'Introduction: The Emerging Field of Pseudotranslation', *Canadian Review of Comparative Literature* 44, no. 4 (2017): 629–36.
22. For more context on this remarkable writer, see Lionel H. C. Thomas, 'The Literary Reputation of Willibald Alexis as an Historical Novelist', *The Modern Language Review* 45, no. 2 (1950): 195–214, and Lynne Tatlock, 'A Timely Demise: The Literary Reputation of Willibald Alexis and the "Reichsgründung"', *Monatshefte* 79, no. 1 (1987): 76–88.
23. See, amongst others, *Lettres Persanes* by Montesquieu (1721), *Histoire de Monsieur Cleveland, fils naturel de Cromwell, écrite par lui-même, et traduite de l'anglais* (1731–9), and *Candide* by Voltaire (1759).

24. Gideon Toury, 'Enhancing Cultural Changes by Means of Fictitious Translations', *Translation and Cultural Change: Studies in History, Norms, and Image-Projection*, ed. Eva Hung (Amsterdam: Johns Benjamins, 2005), 4.
25. Toury, 'Fictitious Translations', 8. On pseudo-translations of Gothic novels, see Daniel Hall, 'The Gothic Tide: *Schauerroman* and Gothic Novel in the Late Eighteenth Century', in *The Novel in Anglo-German Context*, ed. Susanne Stark (Amsterdam: Rodopi, 2000), 51–60.
26. Thomas, 'Literary Reputation of Alexis': 196.
27. Richard Humphrey, *The Historical Novel as Philosophy of History: Three German Contributions: Alexis, Fontane, Döblin* (London: University of London, 1986), 75.
28. Frederick Burwick, 'How to Translate a Waverley Novel: Sir Walter Scott, Willibald Alexis, and Thomas De Quincey', *Wordsworth Circle* 25, no. 2 (1994): 96.
29. *The Eclectic Review* 24 (1825): 16.
30. In addition to the studies cited in the course of this chapter, also see Angela Esterhammer, *Print and Performance in the 1820s: Improvisation, Speculation, Identity* (Cambridge: Cambridge University Press, 2020), 203–6; and Michael Niehaus, *Autoren unter sich: Walter Scott, Willibald Alexis, Wilhem Hauff und andere in einer literarischen Affäre* (Heidelberg: Synchron, 2002).
31. Margaret Russett, *Fictions and Fakes: Forging Romantic Authenticity, 1760–1845* (Cambridge: Cambridge University Press, 2006), 1–12.
32. Bridgwater, *De Quincey's Gothic Masquerade*, 29.
33. WA, 1.vi–vii; 1.xvii–xviii; 1.iii.
34. WA, 3.iii; 3.v.
35. *Literarisches Conversations-Blatt* 12 (1824).
36. *Abendzeitung, Wegweiser* 80 (1824).
37. Willibald Alexis, *Erinnerungen von Willibald Alexis*, ed. Max Ewert (Berlin: Concordia, 1900), 275–6.
38. These plans meet with an exasperated response from his publisher. 'You seem to attach great importance to an English translation and almost to regard this as the main object', the latter writes; but 'I have no such favourable opinion of the idea. It is certainly true that Walladmor has evoked no small interest in England, but we shall have to wait and see whether [*Avalon*] does likewise. However, if I know my English booksellers, I believe that none of them will enter into a contract with me to buy the final proofs.' Cited in Lionel Thomas, *Willibald Alexis: A Biography* (Oxford: Blackwell, 1964), 38.
39. *Blätter für literarische Unterhaltung* 9 November 1826, 429–31; 10 November 1826, 433–5; 11 November 1826, 437–9.
40. Bridgwater, *Masquerade*, 122.
41. W, 4.269.
42. WA, 3.10; 3.291–2; 3.293; 3.296–8.
43. Alexis, *Erinnerungen*, 269.
44. Burwick, 'How to Translate', 94.
45. Ann Rigney, *Imperfect Histories: The Elusive Past and the Legacy of Romantic Historicism* (Ithaca: Cornell University Press, 2001), 21.

46. Ian Duncan, *Scott's Shadow: The Novel in Romantic Edinburgh* (Princeton: Princeton University Press, 2007), 127.
47. Cited in J. Y. W. Macalister and Alfred W. Pollard, *The Library: A Quarterly Review of Bibliography and Library Love* (London: Alexander Morning, 1907), 8.268. See Bridgwater, *Masquerade*, 28 and 114, for conjectures as to the exact identity of this munificent bookseller.
48. WL, 4.221; 4.218; 4.259; 4.218; 4.219.
49. W, 4.269.
50. WL, 4.260.
51. *The Newcastle Magazine* 4, no. 4 (1825): 169.
52. For more context on Defauconpret's translational practice, see Paul Barnaby, 'Restoration and Sentimental Poetics in A.-J.-B. Defauconpret's Translations of Sir Walter Scott', *Translation and Literature* 20, no. 1 (2011): 6–28.
53. W, 4.226–67; 4.267; 4.268; 4.269; 4.268; 4.270.
54. Alexis, *Erinnerungen*, 277.
55. Thomas, 'Walladmor', 229–30. Emphasis mine.
56. W, 4.443; 4.445; 4.444–5; 4.391; 4.402.
57. AB, 10.280.
58. W, 4.270.
59. W, 4.447.
60. W, 4.269; 4.267–9.
61. For an excellent account of hypotyposis in Kant, see Rodolphe Gasché, 'Hypotyposis', *The Idea of Form: Rethinking Kant's Aesthetics* (Stanford: Stanford University Press, 2003), 202–20.
62. WL, 4.220.
63. AB, 10.280.
64. W, 4.444.
65. Walter Scott, *Tales of The Crusaders: The Betrothed* (Edinburgh: Archibald Constable, 1825), 1, i.
66. Scott, *The Betrothed*, iv; viii–ix; x; xi.
67. WA, 3.n.p. [iii].
68. W, 4.271–3; WA, 3.n.p. [iv–v].
69. W, 4.271–2; WA, 3.n.p. [iii–iv].
70. W, 4.446; 4.445.

# Coda: A Yearning for Translation

Think of me as one, even when four [chapters] had passed, still agitated, writhing, throbbing, palpitating, shattered.[1]

The inaugural event of literary theory occurred in the early twentieth century, when a group of formalist critics resolved to centre their scholarship on the Romantic intuition that literature is best defined as a mode of writing that is forever in pursuit of a better understanding and realisation of its own potentialities. Thus construed, the chief duty of literary criticism is the documentation and theorisation of literature's search for itself. Working from its own set of Romantic sources, this book has performed a similar gesture, arguing that a critical theory of translation should attend to those moments where translation begins to examine its status qua translation – when it grows concerned to establish the nature of interlinguistic, interstylistic and interdiscursive transfer in hopes of rendering itself a distinct mode. If the delineation of literariness is difficult, the determination of translativeness must be even more so, translation being a derived force that always adapts to the languages, discourse and disciplines between which it happens to be conducting its business.

The previous chapters have endeavoured to recover the various ways in which De Quincey harnesses translation to redefine what it means to write and to think. They have accordingly granted his translated work pride of place, and have simultaneously endeavoured to trace the ways in which a translative perspective may transform the reading of even ostensibly creative and monolingual texts. Each of this book's four chapters has been themed around a subsidiary of the larger idea of translation that De Quincey seeks to examine in his pursuit of translativeness. In the first chapter, the protagonist was seen to travel in the wake of Wordsworth and Coleridge, negotiating a perilous balance between authorship and translatorship, creativity and imitation, originality and reproduction; ever in search of a mode of writing in which primacy and secondariness might so offset one another as to found a position uniquely De Quincey's own. The second chapter examined the ideal of impassioned prose, tracing how it analogises different languages and different styles by establishing a pseudo-philological hierarchisation of national languages and the two chief components of any one language, form and sense. The third chapter unravelled the construction of an isomorphism between, on the one hand, the Kantian dichotomisation of the noumenal and the phenomenal and, on the other, the divided structures of linguistic and stylistic exchange. Finally, in addition to exploring a reconciliation of textual aesthetics and economics, Chapter 4 studied the processes through which an idealised translation might be practically achieved. Overarching all these analyses is a conception of translation that far exceeds its standard definition of interidiomatic transfer, in that it is intent on determining the fundamental nature of translation that underlies this definition and thence transposing its structuration on all manner of writing and reading. By way of coda, the following paragraphs sketch out an extension of De Quincey's project to refound literature on translation beyond his own idiosyncratic oeuvre, offering an outline of a criticsm of translation that might illuminate Romantic practices and theories of translation up to the present.

In its preface, the present monograph briefly adverted to Berman's incomplete efforts to build a *critique des traductions* by reading individual translators as one might individual authors, inviting critics to study their oeuvres as so many aggregates of acts that separately and together endeavour to effectuate a total norm of translation. To read translation along these lines is to read not in order to assess questions of equivalence or chart relationships of power, but to distil from an oeuvre or a corpus a coherent attitude. To grant this basic layout further specificity, the present book reads its resident translator's texts as objects caught between two irreconcilable desires: one for imaginative autonomy, the other for informative mediation. In so doing, it also offered a theoretical argument, attempting a mediation between translation studies and literary criticism. For his part, so that he might chart a course that was to proceed at right angles with extant frames in translation studies, Berman used for his signposts three unusual suspects: Benjamin, Ricœur and Jauss. In keeping with its differently situated remit, the present book has drawn on a slightly different triad of critics, chosen for their potential as much as their positions vis-à-vis one another, concurring with Berman only in acknowledging the inevitability of Benjamin's essay on 'The Task of the Translator'. The latter was originally published in 1923 as a preface to his translation of Baudelaire's 1857 *Tableaux Parisiens* – Baudelaire himself being so taken with De Quincey's revision of modern authorship that he translated him in 1860. To this inescapable reference this book adds a further two. The first is a somewhat idiosyncratic reading of Benjamin's notoriously difficult text, Paul de Man's response to 'The Task', the final instalment in the series of *Messenger Lectures* he delivered a few months before his death in 1983. A third critic, writing in 1996, contributes a phenomenological view. In his dense commentary on Carlyle's *Sartor Resartus*, described in this book's first chapter, Wolfgang Iser offers a sophisticated analysis of intercultural communication that is highly apposite to a translational study. For each of these writers, translation occupies a relatively marginal position in their broader work: Benjamin, de Man and Iser each devote little more than a single article-length intervention to the problem of translation, and, with the exception of Benjamin, are now therefore rarely hailed for their contributions to translation studies. This seemingly modest role belies the pivotal import with which each endows translation, recognising in its structures and figures an exemplary crystallisation of their ideas.

A thorough critical theorisation of translation as it structures and transforms the writings of Benjamin, de Man and Iser would require a volume unto itself, much of it devoted to explicating the complex textual models informing their perspectives. For the purposes of this concluding section, however, a sketch of their theories in their essential points of disagreement and convergence will suffice. Iser, whose position is most allied to De Quincey's, will claim a position of mediatorship between Benjamin and de Man, who read translation in terms of an orientation that they discern to run in diametrically opposite directions. All three essays do, however, agree on the minimal precondition for a critique of translation. Benjamin starkly states the premise:

> [i]n the appreciation of a work of art or an art form, consideration of the receiver never proves fruitful. [. . .] No poem is intended for the reader, no picture for the beholder, no symphony for the listener.

While it may appear ruthless to exorcise all thoughts of communication from the analysis of translation, Benjamin seeks to apply an epistemological cut necessitated by the extraordinary difficulty of reading translations *as* translations, as texts that might accrue their own interest – that is, *not* as acts of recommunication in whose analysis the consideration of source, target and context ought to predominate. This dramatic expulsion of the audience inaugurates a mode of reading that is interested much less in *what* the translated text might convey about an inaccessible original than its *method* in doing so – that is, the internal structures and performative acts through which the translation frames itself. As Benjamin, de Man and Iser see it, the common characteristic that this style of reading detects in all forms of translation, and does not find in the originals upon which they are grafted, is that they perform and ponder the action of one language on another. It is in the organisation and contemplation of this interlinguistic traffic that all three critics locate the translativeness of translation, the development of which is the key task of the translator, a phrase coined by Benjamin to capture the idea towards which translation finally strives. All three critics, however, delineate this task differently. The Romantic discourse of translation as it is exemplified by De Quincey partakes of each of these stances, switching between them as occasion requires.

Much of Benjamin's essay is preoccupied with determining what it means to argue that translation possesses an energy absent from other types of writing. While not a form unto itself, its uniquely interlinguistic nature does grant it the dignity of a separable 'mode' in that its derived nature also permits it to ask questions that cut to the heart of the original and originary forms of writing with which it is charged to engage. More to the point, translation can be differentiated from those modes of writing which draw on a single language because, in pairing off differences and similarities across languages, it gestures at a dream of total comprehension; a 'pure language' in which all questions of interpretation are confronted and resolved. This ability of translation to imagine the achievement of a total language is what most defines it, in that it

> is a feature of translation which basically differentiates it from the poet's work, because the effort of the latter is never directed at the language as such, at its totality, but solely and immediately at specific linguistic contextual aspects. [...] The intention of the poet is spontaneous, primary, graphic; that of the translator is derivative, ultimate, ideational. [...] There is no muse of philosophy, nor is there one of translation. But despite the claims of sentimental artists, these two are not banausic. For there is a philosophical genius that is characterised by a yearning [*Sehnsucht*] for that language which manifests itself in translation.

The 'pure language' towards which translation moves is to be regarded as a realm of total meaning in which formal and semantic differences within and between idioms are sublated. This, then, is 'the task of the translator' teased by the essay's title – 'to release in his own language that pure language which is under the spell of another, to liberate the language imprisoned in a work in his re-creation of that work', and in so doing, to achieve a 'pure language [...] which no longer means or expresses anything but is, as expressionless and creative Word, that which is meant in all language'.[2] Translation is granted a power that poetry and philosophy lack: it works towards the achievement of a world in which the division of matter and meaning, and all other conflicts that may be calqued onto this basic structure, is overcome through the absorption of the former into the latter.

When Paul de Man reads Walter Benjamin, he develops from him a model of translation whose directionality reverses the latter's projection of an ascent towards meaningful synthesis. De Man's surprising interpretation derives from his focus on a depressive scenario regarding the end point of translation that briefly perturbs Benjamin's serenity. Since translations orchestrate an interlinguistic comparison, Benjamin muses, they inevitably reveal the makeshift nature of language, threatening to explode the empyrean of totalised meaning by infecting practitioners and readers of translation with constant suspicion. Seizing on this quintessentially deconstructive moment, de Man comments that

> [w]e think we are at ease in our own language, we feel a coziness, a familiarity, a shelter in the language we call our own, in which we think that we are not alienated. What the translation reveals is that this alienation is at its strongest in our relation to our own original language, that the original language within which we are engaged is disarticulated in a way which imposes upon us a particular alienation, a particular suffering.[3]

As the work of interpreting progresses, the translator grows unmoored. Meaning touches his work ever more lightly: so much so, Benjamin reflects in his essay's closing lines, that before long, 'meaning' may be seen to 'plunge[] from abyss to abyss until it threatens to become lost in the bottomless depths of language'. Here, however, he interjects a crucial qualification: it is a pivotal part of the translator's task, he insists, that he call 'a stop' lest his writing spiral out of control.[4] Having glimpsed the beginning dissolution of language, the interpreter ought to take a leap of faith that will transport him back into the orderly world of meaning, much as Coleridge's Luther was seen to do in this book's fourth chapter when he banished the demon of linguistic materiality by throwing his inkwell at the apparition. De Man rejects such recuperations as delusional: the descent into disintegration and disillusion which he recognises in translation appears to him irreversible. To de Man, translation always fails in its conversion of one language into another. Moreover, in so doing, it fatally disproves the beliefs to which Benjamin continues to cling, finally disproving any possibility of meaningful communication across inter- and intralinguistic differences. Yet it is precisely in so ignominiously crashing into the reality of unbiddable materiality that translation accomplishes a far higher mission, which properly constitutes the translator's task. 'One of the reasons why [Benjamin] takes the translator rather than the poet' for his model is that the former per definition fails [...] If the text is called 'Die Aufgabe des Übersetzers', we have to read this title more or less as a tautology: Aufgabe, task, can also mean the one who has to give up [from German *aufgeben*].[5]

On de Man's reading, then, translation condemns the translator to a dark parody of the upward mobility envisioned by Benjamin. While it is undertaken in hopes of an ascent to purified meaning, it triggers a vertiginous fall into an unhomed language that wallows in unhinged materiality.

Two irreconcilable theories of translations sit awkwardly alongside one another, their undecidable hierarchy paralysing any advance into a critical theory of translation. Both claim they are in the right, and both cannot simultaneously hold true. So how might one proceed? A path opens in Iser's analysis of Carlyle's *Sartor Resartus*. Even though he does not directly invoke Benjamin or de Man, Iser delineates a scheme of flexible coordination through which their totalising and detotalising readings may both be accommodated. Like de Man and Benjamin, Iser argues that translation serves as a privileged locus through which modern thought hopes to gain an understanding of itself. Modernity, Iser writes, is born of a traumatising rupture that draws a jagged line across all signification, splitting all being and speaking into antinomic structures. Amid this 'experience of crisis', some mechanism of 'repair becomes necessary'. This is the solemn task with which the translator finds himself invested: his professional promise to smooth interlinguistic communication is seen to model a restoration for all forms of cultural production. In essence, this is the Benjaminian model of translation; significantly, however, Iser subjoins a series of comments that move his delineation of translation into de Man's far bleaker territory. In a sobering counterpoint to Benjamin's prophecy of a messianic interpretation, he notes that modern translation is fundamentally unsatisfactory, and the modern translator the very sorriest representative of the modern plight, because he is given a task that exceeds his brief. Translation is expected to heal differences, even as its products continue to be judged according to defunct standards of straightforward recommunication. Since the processes of antinomising fragmentation affect all modern languages – which is to say, *all* languages – a simple transplantation cannot possibly deliver a vision for the future. If translation finds itself paralysed by the paradox that it is 'motivated by the need to cope with a crisis that can no longer be alleviated by the mere assimilation or appropriation of other cultures', it must evolve its way out of its double bind by adapting its methods to suit its ambitions. Rather than create a unidirectional structure of transfer, a modern translation must undertake to establish a discourse whose architecture is designed to replicate the reality into which it seeks to insert itself: a 'cross-cultural discourse', as Iser has it; a style of thought that is not to be equated to any one culture or language, but that maintains itself in a dynamic condition premised on 'a mutual mirroring of cultures'. A modern translation that touches on its ideal shape may be envisaged as

> a network of interpenetrating relationships. These, in turn, allow for a mutual impacting of cultures upon one another [. . .] not motivated by assimilation, appropriation, or even understanding and communication, as each of these [. . .] points to an ulterior purpose.

Those translators who appreciate their mission take it as their task to ensure their work testifies to the divisions that trouble life and thought. The translated text, that is, must be so constructed as to remain visibly divided between competing claims: it is built on the quicksand of a 'constant tilting between mutually exclusive readings'. Far from leading up to a peaceable demesne of purified meaning or down to a fractious collection of uninterpretable detritus, translation has no final orientation to its motions – but it does move, and in moving, it gives itself purpose. *Sartor* thus shuttles from German to English and back again, modelling on these linguistic shifts a vacillation between philosophical and critical perspectives. Rationalism and empiricism assert their dominance in studied alternation, and the same pattern determines even the task that the translator superficially seeks to establish, oscillating between a symbolic, Benjaminian stance and its rhetorical, deManian counter.

The irresolvably dialogic nature of translation renders it a no-thing of no final affiliation: translation specifies itself as the obstinate refusal to forego the usual mechanism through which specificity is attained. It 'liberates its referential control from any pregiven frame of reference in order to generate its own referential control by constantly shifting modes of reference'. Indeed, translation may even be said to be generative of a distinct aesthetics and poetics in its complex negotiations of the native and the foreign. However, it is also condemned to motion, and can accordingly never pin itself down to any one single voice, or style or philosophy: it is prevented 'from turning into an artwork [. . .] [by] its amphibolic nature, as manifested by its inherent duality'. Still, it does generate a cross-cultural philosophy uniquely its own. More importantly, it is precisely as one polar system flips into another that an idea of sorts emerges, briefly flashing up in what appears to Iser 'an empty space around which narrating and arguing revolve'.[6] It is here, at this infinitesimal moment of suspense, that the essence of translation may be glimpsed, and it is as he unfirmly stands on this minimally stable foothold that the translator performs his operations.

Theoretical *and* descriptive, critical *and* functionalist, British *and* German, idealist *and* materialist, licentious *and* literal, Benjaminian *and* deManian – translation has the potential to be all these, and those oeuvre-spanning projects of translation that De Quincey and other Romantic and post-Romantic authors-*cum*-translators undertake seize on this double potential by ensuring that their texts are each of these *by turns*. It is thus, too, that this book has defined Thomas De Quincey: less a man than a set of vectors; less an author than a collection of identities that erupt into each other – in short, less a biographic creature than a writer who takes every care to position himself as a necessary third term, through which other and greater authors, styles and discourse may be mediated into their counters so as to ensure a perfect representation, and perhaps a reparation, of modern writing as in itself really is. While this book has ostensibly treated of De Quincey, he was only ever to be briefly observed, a transient occupant of what only initially appears as central silence voided of conviction: a writer who yearns for translation.

### Notes

1. C 1821, 2.57.
2. Benjamin, 'Task', 70; 71; 77; 80; 75.
3. Paul de Man, '"Conclusions" on Walter Benjamin's "The Task of the Translator": Messenger Lecture, Cornell University, March 4, 1983', *Yale French Studies* 97 (2000): 24–5.
4. Benjamin, 'Task', 82.
5. de Man, 'Conclusions', 20; 21–2.
6. Wolfgang Iser, 'The Emergence of a Cross-Cultural Discourse: Thomas Carlyle's Sartor Resartus', *The Translatability of Cultures: Figurations of the Space Between,* , ed. Sanford Budick and Wolfgang Iser (Stanford: Stanford University Press, 1996), 245; 248; 261; 248; 252; 264; 249.

# Bibliography

Alexander, J. H. 'Learning from Europe: Continental Literature in the *Edinburgh Review* and *Blackwood's Magazine* 1802–1825'. *The Wordsworth Circle* 21, no. 3 (1990): 118–23.
Alexis, Willibald. *Erinnerungen von Willibald Alexis*. Ed. Max Ewert. Berlin: Concordia, 1900.
—. *Walladmor: Frei nach dem Englischen des Walter Scott*. 3 vols, 2nd edn. Berlin: Herbig, 1825.
Bachleitner, Norbert. 'A Proposal to Include Book History in Translation Studies: Illustrated with German Translations of Scott and Flaubert'. *Arcadia: International Journal for Literary Studies* 44, no. 2: 420–40.
Barnaby, Paul. 'Restoration and Sentimental Poetics in A.-J.-B. Defauconpret's Translations of Sir Walter Scott'. *Translation and Literature* 20, no. 1 (2011): 6–28.
Barthes, Roland. *Le plaisir du texte*. Paris: Seuil, 1973.
Baudelaire, Charles. 'Les foules'. In *Petits poèmes en prose*, 31–2. Volume 4 of *Œuvres complètes de Charles Baudelaire*. Paris: Michel Levy, 1869.
—. *Les paradis artificiels, opium et haschisch*. Paris: Poulet-Malassis et de Broise, 1860.
Beiser, Frederick. 'Romanticism and Idealism'. In *The Relevance of Romanticism: Essays on German Romantic Philosophy*, 30–46, ed. Dalia Nassar. Oxford: Oxford University Press, 2014.
Benjamin, Walter. 'The Task of the Translator: An Introduction to the Translation of Baudelaire's *Tableaux Parisiens*'. In *Illuminations*, 70–82, trans. Harry Zorn. London: Pimlico, 1999.
Berman, Antoine. *The Experience of the Foreign: Culture and Translation in Romantic Germany*. Trans. S. Heyvaert. New York: SUNY Press, 1992.
—. *Toward a Translation Criticism: John Donne*. Trans. and ed. Françoise Massardier-Kennedy. Kent, OH: Kent State University Press, 2009.
Bodammer, Eleoma. 'Writing on the Brocken, in the Brocken: The Poetry of the Inn's Albums'. *Publications of the English Goethe Society* 82, no. 1 (2013): 42–64.
Born, Friedrich Gottlob. *Immanuelis Kantii Opera ad philosophiam criticam Latine vertit Fredericus Gottlob Born*. Leipzig: E. B. Schwickert, 1796–8.
Brewster, David. *Letters on Natural Magic: Addressed to Sir Walter Scott, Bart*. London: John Murray, 1832.

Bridgwater, Patrick. *De Quincey's Gothic Masquerade*. Amsterdam: Brill/Rodopi, 2004.
Burwick, Frederick. 'Coleridge and De Quincey on Miracles'. *Christianity and Literature* 34, no. 4 (1990): 387–412.
—. 'How to Translate a Waverley Novel: Sir Walter Scott, Willibald Alexis, and Thomas De Quincey'. *Wordsworth Circle* 25, no. 2 (1994): 93–100.
—. *Knowledge and Power*. London: Palgrave Macmillan, 2001.
—. 'The Dream-Visions of Jean Paul and Thomas De Quincey'. *Comparative Literature* 20, no. 1 (1968).
Byron, George Gordon. *Don Juan*. Ed. A. Cunningham. Philadelphia: Jas. B. Smith & Co., 1859.
Cafarelli, Annette Wheeler. 'De Quincey and Wordsworthian Narrative'. *Studies in Romanticism* 28, no. 1 (1989): 121–47
—. *Prose in the Age of Poets: Romanticism and Biographical Narrative from Johnson to De Quincey*. Philadelphia: University of Pennsylvania Press, 1990.
Carlyle, Thomas. *Lectures on the History of Literature: Delivered by Thomas Carlyle April to July 1838*. Ed. J. Reay Greene. London: Ellis and Elvey, 1892.
—. *Sartor Resartus: The Life and Opinions of Herr Teufelsdröckh in Three Books, The Norman and Charlotte Strouse Edition of the Writings of Thomas Carlyle*. Ed. Mark Engel and Rodger L. Tarr. Berkeley: University of California Press, 2000.
Carlyle, Thomas, and Jane Welsh Carlyle. *The Carlyle Letters Online*. Ed. Brent E. Kinser. Durham, NC: Duke University Press, 2007–16.
Castells, Manuel. *The Information Age*. Vol. 1: *Economy, Society, and Culture: The Rise of the Network Society*. Oxford: Blackwell, 1996.
Clark, David L. 'We "Other Prussians": Bodies and Pleasures in de Quincey and Late Kant'. *European Romantic Review* 14 (2003): 261–87.
Class, Monika. *Coleridge and Kantian Ideas in England: Coleridge's Responses to German Philosophy*. London: Continuum, 2012.
Clej, Alina. *A Genealogy of the Modern Self: Thomas De Quincey and the Intoxication of Writing*. Stanford: Stanford University Press, 1995.
Clément, Bruno. 'Kant est-il mort comme il a vécu? A-t-il vécu comme il a écrit?' In *Vie philosophique et vies de philosophes*, 79–94, ed. Bruno Clément and Christian Trottmann. Paris: Sens & Tonka, 2010.
Coleridge, Samuel Taylor. *Aids to Reflection*. Ed. John Beer. Volume 9 of *The Collected Works of Samuel Taylor Coleridge*. Princeton: Princeton University Press, 1993.
—. *Biographia Literaria: Or Biographical Sketches of My Literary Life and Opinions*. Ed. James Engell and Jackson W. Bate. *The Collected Works of Samuel Taylor Coleridge*. Princeton: Princeton University Press, 1983, 297.
—. *Christabel; Kubla Khan, a Vision; The Pains of Sleep*. London: John Murray, 1816.
—. *Collected Letters of Samuel Taylor Coleridge*. Ed. Earl Leslie Griggs. London: Clarendon, 1956.
—. *Lectures on Shakespeare (1811–1819)*. Ed. Adam Roberts. Edinburgh: Edinburgh University Press.

—. *Literary Remains*. London: William Pickering, 1836.
—. *Specimens of the Table Talk*. London: John Murray, 1836.
—. *Table Talk*. Ed. Carl Woodring. Princeton: Princeton University Press, 1992.
—. *The Annotated Ancient Mariner*. Ed. Martin Gardner. London: Anthony Blond, 1965.
—. *The Friend: A Series of Essays*. London: Gale and Curtis, 1812.
—. *The Poems of Samuel Taylor Coleridge*. Ed. Derwent Coleridge and Sara Coleridge. Leipzig: Bernhard Tauchnitz, 1860.
Condillac, Étiennne Bonnot de. *An Essay on the Origin of Human Knowledge: Being a Supplement to Mr Locke's Essay on the Human Understanding*. Trans. [Thomas] Nugent. London: J. Nourse, 1756.
Crick, Joyce. 'Coleridge's "Wallenstein": Two Legends'. *The Modern Language Review* 83, no. 1 (1988): 76–86.
Dahlmann, [Friedrich Christoph]. *Life of Herodotus Drawn out from His Book*. Trans. G. V. Cox. London: John W. Parker, 1845.
Dayre, Éric. 'Baudelaire, traducteur de Thomas De Quincey, une prosaïque comparée de la modernité'. *Romantisme* 29, no. 4 (1999): 31–51.
—. *L'absolu comparé: littérature et traduction: une séquence moderne: Coleridge, De Quincey, Baudelaire, Rimbaud*. Paris: Hermann, 2009.
—. 'L'impératif tautégorique, de la loi poétique'. In *Une histoire dissemblable: Le tournant poétique du romantisme anglais 1797–1834*, 117–254. Paris: Hermann, 2010.
De Graef, Ortwin. 'Shaft Which Ran: Chinese Whispers with Auerbach, Buck, Woolf, and De Quincey'. In *Fear and Fantasy in a Global World*, 303–22, ed. Susana Araújo, Marta Pacheco Pinto and Sandra Bettencourt. Amsterdam: Brill/Rodopi, 2015.
D'hulst, Lieven. 'La traduction: un genre littéraire à l'époque romantique?' *Revue d'histoire littéraire de la France* 97, no. 3 (1997): 391–400.
De Man, Paul. '"Conclusions" on Walter Benjamin's "The Task of the Translator": Messenger Lecture, Cornell University, March 4, 1983'. *Yale French Studies* 97 (2000): 25–46.
De Quincey, Thomas. 'Kant's Abstract of Swedenborgianism'. In *The Collected Writings of Thomas De Quincey*, vol. xiv, 61–92, ed. David Masson. London: A. & C. Black, 1897.
—. *A Diary of Thomas De Quincey*. Ed. Horace Ainsworth Eaton. London: N. Douglas, 1927.
—. 'Kant on the Age of the Earth'. In *The Collected Writings of Thomas De Quincey*, vol. xiv, 69–93, ed. Masson.
—. *De Quincey Memorials, Being Letters and Other Records Here First Published*. Ed. Alexander H. Japp. London: William Heinemann, 1891.
—. 'Kant on National Character, in Relation to the Sense of the Sublime and Beautiful'. In *The Collected Writings of Thomas De Quincey*, vol. xiv, 46–60, ed. David Masson. London: A. & C. Black, 1897.
—*Die letzten Tage des Immanuel Kant*, trans. Cornelia Langendorf. Berlin: Matthes & Seitz, 1991.
—. 'Notes from the Pocket-Book of a Late Opium-Eater: No. V – Superficial Knowledge'. *The London Magazine* vol. 10 (1824): 25–7.
—. *Recollections of the Lakes and the Lake Poets: Coleridge, Wordsworth, and Southey*. Edinburgh: Adam and Charles Black, 1862.

—. *Selections Grave and Gay: From Writing Published Unpublished*. Edinburgh: James Hogg, 1854.

—. *The Collected Works of Thomas De Quincey*. Ed. Grevel Lindop. 21 vols. London: Pickering & Chatto, 2000–3.

—. *The Posthumous Works of Thomas De Quincey: Edited from the Original Mss., with Introductions and Notes*. Ed. Alexander H. Japp. London: William Heinemann, 1891.

Doyle, Michael. *Ways of War and Peace: Realism, Liberalism and Socialism*. New York: W. W. Norton, 1997.

Duncan, Ian. *Scott's Shadow: The Novel in Romantic Edinburgh*. Princeton: Princeton University Press, 2007.

Eaton, Horace Ainsworth. *A Biography of Thomas De Quincey*. Oxford: Oxford University Press, 1936.

Emerson, Ralph Waldo. *English Traits*. Boston: Ticknor & Fields, 1856.

Esterhammer, Angela. 'Identity Crises: Celebrity, Anonymity, Doubles, and Frauds in European Romanticism'. In *The Oxford Handbook of European Romanticism*, 771–87, ed. Paul Hamilton. Oxford: Oxford University Press, 2016.

—. *Print and Performance in the 1820s: Improvisation, Speculation, Identity*. Cambridge: Cambridge University Press, 2020.

Faflak, Joel. 'De Quincey Collects Himself'. In *Nervous Reactions: Victorian Recollections of Romanticism*, 23–46, ed. Joel Faflak and Julia M. Wright. Albany: SUNY Press, 2004.

Fenzi, Enrico. 'Translatio studii e translatio imperii: Appunti per un percorso'. *Interfaces: A Journal of Medieval European Literature* 1 (2015): 170–208.

Flower, Michael A. 'From Simonides to Isocrates: The Fifth-Century Origins of Fourth-Century Panhellenism'. *Classical Antiquity* 19, no. 1 (2000): 69–76.

Frank, Manfred. *Auswege aus dem deutschen Idealismus*. Frankfurt am Main: Suhrkamp, 2007.

Frey, Anne. 'De Quincey's Imperial Systems'. *Studies in Romanticism* 44, no. 1 (2005): 41–61.

Froude, James Anthony. *Thomas Carlyle: A History of the First Forty Years of His Life, 1795–1835*. London: Longmans, Green, and Co., 1891.

Fulford, Tim. 'De Quincey's Literature of Power'. *The Wordsworth Circle* 31, no. 3 (2000): 158–64.

Gasché, Rodolphe. *Of Minimal Things: Studies on the Notion of Relation*. Stanford: Stanford University Press, 1999.

—. *The Idea of Form: Rethinking Kant's Aesthetics*. Stanford: Stanford University Press, 2003.

—. *The Wild Card of Reading: On Paul de Man*. Cambridge, MA: Harvard University Press, 1998.

Gilfillan, George. *A Gallery of Literary Portraits*. Edinburgh: James Hogg, 1845.

Goldman, Albert. *The Mine and the Mint: Sources for the Writings of Thomas De Quincey*. Carbondale: Southern Illinois University Press, 1965.

Gottlieb, Evan. *Romantic Globalism: British Literature and Modern World Order, 1750–1830*. Columbus: Ohio State University Press, 2014.

Graver, Bruce E. 'Wordsworth and the Romantic Art of Translation'. *The Wordsworth Circle* 17, no. 3 (1986): 169–74.

Gravil, Richard. 'Wordsworth as Partisan'. In *Concerning the Convention of Cintra*, by William Wordsworth, ed. Richard Gravil and W. J. B. Owen. Tirril: Humanities-Ebooks, 2009.
Griggs, Earl Leslie. Introduction to vol. 1 of *Collected Letters of Samuel Taylor Coleridge*, i–l. London: Clarendon, 1971.
Groves, David. 'Thomas De Quincey and the "Edinburgh Saturday Post" of 1827'. *Studies in Bibliography* 55 (2002): 235–63.
Guyer, Paul. 'The Scottish Reception of Kant'. In *Scottish Philosophy in the Nineteenth and Twentieth Centuries*, 118–53, ed. Gordon Graham. Oxford: Oxford University Press, 2015.
Hall, Daniel. 'The Gothic Tide: *Schauerroman* and Gothic Novel in the Late Eighteenth Century'. In *The Novel in Anglo-German Context*, 51–60, ed. Susanne Stark. Amsterdam: Rodopi, 2000.
Hamilton, Paul. *Coleridge and German Philosophy: The Poet in the Land of Logic*. London: Bloomsbury, 2007.
—. *Metaromanticism: Aesthetics, Literature, Theory*. Chicago: Chicago University Press, 2003.
Hay, William Anthony. 'Henry Brougham and the 1818 Westmorland Election: A Study in Provincial Opinion and the Opening of Constituency Politics'. *Albion* 36, no. 1 (2004): 28–51.
Hazlitt, William. *Lectures on the Dramatic Literature of the Age of Elizabeth*. New York: Wiley and Putnam, [1820] 1845.
Herzberg, Max J. 'Wordsworth and German Literature'. *PMLA* 40, no. 2 (1925): 302–45.
Hogg, James. *De Quincey and His Friends: Personal Recollections, Souvenirs and Anecdotes*. London: Sampson Low, Marston & Co., 1895.
Hölderlin, Friedrich. *Sämtliche Werke und Briefe in drei Bänden*. Frankfurt am Main: Deutscher Klassiker Verlag, 1992–4.
Hood, Thomas. *Prose and Verse*. New York: Wiley and Putnam, 1845.
Horrebow, Niels. *The Natural History of Iceland*. London: Linde, 1758.
Hume, David. *An Enquiry Concerning Human Understanding: And Other Writings*. Ed. Stephen Buckle. Cambridge: Cambridge University Press, 2007.
Humphrey, David. *The Historical Novel as Philosophy of History: Three German Contributions: Alexis, Fontane, Döblin*. London: University of London, 1986.
Hutchinson, Sara. *The Letters of Sara Hutchinson, 1800–1835*. Ed. Kathleen Coburn. London: Routledge, 1954.
Iser, Wolfgang. 'The Emergence of a Cross-Cultural Discourse: Thomas Carlyle's Sartor Resartus'. In *The Translatability of Cultures: Figurations of the Space Between*, 245–64, ed. Sanford Budick and Wolfgang Iser. Stanford: Stanford University Press, 1996.
Jackson, H. J. 'Coleridge, Etymology and Etymologic'. *Journal of the History of Ideas* 44, no. 1 (1983): 75–88.
Jordan, John E. 'De Quincey on Wordsworth's Theory of Diction'. *PMLA* 68, no. 4 (1954), 764–78.
—. *De Quincey to Wordsworth: A Biography of a Relationship*. Berkeley: University of California Press, 1962.
Kant, Immanuel. *Critique of Judgment*. Trans. J. H. Bernard. New York: Macmillan, 1951.

—. 'The Conflict of the Faculties'. In *Religion and Rational Theology*, 233–327, trans. and ed. Allen W. Wood and George di Giovanni. Cambridge: Cambridge University Press, 1996.

—. *The Metaphysics of Morals*. In *Practical Philosophy*, 422–37, trans. Mary J. Gregor. Cambridge: Cambridge University Press, 1996.

Keats, John. *Letters of John Keats*. Ed. Stanley Gardner. London: University of London Press, 1965.

Kuehn, Manfred. *Kant: A Biography*. Cambridge: Cambridge University Press, 2002.

Lallier, François. 'Traduire *Les confessions d'un anglais mangeur d'opium*'. In *Traductions, passages: Le domaine anglais*, 69–75, ed. Stephen Romer. Tours: Presses Universitaires François-Rabelais, 1993.

Leask, Nigel. '"Murdering One's Double": De Quincey's "Confessions of an English Opium-Eater" and S. T. Coleridge's *Biographia Literaria*'. *Prose Studies* 13, no. 3 (1990): 78–98.

Lindop, Grevel. *The Opium Eater: A Life of Thomas De Quincey*. London: J. M. Dent, 1981.

—. *The Opium Eater: A Life of Thomas De Quincey*. Oxford: Oxford University Press, 1985.

Lockhart, John Gibson. *Memoirs of the Life of Sir Walter Scott*. Edinburgh: A. & C. Black, 1851.

Lohmann, Johannes. *Philosophie und Sprachwissenschaft*. Berlin: Duncker and Humblot, 1965.

Lynch, Deirdre. '"Wedded to Books": Bibliomania and the Romantic Essayists'. *Romantic Circles Praxis Series*, February 2004, <https://romantic-circles.org/praxis/libraries/lynch/lynch.html> (last accessed 10 March 2019).

Macalister, J. Y. W., and Alfred W. Pollard. *The Library: A Quarterly Review of Bibliography and Library Love*. London: Alexander Morning, 1907.

McDonagh, Josephine. 'De Quincey and the Secret Life of Books'. In *Thomas De Quincey: New Theoretical and Critical Directions*, 123–42, ed. Robert Morrison and Daniel Sanjiv Roberts. London: Routledge, 2008.

McFarland, Thomas. *Romanticism and the Forms of Ruin: Wordsworth, Coleridge, the Modalities of Fragmentation*. Princeton: Princeton University Press, 1981.

Macfarlane, Charles. *Reminiscences of a Literary Life*. London: Murray, 1917.

Macfarlane, Robert. *Original Copy: Plagiarism and Originality in Nineteenth-Century Literature*. Oxford: Oxford University Press, 2007.

Martens, David, and Beatrijs Vanacker. 'Scenographies of the Pseudo-Translation I: Literary Issues of a Marginal Device'. *Lettres Romanes* 67, nos. 3–4 (2013): 347–58.

Maniquis, Robert. 'Lonely Empires: Personal and Public Visions of Thomas De Quincey'. In *Literary Monographs* 8, 47–127, ed. Eric Rothstein and J. A. Wittreich. Madison: University of Wisconsin Press, 1976.

Mazzeo, Tilar J. 'Coleridge, Plagiarism, and the Psychology of Romantic Habit'. *European Romantic Review* 15, no. 2 (2004): 335–41.

—. *Plagiarism and Literary Property in the Romantic Period*. Philadelphia: University of Pennsylvania Press, 2007.

McGrath, Brian. 'Thomas De Quincey and the Language of Literature: Or, on

the Necessity of Ignorance'. *Studies in English Literature, 1500–1900* 47, no. 4 (2007): 847–62.
Merritt, Mark D. 'De Quincey's Coleridge and the Dismantling of Romantic Authority'. *a/b: Auto/Biography Studies* 20, no. 2 (2005): 195–229.
Meschonnic, Henri. 'Propositions pour une poétique de la traduction'. *Langages* 7, no. 28 (1972): 49–54.
Millan-Zaibert, Elizabeth. *Friedrich Schlegel and the Emergence of Romantic Philosophy*. Albany: SUNY Press, 2007.
Miller, J. Hillis. *The Disappearance of God: Five Nineteenth-Century Writers*. Cambridge, MA: Harvard University Press, 1975.
Milligan, Barry. 'Brunonianism, Radicalism, and "The Pleasures of Opium"'. In *Thomas De Quincey: New Theoretical and Critical Directions*, 45–63, ed. Robert Morrison and Daniel Sanjiv Roberts. London: Routledge, 2008.
Mole, Tom. *What the Victorians Made of Romanticism: Material Artefacts, Cultural Practices, and Reception History*. Princeton: Princeton University Press, 2017.
Morrison, Robert. 'De Quincey and the Opium-Eater's Other Selves'. *Romanticism* 5, no. 1 (1999): 87–103.
—. 'Opium-Eaters and Magazine Wars: De Quincey and Coleridge in 1821'. *Victorian Periodicals Review* 30, no. 1 (1997): 27–40.
—. 'Red De Quincey.' *The Wordsworth Circle* 29, no. 2 (1998): 131–6.
—. '"The 'Bog School"': Carlyle and De Quincey'. *Carlyle Studies Annual* (1995): 13–20.
—. *The English Opium-Eater: A Biography of Thomas De Quincey*. London: Weidenfeld & Nicolson, 2009.
Morrison, Robert, and Daniel Sanjiv Roberts. '"I was Worshipped; I was Sacrificed": A Passage to Thomas De Quincey'. *New Theoretical and Critical Directions*, 1–18, ed. Robert Morrison and Daniel Sanjiv Roberts. London: Routledge, 2009, 14.
Mortensen, Peter. 'Robbing *The Robbers*: Schiller, Xenophobia, and the Politics of British Romantic Translation'. *Literature and History* 11, no. 1 (2002): 41–61.
Niehaus, Michael. *Autoren unter sich: Walter Scott, Willibald Alexis, Wilhem Hauff und andere in einer literarischen Affäre*. Heidelberg: Synchron, 2002.
Nitsch, Friedrich. *A General and Introductory View of Professor Kant's Principles Concerning man, the World and the Deity, Submitted to the Consideration of the Learned*. London: J. Downes, 1796.
—. 'A Sketch of the Philosophy of Dr Kant, Professor of Philosophy at the University of Konigsberg in Russia: By a Disciple of Kant's'. *English Review* 27 (1796): 106–11; 354–7.
—. 'To the Editor of the Monthly Magazine and British Register'. *Monthly Magazine* 9 (1796): 702–5.
North, Julian. 'Intertextual Sociability in Victorian *Lives* of the Romantic Poets: Thomas De Quincey's "Lake Reminiscences" and Edward John Trelawny's *Recollections of the Last Days of Shelley and Byron*'. *Life Writings* 14, no. 2 (2017): 155–69.
Parrish, Stephen Mayfield. *The Art of the Lyrical Ballads*. Cambridge, MA: Harvard University Press, 1973.
Pollitt, Charles. *De Quincey's Editorship of the Westmorland Gazette, with*

Selections from his Work on that Journal, from July 1818 to November, 1819. London: Simpkin, Marshall, Hamilton, Kent & Co., 1890.
Poulet, Georges. 'Timelessness and Romanticism'. *Journal of the History of Ideas* 15, no. 1 (1954): 3–22.
Proescholdt-Obermann, Catherine Waltraud. *Goethe and His British Critics: The Reception of Goethe's Works in British Periodicals, 1779–1855*. Berlin: Peter Lang, 1992.
Rajan, Tilottama. *Dark Interpreter: The Discourse of Romanticism*. Ithaca: Cornell University Press, 1980.
—. 'Romanticism and the Unfinished Project of Deconstruction'. *European Romantic Review* 23, no. 3 (2013): 293–303.
Reid, Nicholas. 'Coleridge and Schelling: The Missing Transcendental Deduction'. *Studies in Romanticism* 33, no. 3 (1994): 451–79.
Rener, Frederick M. *Translatio: Language and translation from Cicero to Tytler*. Amsterdam: Rodopi, 1989.
Richter, Jean Paul. *Horn of Oberon: Jean Paul Richter's School for Aesthetics*. Trans. Margaret Hale. Detroit: Wayne State University Press, 1973.
Rigney, Ann. *Imperfect Histories: The Elusive Past and the Legacy of Romantic Historicism*. Ithaca: Cornell University Press, 2001.
Roberts, Daniel Sanjiv. 'Exorcising the Malay: Dreams and the Unconscious in Coleridge and De Quincey'. *The Wordsworth Circle* 24, no. 2 (1993): 91–6.
—. *Revisionary Gleam: De Quincey, Coleridge, and the High Romantic Argument*. Liverpool: Liverpool University Press, 2000.
Robinson, Henry Crabb. *Books and Writers*. Ed. Edith J. Marley. London: J. M. Dent and Sons, 1938.
Ross, George McDonald Ross, and Tony McWalter (eds), *Kant and His Influence*. London: Continuum, 2005.
Russett, Margaret. *De Quincey's Romanticism: Canonical Minority and the Forms of Transmission*. Cambridge: Cambridge University Press, 1997.
—. *Fictions and Fakes: Forging Romantic Authenticity, 1760–1845*. Cambridge: Cambridge University Press, 2006.
—. 'Wordsworth's Gothic Interpreter: De Quincey Personifies "We Are Seven"'. *Studies in Romanticism* 30, no. 3 (1991): 345–65.
Rzepka, Charles. 'Bang-up! Theatricality and the "Diphrelatic Art" in De Quincey's English Mail-Coach'. In *Selected Studies in Romantic and American Literature, History, and Culture: Inventions and Interventions*, 63–80. Farnham: Ashgate, 2010.
—. 'De Quincey and Kant'. *PMLA* 115, no. 1 (2000): 93–4.
—. 'De Quincey and the Malay: Dove Cottage Idolatry'. *The Wordsworth Circle* 24, no. 3 (1993): 180–5.
Sackville-West, Edward. *A Flame in Sunlight: Life and Work of Thomas De Quincey*. London: Cassell, 1936.
Saglia, Diego. *European Literatures in Britain, 1815–1832: Romantic Translations*. Cambridge: Cambridge University Press, 2019.
Saintsbury, George. 'The Historical Novel'. In *Macmillan's Magazine* 70, no. 10 (1984): 1–23.
Schelling, Friedrich Wilhelm Joseph von. *Sämmtliche Werke*. Stuttgart and Augsburg: J. G. Cotta'scher Verlag, 1856.

Schiller, Friedrich. *Briefwechsel zwischen Schiller und Körner*. Stuttgart: J. G. Cotta, [1892–6].
—. *On the Aesthetic Education of Man in a Series of Letters: English and German Facing*. Ed. and trans. Elizabeth M. Wilkinson and L. A. Willoughby. Oxford: Clarendon, 1982.
Scott, Walter. *Familiar Letters of Sir Walter Scott*. Boston: Houghton Mifflin, 1894.
—. 'Prefatory Memoir of the Life of the Author'. In *The Novels of Mrs Ann Radcliffe: Complete in One Volume: To which is Prefixed, a Memoir of the Life of the Author*, i–xxxix. London: Hurst, Robinson, & Co., 1824.
—. *Tales of the Crusaders: The Betrothed*. Edinburgh: Archibald Constable, 1825.
Sheridan, Richard Brinsley. *The Critic: Or, a Tragedy Rehearsed: A Farce*. Ed. G. A. Aitken. London: J. M. Dent, 1897.
Simpson, David. 'The Limits of Cosmopolitanism and the Case for Translation'. *European Romantic Review* 16, no. 2 (2005): 141–52.
— (ed.). *The Origins of Modern Critical Thought: German Aesthetic and Literary Criticism from Lessing to Hegel*. Cambridge: Cambridge University Press, 1988.
Smith, Christopher. 'Robert Southey and the Emergence of *Lyrical Ballads*'. *Romanticism on the Net* 9 (February 1998), <https://id.erudit.org/iderudit/005792ar> (last accessed 8 December 2020).
Smith, J. Mark. 'De Quincey, Dictionaries, and Casuistry'. *ELH* 84, no. 3 (2017): 689–713.
Sorensen, Janet. *The Grammar of Empire in Eighteenth-Century British Writing*. Cambridge: Cambridge University Press, 2000.
Southey, Robert. *Letters of Robert Southey: A Selection*. Ed. M. H. Fitzgerald. Oxford: Oxford University Press, 1912.
Spice, Nicholas. 'Little Mr De Quincey'. *London Review of Books*, 18 May 2017: 3–8.
Stanback, Emily. 'Peripatetic in the City: De Quincey's *Confessions of an English Opium-Eater* and the Birth of the *Flâneur*'. *Literature Compass* 10, no. 2 (2013): 146–61.
Stephen, Leslie. 'De Quincey'. In *Hours in a Library*, vol. 1, 237–68. London: Smith, Elder, & Co., 1892.
Stirling, J. H. *Jerrod, Tennyson and Macaulay, With Other Critical Essays*. Edinburgh: Edmonston & Douglas, 1886.
Stokoe, F. W. *German Influence in the English Romantic Period, 1788–1818*. Cambridge: Cambridge University Press, 1926.
Tatlock, Lynne. 'A Timely Demise: The Literary Reputation of Willibald Alexis and the "Reichsgründung"'. *Monatshefte* 79, no. 1 (1987): 76–88.
Thomas, Lionel H. C. 'The Literary Reputation of Willibald Alexis as an Historical Novelist'. *The Modern Language Review* 45, no. 2 (1950): 195–214.
—. '"Walladmor": A Pseudo-Translation of Sir Walter Scott'. *The Modern Language Review*, vol. 46, no. 2 (1951): 218–31.
—. *Willibald Alexis: A Biography*. Oxford: Blackwell, 1964.
Thomson, William. *Outline of the Laws of Thought*. London: William Pickering, 1842.

Toremans, Tom and Beatrijs Vanacker. 'Introduction: The Emerging Field of Pseudotranslation'. *Canadian Review of Comparative Literature* 44, no. 4 (2017): 629–36.

—. '*Sartor Resartus* and the Rhetoric of Translation'. *Translation and Literature* 20 (2011): 61–78.

Toury, Gideon. 'Enhancing Cultural Changes by Means of Fictitious Translations'. In *Translation and Cultural Change: Studies in History, Norms, and Image-Projection*, 3–18, ed. Eva Hung. Amsterdam: Johns Benjamins, 2005.

—. *In Search of a Theory of Translation*. Tel Aviv: Porter Institute for Poetics and Semitics of Tel Aviv University, 1980.

Turley, Richard Margraf. *The Politics of Language in Romantic Literature*. Basingstoke: Palgrave Macmillan, 2002.

Vardy, Alan D. *Constructing Coleridge: The Posthumous Life of the Author*. London: Palgrave Macmillan, 2010.

Venuti, Lawrence. *The Translator's Invisibility: A History of Translation*, 2nd edn. London: Routledge, 2008.

Vigus, James. Introduction to *Essays on Kant Schelling, and German Aesthetics*, by Henry Crabb Robinson, 1–27, ed. James Vigus. London: Modern Humanities Research Association, 2010.

Warminski, Andrzej. *Readings in Interpretation: Hölderlin, Hegel, Heidegger*. Minneapolis: University of Minnesota Press, 1987.

Wasianski, Ehregott Andreas Christoph. *Immanuel Kant in seinen letzten Lebensjahren: Ein Beytrag zur Kenntniß seines Charakters und häuslichen Lebens aus dem täglichen Umgange mit ihm*. Vol. 3 of *Über Immanuel Kant*. Königsberg: Friedrich Nicolovius, 1804.

—. *Les derniers jours d'Emmanuel Kant*, trans. Marcel Schwob. Paris: L'Herne, 2013.

Wellek, René. 'De Quincey's Status in the History of Ideas'. *Philological Quarterly* 23 (1944): 248–72.

—. *Immanuel Kant in England 1793–1838*. Princeton: Princeton University Press, 1931.

Wells, John Edwin. 'The Story of Wordsworth's "Cintra"'. *Studies in Philology* 18, no. 1 (1921): 15–76.

—. 'Wordsworth and de Quincey in Westmorland Politics, 1818'. *PMLA* 55, no. 4 (1940): 1080–128.

Wheeler, Kathleen M. 'Kant and Romanticism'. *Philosophy and Literature* 13, no. 1 (1989): 42–56.

Wilkie, Brian. 'Wordsworth and the Tradition of the Avant-Garde'. *The Journal of English and Germanic Philology* 72, no. 2 (1973): 194–222.

Wilkinson, Elizabeth M., and L. A. Willoughby. Appendices to *On the Aesthetic Education of Man in a Series of Letters: English and German Facing* by Friedrich Schiller, 348–51, ed. and trans. Elizabeth M. Wilkinson and L. A. Willoughby. Oxford: Clarendon, 1982.

Willich, Anthony Florian Madinger. *Elements of the Critical Philosophy: Containing a Concise Account of its Origin and Tendency; a View of All the Works Published by its Founder, Professor Immanuel Kant; and a Glossary for the Explanation of Terms and Phrases*. London: T. N. Longman, 1798.

—. *Kant's Essays and Treatises on Moral, Political, and Various Philosophical Subjects*. London: William Richardson, 1798–9.
Willoughby, L. A. 'English Translations and Adaptations of Schiller's *The Robbers*'. *Modern Language Review* 27 (1921): 297–315.
Wilson, Frances. *Guilty Thing: A Life of Thomas De Quincey*. London: Bloomsbury, 2016.
Wilson, John, et al. *Noctes Ambrosianae*. New York: W. J. Widdleton, 1867.
Wirgman, Thomas. 'Moral Philosophy Reduced to a Complete and Permanent Science, On the Principles of Transcendental Philosophy, As Contained in Kant's "Critic of Practical Reason"'. In volume 15 of *Encyclopaedia Londinensis*: 763–83. London: Encyclopaedia Londinensis, 1817.
Wolfreys, Julian. 'Otherwise in London or, the Essence of Things: Modernity and Estrangement in the Nineteenth-Century Cityscape'. *Victoriographies* 5, no. 1 (2015): 17–35.
Woolf, Virginia. 'De Quincey's Autobiography'. In *Collected Essays*, vol. 4, 1–11, ed. L. Woolf. London: Hogarth, 1967.
—. 'Impassioned Prose'. In *Collected Essays*, vol. 1,167, ed. L. Woolf. London: Hogarth, 1966.
Wordsworth, Christopher. *Memoirs of William Wordsworth*. Ed. Henry Reed. Boston: Ticknor & Fields, 1851.
Wordsworth, Dorothy, and William Wordsworth. *The Letters of Dorothy and William Wordsworth: The Middle Years*. Ed. Ernest de Selincourt. Oxford: Clarendon, 1967.
Wordsworth, William. *Lyrical Ballads, and Other Poems. 1797–1800*. Volume 6 of *The Cornell Wordsworth*. Ed. James Butler and Karen Green. Ithaca: Cornell University Press, 1992.
—. *Poems, in Two Volumes, and Other Poems, 1800–1807*. Volume 7 of *The Cornell Wordsworth*. Ed. Jared Curtis. Ithaca and London: Cornell University Press, 1983.
—. *Translations of Chaucer and Virgil*. Ed. Bruce E. Graver. Ithaca: Cornell University Press, 1998.
Youngquist, Paul.'De Quincey and Kant'. *PMLA* 115, no. 1 (2000): 93–4.
—. 'De Quincey's Crazy Body'. *PMLA* 114, no. 3 (1999): 346–58.

# Index

*Abendzeitung, Wegweiser*, 176n, 177n
addiction, 23, 25, 27, 29, 37, 40, 121–3; *see also* opium
Adelung, Johann Christoph, 57, 142n
aesthetic ideology, 12, 78, 115
Alexander, J. H., 141n
Alexis, Willibald, 152–6, 159–74
  *Erinnerungen*, 155, 159, 165
  *Schloß Avalon*, 155, 177n
  *Walladmor*, German original, 147–75
allegory, 2, 10, 16, 20, 35, 58, 68, 82, 87, 121, 124, 130, 134, 135, 156–7, 168–70
*Allgemeine Literatur-Zeitung*, 148–9, 151
antinomy, 58, 114, 116, 119, 130–1, 134–5, 184
Aristotle, 72, 128
Asensi, Manuel, 38
authorship, 5–6, 14–15, 27, 30, 38–9, 46–7, 58, 78, 88, 118, 120, 123–4, 126, 132, 138–40, 147, 150–1, 154–5, 157, 160, 172, 175, 179

Bachleitner, Robert, 175n
Barnaby, Paul, 178n
Barthes, Roland, 1
Baudelaire, Charles, 15, 132, 180–1
Beiser, Frederick, 141n
Benjamin, Walter, 4, 6, 180–6
Berman, Antoine, 6–9, 72, 75–6, 180–1
bibliomania, 17–19
biography, 26, 28–9, 40, 41, 51n, 119, 121–4, 127–32, 137, 155, 167, 170
*Blackwood's Magazine*, 17, 29, 41, 103, 104, 107, 110, 119
*Blätter für literarische Unterhaltung*, 177n

Bodammer, Eleoma, 112n
body/mind dichotomy, 18, 37, 51n, 52n, 114–15, 121–9
Bog School, 40–1
Born, Friedrich Gottlob, 142n
Borowski, Ludwig Ernst von, 119–20, 144n
Bourdieu, Pierre, 7
Brewster, David, 132–6
Bridgwater, Patrick, 53–4n, 178n
Britain, 28, 44, 46, 56, 59–62, 66, 68, 73–4, 76, 78–9, 84–5, 92, 97n, 100–1, 106, 108, 110, 134, 151, 156, 165, 167
  national destiny, 63, 65, 74–6, 78
Brocken Spectre, 132–8, 145n
Brown, Thomas, 107
Browne, Sir Thomas, 34, 92
Bürger, Gottfried August, 100
Burwick, Frederick, 3, 93n, 98n, 143n, 145n, 160
Byron, George Gordon Lord, 105

Cafarelli, Annette Wheeler, 51n, 53n
Carlyle, Thomas, 39–41, 47, 87, 110–11, 129, 130, 169
  *Lectures on the History of Literature*, 114–15
  *Letters*, 40–1, 50n
  *Sartor Resartus*, 34–6, 41, 104, 181, 184–5
  translation of *Wilhelm Meister*, 39–40
Castells, Manuel, 74
Chatterton, Thomas, 16
chiasmus, 76–81, 96n, 136
  as a critique of Kantian dichotomies, 114, 129
Cicero, 71–5, 90, 118

Clark, David L., 116, 123
Class, Monika, 141n, 142n
Clej, Alina, 49n
Clément, Bruno, 144n
Coleridge, Hartley, 37, 42, 55n
Coleridge, Samuel Taylor, 14, 19–23, 27–31, 34–7, 51n, 59, 62–3, 66, 77, 80, 88, 94n, 104, 106, 115–16, 129, 131–40, 148, 162, 179, 183
  *Aids to Reflection*, 134
  *Biographia Literaria*, 34–6, 42–4, 62, 105–6, 111, 116, 135
  'Christabel', 27
  'Constancy to an Ideal Object', 134–6
  imagination/fancy dichotomy, 34–6, 62, 102
  *Lectures on Shakespeare*, 135
  *Letters*, 27, 52n
  personal relationship with De Quincey, 21, 27–30, 37, 39–47, 52n
  plagiarism, 41–6, 111
  suspension of disbelief, 135
  'The Ancient Mariner', 30–1, 132
  *The Friend*, 138–40
  as a translator, 39–47, 66, 84–6, 90, 98n, 106–7, 111
Coleridge, Sara, 41
Condillac, Etienne de, 62–6, 70–1, 102
Cosmopolitanism, 3, 6, 62, 71, 103
Crabb Robinson, Henry, 27–8, 104, 141n
creativity, 16, 18–19, 61, 63, 88, 116, 118, 125, 131, 152, 155, 159, 169–70, 175, 182; *see also* imitation; originality
crisis, 36, 39, 65–6, 70, 73, 84, 87, 117, 184
crowds, 15–16

Dayre, Éric, 48n, 55n, 75
de Graef, Ortwin, 48n
de Man, Paul, 96n, 181–4, 186
De Quincey, Thomas
  'Abstract of Swedenborgianism', 109
  'Autobiography of an English Opium-Eater', 22, 83, 113, 115, 167, 170
  Coleridge, essays on, 28–9, 37, 39, 41–3, 45–6, 116
  *Concerning the Convention of Cintra* see Wordsworth, William
  'Confessions', 1, 5, 15–18, 23, 25–6, 29, 47n, 56–8, 81–2, 104–5, 117–18
  'Conversation', 93n
  'Danish Origin of the Lake-country Dialect', 94n
  dark interpreter, the, 1–2, 128, 132, 137–8, 175
  *Diary*, 18–19, 20–2, 30–1, 32–3, 47n, 52n
  'Elements of Rhetoric', 59–60, 79, 93n, 112
  'English Dictionaries', 93n
  finances, 17–18, 28
  'How to Write English', 61–2, 73–4, 93n
  'Idea of a Universal History', 109
  'Jean Paul Richter', 16, 81–4, 88–92, 93n
  'Kant in his Miscellaneous Essays', 108–13
  'Kant on National Character', 109–10, 140–1n
  'Kant on the Age of the Earth', 103
  *Klosterheim*, 30, 52–3n
  'Last Days of Immanuel Kant', 119–26, 144n, 168
  'Letters to a Young Man', 81–4, 91–3, 93n, 103, 106–7
  'Notes from the Pocket-Book of a Late Opium-Eater', 86–7
  'On Languages', 93n
  'On the Common Saying', 109–10
  'On the Knocking at the Gate in MacBeth', 31–2, 93n
  'On the Present State of the English Language', 60, 64–72, 74, 93n, 96, 112–15
  politics, 17, 29, 37, 61, 99–101, 110, 140n
  pseudonyms and alternative spellings for, 16, 19
  *Recollections*, 26, 28–9, 37, 41, 51n
  'Secret Societies', 46
  *Selections Grave and Gay*, 33–4
  'Sir William Hamilton', 127–31
  'Style', 19–20, 65–6, 68, 71, 73–4, 76, 79–80, 93n, 113
  'Suspiria de Profundis', 1–2, 15, 37, 54–5, 132–7, 134–5, 136–8, 145–6n
  *Table Talk*, 29
  'The English Language', 59, 61, 67, 75, 80–1

De Quincey, Thomas (*cont.*)
  'The English-Mail Coach', 14, 47n, 61, 82, 94n
  'The German Language', 142n
  translations of Kant, 9–19
  *Walladmor*, English translation, 148, 150, 155–6, 160–75
  'Walladmor: Sir Walter Scott's German Novel', 147–8, 155–6, 160–2, 170
  'Wilhelm Meister', 39–40, 84
  Wordsworth, essays on, 26
Defauconpret, A. J. B., 163–4, 178n
desynonymisation, 62–3, 66
D'Hulst, Lieven, 95n
dictionaries, 57, 59, 79, 94n, 112, 129
Dove Cottage, 22–4, 56–7
drama, 18, 21, 31–3, 84–5
Duncan, Ian, 178n
Dutch, 66, 152

*Eclectic Review, The*, 153
*Edinburgh Review*, 104, 108, 142n
*Edinburgh Saturday Post, The*, 142n
eloquence, 63–5, 68, 80, 92
Emerson, Ralph Waldo, 54
empire, 40, 47n, 62, 72, 74–6
empiricism, 35–6, 101, 110, 112, 130, 133–7, 185
England, 29, 44, 61–2, 65, 76, 81, 90, 104, 107–8, 110, 148–9, 163, 169, 177n
English, 25–6, 33, 36, 59–67, 73–6, 78–81, 83–4, 90–3, 93n, 94n, 100, 102, 105, 122, 129, 134, 137, 161–7, 174, 185
  crises of, 65, 70
  nature of, 57–8, 64–5, 70
  see also Britain
Enlightenment, 11–12, 71, 104, 121, 135–7
Esterhammer, Angela, 148, 176n, 177n, 178n
etymology, 82, 132, 174; see also philology

Faflak, Joel, 47
Fenzi, Enrico, 96n
Fichte, Johann Gottlieb, 98n, 104
*flânerie*, 15–16, 48n
Flower, Michael A., 96n
footnotes, 109, 120, 124, 129–30, 159, 172
Frank, Manfred, 141n

French, 25–6, 60, 64, 66–7, 75–6, 78–85, 95n, 97n, 101–2, 104, 106–10, 112, 148, 152, 163
  distinct style of, 79–81
  talents for translation, 62
Frey, Anne, 94n
fugue, 92, 169
Fulford, Tim, 143n

Gasché, Rodolphe, 78, 96n
German, 16, 21, 25–8, 30, 34, 36, 39–46, 58, 66, 76–93, 99–117, 119–20, 124–6, 132, 139, 142n, 147–52, 156, 159–69, 171–3, 185–6
  distinct style, 76, 78–81, 83–4, 113–15
Gilfillan, George, 37–8, 53n
Goethe, Johann Wolfgang von, 39–40, 54n, 84, 100, 132, 165n
  *The Sorrows of Young Werther*, 84
  see also Carlyle: translation of *Wilhelm Meister*; De Quincey: 'Wilhelm Meister'
Goldman, Albert, 17
Gothic, the, 19, 32–3, 52–3n, 133, 152
Gottlieb, Evan, 3
Graver, Bruce, 54n
Gravil, Richard, 50n
Greek, 20, 38, 56–7, 66–78, 87, 89
Grimm brothers, 94n
Grosse, Carl, 30

Hamilton, Paul, 6, 55n
Hamilton, William, 55n, 127–31, 139
Häring, Georg Wilhelm Heinrich see Alexis, Willibald
Hazlitt, William, 53n, 84, 98n
Hebrew, 66–71, 76, 80, 139
Heine, Heinrich, 121
Herbig, 151–2, 177n
Herder, Johann Gottfried, 103, 143n
Herodotus, 19, 34, 73–5, 90, 96n, 118
Herschel, Sir John, 103
hoaxing, 147–62, 166–8, 171
Hogg, James, 49n, 132
Hölderlin, Friedrich, 9, 11, 77–8, 96n
Hood, Thomas, 50n, 55n
Horrebow, Niels, 97n
hospitality, 59, 66, 85, 165; see also insularity
Hume, David, 114, 133–5, 145n
Hutchinson, Sara, 24–5, 134
hypotyposis, 169, 178n

idealism, 6, 16–17, 28, 34–5, 41–4, 76–7, 81, 88, 93, 96n, 101–11, 114–18, 121, 123, 125, 129–30, 136, 138, 140, 169, 175, 186
imitation, 10, 18–19, 39, 54n, 56, 58–9, 78, 118, 126, 131, 136, 148, 153, 174–5, 179–80; *see also* creativity; originality
impassioned prose, 4, 11–12, 33–5, 38, 73, 132
  philosophy and, 114, 119, 127–9
  rhetorical manifestation of the sublime, as a, 30–3
  style and, 33–5, 88, 90–2, 113–15, 118
  translation and, 81, 91–3, 118–19
improvisation, 129–30
inoculation, 75, 81–6, 97n, 102, 166, 168–9
insularity, 59, 70, 75–6, 81, 83, 85, 90; *see also* hospitality
Ireland, 51, 57
Irving, Washington, 148
Iser, Wolfgang, 181–2, 184–6
Israel *see* Hebrew
Italian, 58, 66

Jachmann, Reinhold Bernhard, 119–20, 124, 144n
Japp, Alexander H., 38, 145n
Jauss, Hans Robert, 180
Jean Paul, 6, 11, 19, 40, 76, 81, 88–93, 98n, 102, 103
  *Vorschule*, 88–91, 98n
Johnson, Samuel, 94n
Jordan, John, 22, 38, 49n, 50n, 51n

Kant, Immanuel, 34–5, 43, 83–4, 91, 93, 99–131, 136, 140n, 168–9, 172, 180
  *Critiques*, 91, 105, 112, 117, 128
  *Dreams of a Spirit-Seer*, 103, 109
  'Idea of a Universal History', 103
  *Last Days see* Wasianski
  *Metaphysics of Morals*, 121, 125
  noumenon/phenomenon dichotomy, 59, 93, 102–2, 116
  *Observations*, 101–3, 109–10, 140–1n
  'On the Common Saying', 103, 109–10
  *Perpetual Peace*, 103, 109
  'The Conflict of the Faculties', 121, 123

translated to English, 106–8, 142n, 168–9
  *Universal Theory and Natural History of the Heavens*, 100
Keats, John, 16, 53n
*Kendal Chronicle*, 99–101
Kleist, Heinrich von, 117
knowledge/power dichotomy, 37–8, 112–13, 127, 143n
Kuehn, Manfred, 123

Lake School, 21, 26, 40–1
Latin, 16, 28, 71, 74–6, 84, 137
laudanum *see* opium
Leask, Nigel, 52n, 105
Lessing, Gotthold Ephraim, 90–1, 119
Lichtenberg, Georg Christoph, 90
Lindop, Grevel, 116, 145–6n
linguistics *see* philology
*Literarisches Conversations-Blatt*, 177n
*Literary Gazette, The*, 99, 151–2
Lloyd, Charles, 20, 49n
Locke, John, 62, 101
Lockhart, John Gibson, 149, 161, 176n
Lohmann, Johannes, 72, 95n
*London Magazine, The*, 103, 110, 143n, 160–1
Lucian of Samosata, 96n
Luther, Martin, 101, 138–40, 183
Lynch, Deirdre, 49n

McDonagh, Josephine, 49n
Macpherson, James, 16
Malay, the, 56–9, 82, 93n
Maniquis, Robert, 38–9
Martens, David, 176n
Masson, David, 38
medicine, 51n, 82–5, 97n, 122–5, 166
Mendicino, Kristina, 6
Merritt, Mark, 52n
Meschonnic, Henri, 13
metaphysics *see* idealism
Millan-Zaibert, Elizabeth, 141n
Miller, J. Hillis, 38–9
Milligan, Barry, 51n
Milton, John, 19, 21, 26, 31, 84–5
minority, 5, 9, 14–15, 18–20, 23, 47, 159, 179–80
Mole, Tom, 49n
Montesquieu, Charles, 176n
*Monthly Critical Gazette, The*, 176n
*Monthly Magazine, The*, 142n

Morrison, Robert, 23, 48n, 49n, 50n, 51n, 52n, 53n, 54n, 131n
Mortensen, Peter, 98n

nationalism, 23, 59, 61–2, 71, 94n, 100
neologism, 60–4
*New Monthly Magazine, The*, 145n
*Newcastle Magazine*, 163
Niehaus, Michael, 30n
Nitsch, Frederic, 104, 107, 142n
*Noctes Ambrosianae*, 29, 41
North, Julian, 50n

opium, 15–16, 18, 23, 26–9, 36–7, 40–1, 44, 51n, 52n, 57, 81–2, 86, 104–5, 116–19, 124–6, 167
originality, 18, 34, 54n, 83, 111, 127, 173, 179–80; *see also* creativity; imitation
orthography, 19, 24, 59–60, 112, 143n

paradox, 5, 59, 71, 77–8, 120, 126, 130–1, 136–7, 150, 184
paratext, 120, 147, 150, 153–5, 160–1, 166–7
Parrish, Stephen Mayfield, 22
performativity, 15–16, 24, 28, 33, 37, 40–1, 44–5, 57, 74, 91, 105, 121, 127–8, 138–9, 163, 168–9, 172, 181
philology, 59–67, 73, 76–7, 85–7, 92, 94n, 95n, 115, 126, 180
philosophy, 2, 5, 17, 25, 27, 34–7, 40–4, 47, 59, 64–5, 68, 77–9, 90–1, 94n, 99–119, 121–30, 133–4, 136, 143n, 148, 152–3, 162, 168–70, 172–3, 182, 185; *see also* empiricism; idealism; rationalism
plagiarism, 17, 41–6, 111
poetry, 4, 18, 21, 26–7, 31–4, 39, 41, 44, 52–3n, 66–9, 73, 75, 78–81, 88–90, 92, 100, 102, 109, 112, 118–19, 182; *see also* impassioned prose
Politt, Charles, 140n
Pope, Alexander, 90
Poulet, Georges, 38, 53n
prescriptivism, 59–61, 62–3, 65
print, 24, 147, 150, 152, 154–5, 161–2, 170–2, 174–5, 176n
prose, 4, 11–12, 33–5, 38, 65–9, 73–4, 76, 78–81, 83, 84, 87–8, 90–2, 100, 102, 111–14, 118–19, 127–9, 132, 180; *see also* impassioned prose
pseudonymy, 16, 19, 152–9
pseudotranslation, 125, 151–6, 159, 164, 168, 176n, 177n

Radcliffe, Ann, 33–4, 152, 154
Rajan, Tilottama, 1–4
rationalism, 35–6, 101, 112, 123, 130, 137, 185
Rener, Frederick M., 95–6n
rhetoric, 5, 15, 19, 32, 37–9, 51n, 63–5, 68, 71–2, 79–81, 83–4, 92–3, 128, 185; *see also* chiasmus; hypotyposis
Richardson, Charles, 94n
Richter, Jean Paul *see* Jean Paul
Ricœur, Paul, 180
Rigney, Ann, 160
Rink, Friedrich Theodor, 119, 144n
Roberts, Daniel Sanjiv, 49n, 51n, 52n, 53n, 93n, 95n, 141n
Russett, Margaret, 14–15, 49n, 51n,153
Rzepka, Charles, 93n, 94n, 125–7

Sackville-West, Edward, 51n
Saglia, Diego, 6
Saintsbury, George, 176n
Schelling, Friedrich, 43–5, 55n, 90, 104
Schiller, Friedrich von, 40, 76–7, 84–90, 93, 96n, 130
 *Aesthetic Education*, 86–7
 *The Robbers*, 84
 *Wallenstein*, 84, 86, 98n
Scotland, 61–2, 148, 159
Scott, Walter, 14, 30, 147–74
 Radcliffe and, 33
 *St Ronan's Well*, 149, 151, 155, 176n
 *The Betrothed*, 171, 176n
 the Great Unknown, 147, 150–1, 155–6, 158–60, 163, 165, 172
 *Walladmor* and, 150–1, 171–2
 *Waverley*, 148–51, 153, 156, 158, 171–2
Shakespeare, William, 21, 31–3, 135
Shelley, Percy Bysshe, 7, 17, 75
Simpson, David, 6, 98n
Smith, Adam, 171
Smith, Christopher, 49n
Smith, Mark J., 94n
Sorensen, Janet, 94n
Southey, Robert, 18–19, 21, 31–4, 50n, 51n, 53m, 84

Spanish, 66
Spice, Nicholas, 50n
Staël, Madame Germaine de, 80, 107, 143n
Stanback, Emily, 48n
Stephen, Leslie, 24, 33–4
Stewart, Dugald, 107
Stirling, J. H., 16–17
style, 63–5, 67–71, 73–4, 79–81, 91–3, 113–15, 120–1, 139
sublime, the, 30–2, 37, 101–3, 109, 132, 169
  absence of, 134
  negative forms of, 15, 17
  see also impassioned prose: rhetorical manifestation of the sublime, as a

Tait's Edinburgh Magazine, 17, 29, 37, 52n, 53n, 102, 142n, 167
Taylor, Jeremy, 92
tertium aliquid, 34–6, 87–8
Thomas, Lionel H. C., 175n, 176n, 177n
Thomson, William, 142n
Tooke, John Horne, 94n
Toremans, Tom, 5, 176n
Toury, Gideon, 7, 152
transcendentalism see idealism
translation
  classical history of, 68–72
  commercial aspects of, 91, 103, 152, 161, 164, 170, 172–5
  mode, as a, 4–7, 11–13, 33, 38, 47, 72–5, 88, 102, 114, 129–31, 159, 170, 175, 179–82
  national ideal, as a, 62–5, 74, 101–2
translatorship, 4, 8, 38–9, 47, 128–9, 138–9, 179
Turley, Richard Margraf, 94n

Vanacker, Beatrijs, 176n
Vardy, Alan, 54–5n
Venuti, Lawrence, 3

Victorianism, 14, 37, 49–50n
Vigus, James, 141n
Voltaire, 90, 176n

Wales, 23, 56, 61, 154–6, 158–9, 165, 176n
Warminski, Andrzej, 77, 96n
Wasianski, Ehregott Andreas, 119–27
  *Immanuel Kant in seinen letzten Lebensjahren*, 119, 121–3
Webster, Noah, 94n
Wellek, René, 3, 6, 16–17, 95n, 101, 108, 117, 142n
Wells, John Edwin, 51n, 140n
*Westmorland Gazette*, 25, 62
  De Quincey's editorship of, 47n, 62, 99–103, 140n
Wheeler, Kathleen, 104
Wieland, Christoph Martin, 100
Wilkie, Brian, 54n
Willich, Anthony Madinger, 107, 142n
Wilson, Frances, 48n, 49n
Wilson, John, 54n
Wirgman, Thomas, 104, 107–8, 142n
Wolff, Christian, 100
Wolfreys, Julian, 48n
Woolf, Virginia, 16
Wordsworth, Dorothy, 23–6, 51n
Wordsworth, William, 19–31, 34, 45, 47, 47n, 54n, 56, 102, 110, 115, 129, 131, 140n
  *Concerning the Convention of Cintra*, 23–4, 28, 50–1n, 120
  *Letters*, 22–4, 29, 50n
  *Lyrical Ballads*, 18, 21–3, 25
  personal relationship with De Quincey, 20–30, 37, 50n, 51n, 52n, 93n
  *The Excursion*, 26
  as a translator, 39, 54n

Youngquist, Paul, 116, 125–7

EU representative:
Easy Access System Europe
Mustamäe tee 50, 10621 Tallinn, Estonia
Gpsr.requests@easproject.com

www.ingramcontent.com/pod-product-compliance
Lightning Source LLC
Chambersburg PA
CBHW070355240426
43671CB00013BA/2512